PRAISE FOR

The Forensic Science of C.S.I.

"With the mind of a true investigator, Katherine Ramsland demystifies the world of forensics with authentic and vivid detail."

—John Douglas, former FBI profiler and coauthor of
Mindhunter: Inside the FBI's Elite Serial Crime Unit

"Fascinating . . . this book is a must for anyone who wonders how the real crime-solvers do it."

—Michael Palmer, *New York Times*
bestselling author of *The Patient*

THE
C.S.I.
EFFECT

Katherine Ramsland

BERKLEY BOULEVARD BOOKS, NEW YORK

THE BERKLEY PUBLISHING GROUP
Published by the Penguin Group
Penguin Group (USA) Inc.
375 Hudson Street, New York, New York 10014, USA
Penguin Group (Canada), 90 Eglinton Avenue East, Suite 700, Toronto, Ontario M4P 2Y3, Canada
(a division of Pearson Penguin Canada Inc.)
Penguin Books Ltd., 80 Strand, London WC2R 0RL, England
Penguin Group Ireland, 25 St. Stephen's Green, Dublin 2, Ireland (a division of Penguin Books Ltd.)
Penguin Group (Australia), 250 Camberwell Road, Camberwell, Victoria 3124, Australia
(a division of Pearson Australia Group Pty. Ltd.)
Penguin Books India Pvt. Ltd., 11 Community Centre, Panchsheel Park, New Delhi—110 017, India
Penguin Group (NZ), Cnr. Airborne and Rosedale Roads, Albany, Auckland 1310, New Zealand
(a division of Pearson New Zealand Ltd.)
Penguin Books (South Africa) (Pty.) Ltd., 24 Sturdee Avenue, Rosebank, Johannesburg 2196,
South Africa

Penguin Books Ltd., Registered Offices: 80 Strand, London WC2R 0RL, England

THE C.S.I. EFFECT

This book was not authorized, prepared, approved, licensed, or endorsed by any entity involved in creating or producing the *C.S.I.* television series.

While the author has made every effort to provide accurate telephone numbers and Internet addresses at the time of publication, neither the publisher nor the author assumes any responsibility for errors, or for changes that occur after publication. Further, publisher does not have any control over and does not assume any responsibility for author or third-party websites or their content.

PRINTING HISTORY
Berkley Boulevard trade paperback edition / September 2006

Berkley Boulevard trade paperback ISBN: 0-425-21159-2

An application to register this book for cataloging has been submitted to the Library of Congress.

PRINTED IN THE UNITED STATES OF AMERICA

10 9 8 7 6 5 4 3 2 1

In memory of Ethan Jensen

Always enthused, supportive, and dedicated to justice

CONTENTS

Acknowledgments

Covering so many areas of forensic science would be difficult without the assistance of professionals working in this field who gave freely of their time to answer questions or tell me about cases. Thanks specifically to Frank Bender, Dr. Tom Crist, Dr. Carole Chaski, Vernon Geberth, Mack House, Dr. Tim Palmbach, James E. Starrs, Karen Taylor, Steven Teppler, John Trestrail, Joyce and David Williams, and Zachary Lysek. In addition, there are many people whom I've met at various conferences who often explained their work to me, inspired me to go in a certain direction, or suggested good books.

I'd like to also thank friends, relatives, and associates who offered other kinds of assistance, from research to resources to creative ideas, including Ruth Osborne, Dana DiVito, Dr. Scott Paul, Gregg McCrary, Dr. Richard Noll, Kim Lionetti, and Al Sproule.

The enthusiasm of Ginjer Buchanan and Leslie Gelbman at Berkley for this second volume made it happen, and my agent, John Silbersack, has always been my most significant support in publishing and good friend. I'm grateful to them all.

Introduction:
The *C.S.I.* Effect

On October 27, 2001, a battered male body was discovered in a park in Fort Worth, Texas. Investigators initially believed the thirty-seven-year-old homeless man, Gregory Biggs, had been the unfortunate victim of a hit-and-run. His death was declared an accident.

Four months later, a bizarre story emerged. It seems that as a woman named Chante Mallard drove home one night under the influence of drugs and alcohol, she struck Biggs, who was walking along the road. She'd eventually confided this to an acquaintance, who then notified the police. Under questioning, Mallard admitted that she had hit the man and insisted it was an accident. Authorities were not so certain, but the forensic challenge was to find enough evidence from months earlier, after known and unknown tampering, to reconstruct the incident in a way that would reveal the real story: accident . . . or felony murder?

Detectives searched Mallard's home and found her Chevrolet Cavalier, clearly damaged, still in her garage. But someone had tried to hide or remove evidence. The windshield had been mostly knocked out and a seat removed, so it would be difficult to reconstruct the incident. Nevertheless, crime scene investigators with special tools got to work on the interior and soon found what they needed.

Blood spatter inside the car proved to be from Biggs, as was the blood that filled a side-door pocket compartment. Not only did it prove he had been in the car but the various stains also offered a map of what had occurred that night. One area of blood was consistent with spatter that had been wheezed or coughed out, and there were fragments of hair and flesh from a Caucasian on remaining edges of the shattered windshield. In addition, a hammer left in the backseat was proven with trace analysis to have been used against glass, an indication of evidence tampering. It all added up, as carefully described by an analyst in court, to a living man struggling and bleeding substantially in that space. The blood-smear patterns even indicated how his body was twisted as he bled.

The medical examiners on both sides agreed that Biggs had died from loss of blood. From the accident, he'd sustained several broken bones and a nearly severed leg. The points of discrepancy involved his actual time of death, his degree of suffering, and whether Ms. Mallard could have helped him. The ME who'd conducted the autopsy stated that none of the injuries was consistent with instantaneous death, which meant that with medical assistance Biggs could have survived. He believed that Biggs had struggled for several hours and that Mallard, a nurse's assistant, had enough expertise to have saved him. At the very least, she knew how to call for help. (The defense's medical expert thought Biggs might have been unconscious, although Mallard reported that he'd been moaning and moving around.)

Between testimony from the different parties who saw the victim,

Mallard's confession, and the crime reconstruction from physical evidence, the scenario appeared to have occurred thus: Mallard was high on a mixture of drugs and alcohol that night while driving. As she hit him, Biggs came through her windshield headfirst and lodged there, his arms pinned to his sides. Rather than stop to get him out, she drove eight miles to her home and parked her damaged car in her garage, leaving Biggs struggling and bleeding in her windshield.

Too scared to do the right thing, Mallard called friends, who agreed to help. (One person said that Mallard had refused to call 911 when urged to.) As the terrified Biggs slowly expired over the course of an hour or two, probably suffering excruciating pain, Mallard checked him and actually apologized. When she found him dead, she and two male friends dumped him in the park.

It was a story that stunned the nation. Given the evidence against her, Mallard was convicted of murder and sentenced to fifty years, with another ten-year sentence for tampering with evidence. Her two friends received sentences for tampering as well. Not surprisingly, because it was startling, bizarre, and required the expertise of crime scene analysts for accurate interpretation and successful prosecution, this is among the cases that have inspired the writers of C.S.I., Crime Scene Investigation. They took it on as a framework for "Anatomy of a Lye." Other actual cases, such as Michael Peterson's murder of his wife in a stairwell, the Georgia crematory incident with corpses left to decompose outside, and the investigation of ground-based lasers aimed at planes overhead, have spawned C.S.I. episodes as well, and while the writers generally apply their own special twist, the line between fiction and fact can blur. Thus, thanks to the way such cases get absorbed into the programs, legal professionals now worry about what's been dubbed the "C.S.I. Effect."

What they mean is this: Through a proliferation of forensic television programs, the mass media has offered the public an education of sorts about forensic science and investigation, with a threefold effect. Until recently, a key issue in the legal process has been how to translate scientific testimony to laypeople on a jury, but these television shows have made potential jurors somewhat savvier about scientific methods and evidence. As a result, they often expect it and even look for better results than can be produced or techniques that may not exist. Thus, they may translate testimony from imperfect or technologically unsophisticated investigations into "reasonable doubt" and decline to convict.

In sum, the *C.S.I.* Effect is alleged to be this: Thanks to these programs, people on juries believe they know all about forensic science and investigation. They're wrong, but they don't know that, and their errors can impact the outcome of a case.

While some judges claim there's no evidence for this, and to date no studies prove its existence, many attorneys are nevertheless concerned and they may say so in opening statements and closing arguments. Few cases have all the pieces of the puzzle, but *C.S.I.*, they say, makes the process of getting these pieces look rather effortless. And there's another, more potent, concern as well: The public has viewed shows that have hypothetically solved real-life cases before the actual cases have gotten to trial, so some jurors believe they have gained "insight" from the media's amateur sleuthing. In other words, a person's guilt or innocence may be decided before the evidence is even heard. Even if it's not *C.S.I.* specifically that has influenced this, the entire spectrum of television shows that offer crime investigation techniques are judged to be part of the *C.S.I.* Effect.

U.S. News and World Report attributed the show's influence to its ability to attract 60 million viewers to a presentation of science that is "sexy, fast, and remarkably certain." In other words, murders get solved quickly, the lab scientists are always right, and the crime technicians are keenly intuitive (not to mention fit, stylish, and attractive). But even when the show is not "sexy," it has a way of showing a step-by-step process that makes viewers feel in the know about behind-the-scenes brainpower—especially when the good guys inevitably come out on top.

To be fair, there's something positive as well in the *C.S.I.* Effect. Increased jury awareness of the investigative process has helped to make it more accountable, and thus, investigators and evidence handlers are more conscious of what must be done to impress a jury. Nevertheless, the bar may be set so high at times—typically based on flawed ideas—that legal professionals despair. Few police departments have access to high-tech gadgets and expensive experts, so prosecutors find themselves at pains to de-educate juries, i.e., correct their misperceptions. The levels of certainty in the forensic sciences aren't generally as they're portrayed on television, and the evidence processing certainly is not that fast. Sometimes the *C.S.I.* shows acknowledge that. Mistakes and miscalculations are made as part of the plot . . . but are usually corrected before someone gets hurt, goes to prison, or is wrongly freed. Only occasionally is human error acknowledged, and even less frequently are cases left with loose ends.

Yet while legal professionals are justified in their concern over the *C.S.I.* Effect (especially when some procedures are simply misrepresented or fictionalized altogether), it's gratifying to know that people on juries do try to utilize the available tools. Just as scientific expertise has gradually improved the legal process over the past two centuries, it's also possible that greater attentiveness among all participants may eventually have the same result. In the meantime, it's important for TV viewers to understand that television is not real life, no matter how "real" the science seems or how closely the plots may mimic actual cases. It's fiction.

Nevertheless, the techniques and cases have brought a lot of attention to the field of forensic investigation. Around the country, high school and college courses on any forensic subject fill up, new graduate programs have been developed to accommodate this interest, and even grade-school teachers are presenting hands-on crime labs for students. In addition, there are many more certification programs offered through colleges or online than ever before, from one-day to weeklong seminars. Since the first volume of *The Forensic Science of C.S.I.* was published, many people have asked me what it takes to become a crime scene technician or investigator. I'll just say a few things about them here.

First, the C.S.I.s are not really detectives, although they're portrayed on the programs as such. Their primary job is to identify, collect, and document potential physical evidence from a crime scene. Different jurisdictions require different levels of education and expertise, and people interested in this occupation ought to consult their state guidelines before signing up for one of the certification programs for crime scene technicians. It may or may not be necessary to become a police officer first, and may or may not require a four-year college degree. They should also learn how the police departments for which they'd like to work define the C.S.I.'s duties.

In general, a crime scene technician will need some experience with photography, fingerprints processing, footwear impressions, sketching diagrams, lifting and preserving trace evidence, handling biological fluids, and perhaps assisting with collecting evidence during an autopsy. They should be able to take good notes and write clear and comprehensive reports. Along with that, they must be familiar with courtroom protocol and admissibility standards. They may have to lift or move heavy objects, and will likely have to be able to communicate well with other members of the investigative team. They ought to have a good working knowledge of the various areas of a crime lab and how the evidence gets processed. In fact, some professionals advise prospective students in this area to get undergraduate degrees in chemistry or biology, because it will help with job advancement. So will keeping up with the field's progress and knowing about some of the more refined and sophisticated developments. If you see something on *C.S.I.* that appears groundbreaking, look it up and find professionals who do it.

INSIDE

This second volume of forensic science utilized in the *C.S.I.* programs goes beyond the basics covered in the first volume. With three shows now in production, set in Las Vegas, New York, and Miami, innovations had to be found to keep them edgy and popular. Partly, that comes with the diverse settings. Las Vegas is a high-powered desert town full of casinos, sex, and high stakes; Miami adds oceans, gators, and C.S.I.s who are also cops; while New York, the only city of the three with a true winter, takes on the gritty, high-rise, old-money feel of an established East Coast hub. The crimes are somewhat different from one setting to another, and the approach to them differs as well, especially in light of the leadership styles unique to each unit chief.

In Vegas, Gil Grissom, a literary scientist/guru who loves bugs, is fairly low-key; he focuses on the physical evidence. Miami's Horatio Caine feels deep compassion for crime victims and flashes a fierce anger toward offenders. In New York City, Mac Taylor believes that everything is connected, indicating his affinity with quantum physics and setting the stage for the high-tech approach taken by the ethnically diverse Manhattan-based investigators. The choice of a nearly black-and-white cinematic look there supports the abrupt, no-nonsense style of a typical New Yorker. In addition, this city was the target of the 9/11 terrorist attacks, which had a profound impact on all city law-enforcement personnel, because many lost friends on that black day and they now live in anticipation of future threats.

The chapters that follow describe many of the procedures demonstrated on any of the three shows, with real-life cases to illustrate them and interviews with key forensic scientists or technicians to further explain how their parts in an investigation works. Even so, with innovations happening at a rapid pace, a book like this cannot cover them all, or even keep up. My hope is that I've covered vital areas and offered sufficient detail for readers to see how some of these techniques work. To make things easier, when I refer to one of the *C.S.I.* programs, I use *CSI-LV* for the one set in Vegas, *CSI-M* for Miami, and *CSI-NY* for New York.

Since computers are showing up more often on the show and in a greater variety of ways, let's start there.

CHAPTER ONE

Whodunit.com

All three *C.S.I.* shows rely on the fast-developing field of computer forensics, from an incident simulation in "Ashes to Ashes" to 3-D geographic orientation in "Officer Blue" to digital manipulation in "The Closer." The nature of digital evidence is a concern for the courts, as is Internet crime, identity theft, and cyber-victimology. While not all of the techniques used on television are viable for criminal investigation, we'll cover some of the basics here.

Computer forensics is the application of legal concerns and activities to the computer arena for the purpose of developing evidence. Investigators must collect information the way they do in other potential crimes, but they often need specialized knowledge to do so. The realm of computer forensics, also known as cyber-forensics or forensic informatics, has developed in many directions, and computers have brought greater precision into investigations, even when investigators aren't entirely sure how a program works. In "Crime and Misdemeanor," for example, the New York team was able to measure body parts of a human pretending to be a statue to use subtle differences to prove that the "statue" in the two videos was in fact two different people.

Some professionals doubt that "computer science" can actually be called a science, but informatics is heavily systematic, involving the processes of gathering, storing, classifying, manipulating, and retrieving information. It's an application of statistical techniques to the management of information and includes methods for searching databases quickly and effectively, without information distortion. To some extent, that involves interpretation, but the attitude remains objective and oriented toward measured and replicable data analysis.

OVERVIEW

Informational organization works for both criminals and law enforcement. The Internet has made some crimes easier to commit, but it has also provided police with new ways to detect a crime and collect evidence. One of the earliest investigations to involve computers was for the so-called Boston Strangler in 1964. The "Strangler Bureau" had to organize, compare, and analyze over 37,000 documents from the various police jurisdictions involved, which reportedly totaled more than 800,000 pieces of paper. A company donated a computer to help keep track.

As early as 1958, in Los Angeles, Detective Pierce Brooks had already recognized the value of computers for linking one crime to another to pin several on a single offender. The year before, the police came across a woman along a roadside near Los Angeles struggling with a man so they

otoppod, and oho boggod for holp. Sho olaimod that tho man, Harvey Glatman, had told her he was a photographer. The police arrested him and in
his apartment found photographs of three women who had disappeared.
All had been posed bound and gagged. Glatman confessed that he had
killed them, and was convicted in 1958 and executed.

Glatman's crime spree inspired Brooks to consider the viability of a
nationwide computerized databank on violent crimes. As he'd studied one
of the murders, he'd come to believe that the offender had killed before.
Then he was assigned to an unrelated case that struck him the same way.
Brooks spent many hours in the library looking for similar incidents as a
way to link these crimes to a repeat offender. The tedious task initially
seemed hopeless, but then he found a similar murder. He made a fingerprint match between the two cases and found a good suspect. But the
process had consumed a lot of time, so he went to his chief to ask about
purchasing a computer.

At the time, his request seemed absurd: A mainframe was vastly expensive and gigantic in proportion. Nevertheless, Brooks proved to have
been a visionary, and once computers came on the scene decades later,
law enforcement soon realized their value and necessity.

Computer applications in a forensic investigation or proceeding may
take any of the following forms:

- Using computer databases

- Developing crime scene simulation/animation

- Enhancing images or filtering noises

- Networking with other agencies

- Recovering digital evidence

- Decoying and ambushing cyber criminals

- Proving computer fraud

The first forensic database was developed for fingerprints. Previously stored on cards, fingerprints lifted at a crime scene could be compared with stored prints from a suspect only with painstaking analysis that required days or weeks. Then the Automated Fingerprint Identification System (AFIS) was developed in each state and at the FBI, and with improved digital technology, operators were able to make the same type of comparison in a matter of hours, even minutes (or, on *C.S.I.*, a few seconds). But the computer doesn't make the final call; the technician does. Images of fingerprints are taken from a person or surface and scanned into the program. The print features are extracted from the unique pattern and stored as specific formulas or algorithms. That makes them available as digital data for comparison. It wasn't long before databases for other types of evidence followed, and the investigators in all three *C.S.I.* programs rely on them to make comparisons and learn sources of origin of their own evidence.

In 1985, the FBI's National Center for the Analysis of Violent Crime had the Violent Crime Apprehension Program (VICAP) system up and running (in response to Pierce Brooks's persistent plea) to provide a national database for associating several crime scenes, identifying missing persons via discovered homicide victims, and linking victims to offenders.

A computerized database, the Combined DNA Index System (CODIS), was later developed for DNA, but collection of samples has been controversial. The database itself is limited to the DNA codes of whatever population the law in a given country or state allows, such as known sex offenders.

Databases also exist for a number of key evidence items, sometimes specifically for forensic use and other times the forensic application is incidental:

- Handwriting analysis—A subject's handwriting is digitized via a scanner and the strokes, slants, letter heights, and distances between lines and words are analyzed with standardized systems.

- Paint chips—The formula for paint used by car manufacturers differs, so a paint chip from a crime scene can be analyzed for its elemental composition and compared against these databases.

- Tool marks—The entries into this database come from tools the police have picked up at crime scenes. A three-dimensional image can be developed and compared to an earlier crime where a tool was used, which may link it to the same person or team.

- Cartridge cases—The parts of firearms that contact a cartridge when it's fired leave distinct marks. Irregularities in the barrel also leave an impression, as do the lands and grooves. These marks are computerized as images and can be compared against a test-fired bullet. DRUGFIRE and the Integrated Ballistics Information System (IBIS), have been the typical databases used for making such comparisons, but IBIS is now the U.S. standard.

- Shoes—A large database of footwear on the market can be useful if a clear shoeprint impression is left at a crime scene, to determine which brand and model the person was wearing.

All of the databases are searched through a "query by example," which means that they follow a protocol for querying the database about similarities. First, investigators acquire the image and put it into the system. The program extracts the relevant features, uses a matching algorithm, and makes a decision about authentication. It presents several close matches and the analyst makes the final decision.

ONLINE INVESTIGATIONS

Knowing how to navigate the Internet can be a real boon for law enforcement, and but for this skill some crimes might have gone unsolved. While they rarely make reference to the Internet on *C.S.I.*, they clearly use it for research, resources, directories, sending queries to state and national databases, and learning about local businesses. At times, real-life investigators must utilize this skill to fully track down the evidence they need to make a case, and in recent years many more have been trained in online technology. Let's look at a case in which the most efficient resource was the Internet.

In Etna, New Hampshire, Half Zantop, sixty-two, and his wife, Susanne, fifty-five, were found savagely murdered on January 27, 2001. Both were professors at Dartmouth University, well-regarded, and appeared to have no enemies.

It was clear to the police from evidence at the scene that there had likely been two killers involved, because two large knife sheaths were left behind. Key evidence was a boot print and several fingerprints on the knife sheaths, but the police needed suspects to make these viable. They had to learn more about the knives used.

Trooper Charles West and Detective Frank Moran doggedly tracked down the company that made the SEAL 2000 commando-type weapons, tracing them to SOG Specialty Knives and Tools in Washington State. The knife model had been sold over the past five years, but the company had customers worldwide via a large number of dealers. In that space of time, the dealer estimated, there may have been five thousand sold, without serial numbers or ways to track them. Indeed, they could have been sold from one owner to another and the killers might have purchased them second- or thirdhand.

The manufacturer offered a list of catalogues that carried the knives, as well as a list of merchants in the New England area. West and Moran called the dealers, one by one, but they got nowhere, so they turned to deals made via the Web. Neither was an expert in this area, but they knew that the purchase could have been accomplished online, so they had to learn how to maneuver through the Internet. West found numerous sites that sold knives, and contacted the site owners. He identified the sales of pairs of knives close to the crime scene and not long before the murders.

West came across a dealer in Massachusetts who had ordered a large number of the knives, and according to his computerized list of customers, had sold two via the Internet to a Jim Parker, who resided about thirty miles from the scene of the crime. The order had come just a month before the murders.

On February 15, the police asked James Parker, sixteen, to come to the police department to give fingerprints and answer questions. On the same day, Parker's friend James Tulloch, seventeen, was also fingerprinted. They realized they had left the sheaths at the Zantop home, so they fled. Within days, they were caught and returned to New Hampshire. Tulloch tried an insanity plea, but Parker made a deal to tell everything and to testify against Tulloch in exchange for a second-degree murder conviction. He said that Tulloch had instigated the plan of killing people to get money for a trip. Tulloch then pled guilty to two counts of first-degree murder and one count of murder conspiracy and received a life sentence, without parole.

The case was solved because detectives learned the technology. More dramatically, an investigation that stretched across three decades and utilized both FBI and task force resources was finally resolved because of the way computer technology made the killers' tracks evident as "digital footprints."

Often, people believe that when they've deleted a file, they've removed it from a disk, CD, or hard drive. In fact, they've only removed the link to it. The data itself remains until the computer needs the space. If they know how, they might use a "logic bomb," or delayed-action virus code designed to execute under specified circumstances, such as the failure of a user to respond to a program command. They might also use some device that defies detection procedures, but that requires some sophistication. Yet in the following case, a serial killer who didn't know much about computers made a mistake that gave the police all they needed to find him and make a solid case against him.

In Wichita, Kansas, someone had killed a family of four early in 1974, singling out the daughter for torture and strangulation by hanging. Six months later, a young woman was murdered in her home. The local newspaper received a letter with crime scene details of the family massacre, and while arrests were made, no one was identified as the killer. Then two women were murdered in the area in 1977. Following the murders, a poem was sent to the press referring to the family massacre. The killer had also called from one crime scene to direct police to it. FBI profilers had suggested downplaying the murders and dispensing with all the glitzy media, which apparently angered the offender.

He sent a letter to a local television station claiming responsibility for the murders and referring to himself as "BTK" for "bind, torture, kill." He indicated that he had not gotten the media attention he deserved and that he was already stalking victim number eight. How many people had to die, he asked, before his work would be recognized? The city of Wichita felt terrorized, wondering who might be killed next. But BTK had stopped communicating.

Years passed and computers became part of the communication system. Then in 2004, BTK returned, offering proof that he'd committed an as-yet-unsolved murder not initially linked to him. While many profiles were offered, one was generated by a computer program. A Virginia-based company called EagleForce Associates gathered the evidence and weighted different items for their significance. The analysts then cross-correlated all the data, showing that BTK was likely a white male around sixty, with military experience and a connection to the local university. That still left thousands of potential suspects, but a surveillance video caught a man who'd left a package for the police. EagleForce saw from the video that he drove a black Jeep Cherokee. The pool of suspects was further narrowed, and then something else happened to close the case.

BTK's package included a computer diskette. On it, the police found the name DENNIS, and by recreating data on it that had been overwritten ("erased" and reused) they were able to trace it back to a computer at Christ Lutheran Church. (Some reports indicated that there was also a hidden electronic code on it that tied it to the church computer.) The president of the congregation, confirmed by an online search via Google, was Dennis Rader, and when questioned, the pastor admitted that he had shown Rader how to use the computer to print out notes from a meeting. Digital footprints were found on the hard drive that indicated this computer had been used to write one of the BTK messages to a local media station. A search of Rader's office turned up a stack of BTK communications in a locked file cabinet: they contained the originals of the letters he had sent over the years to the media and police. In July 2005, he confessed to ten murders and said he'd already targeted his next victim. He received ten life sentences.

It's not just about what investigators can do, either. Criminal attorneys can also benefit from knowing Internet technology; if they don't, they may find their cases in the toilet. In a Canadian incident, a witness undermined an ongoing trial by failing to understand how her online musings could become evidence. She ended up being charged with perjury, which had an adverse effect on information that had already become part of jury deliberations. It was the first time, said newspapers, that electronic evidence was discovered during a trial, and since it revealed a new side to the witness, it had to be considered.

In Toronto on November 25, 2003, a twelve-year-old boy was found in the crawl space of the basement of his home, murdered and nearly drained of blood. He had been bludgeoned, stabbed, and hacked seventy-one times, and his older brother, sixteen, and two friends were arrested and tried for first-degree murder. The victim was known in the press as "Jonathan" and the three alleged perpetrators, who were juveniles, were not named. The trial had run for three months, with testimony from the girlfriend of one of the accused, and was already in jury deliberations when new evidence was discovered.

The girl had described the boys' affiliation with a vampire subculture, including her statement that the grisly murder had been planned as part of their gruesome role-playing. According to a taped phone call to her by one of the accused, they had planned to kill the entire family and two of them had apparently made an attempt on the stepfather with a baseball bat half an hour after attacking Jonathan. The brother and another young man were also charged with attempted murder.

Defense attorneys for the two accomplices insisted that the phone call had not been serious, and the fact that the murder had occurred shortly thereafter was only a coincidence. They contended that Jonathan's brother had acted alone in a fit of rage. The accomplice, whose former girlfriend had testified against the boys, said that his call to her to discuss the killing was an attempt to impress her, because she wanted to break up with him. He claimed that he'd said similar things to impress other girls, and he was only joking when he referred to himself as a vampire.

As the trial wore on, the witness made entries on her Web log and a Website, vampirefreaks.com, which a reporter revealed in a story in the *National Post*. Neither attorney had been aware of the teen's Internet commentary. While she had testified that she had gone along with the vampire fetish to be involved with her boyfriend but thought it childish, her writings gave a different story: Her online comments indicated that in fact she bore a fondness for blood, pain, and cemeteries, and hated people.

When defense attorneys raised an issue with the Website's contents, the judge said it put the witness's testimony in doubt and he declared a mistrial. Afterward, legal commentators said that Internet Web logs (known as blogs) could add a new dimension to criminal trials. Things get exposed in the public arena that can affect evidence or deliberations. Prior to seeking a new trial, the prosecutors in this case will have to evaluate whether the girl's Web postings are sincere and thus damaging to her testimony.

The popularity of blogs has increased exponentially in recent years. Because blogs are easy to learn, quick to create via online services, and allow people to express themselves to an audience on any subject of their choosing, blogging has taken over the Internet. A blog is an online diary, simple to create and update. It offers people a way to post text, photos, and links to other sites. More than twelve million people interact in this format daily on specific topics ranging from politics to pets to pedophilia. There are even Websites that track blogs, noting how many are added each day to the "blogosphere" and how many comments are posted to them. Bloggers can create whole communities around their blogs from people they have never met, or restrict it to friends and family. Authors can find new readers; movie fans, one another; and entrepreneurs, new customers.

In general, people find it fulfilling to have others read their expressions. Some people use blogs to blow off steam, which may constructively channel aggression, but just in case, authorities monitor both blogs and online chatrooms to watch for troubled people spouting threats who might eventually become violent—especially known or potential terrorists, people fascinated with bombs, or predators.

A Web diary labeled "Blogging the Fifth Nail," was kept by sex offender Joseph Edward Duncan III, who used the Internet over a period of several months to document his struggles with "demons." He wrote, "The demons have taken over," four days before two children, Dylan and Shasta Groene, turned up missing in Idaho. In the family's home, their mother, brother, and a family friend were found bludgeoned to death, and a few days later Shasta turned up in Duncan's company, while Dylan's remains were found in Montana. In Duncan's blog he'd discussed the idea of right and wrong, and his awareness that he did not know the difference. "God has shown me the right choice," he wrote in April 2005, "but the demons have tied me to a spit and the fire has already been lit." The title of his blog was a reference to the nails used in the crucifixion of Jesus Christ. During the investigation, the police identified the blog, signed only as "Joe," as Duncan's after they traced the Internet address to the computer used to set up the blog and make the entries. Many of Duncan's complaints evidenced anger over his social isolation, which had occurred subsequent to a sex offender conviction. He has been charged with several counts of first-degree murder and kidnapping, and his trial is still pending.

DIGITAL DATA

It's all about digital data. We can watch the investigators on the *C.S.I.* programs type in commands and manipulate information to get results, as Stella did on "The Closer" to clarify the resolution of a photo of a smeared ink stamp on a victim's hand. Investigators utilize many different types of programs for better imagery, sound, and perspective, but all of it is vulnerable. Information has become a digital asset, translated into machines and networks and guarded by software systems, passwords, and database access. The cyber world connects to the real world via a vast and complicated network of simulations. Thanks to the relentless development of computer technology, forensic science and investigation have become more sophisticated. Crime scene processing is now information-heavy, and that has amplified the demand for high-speed organization.

Forensic computer specialists know how to access a computer to track whatever a user has done on it. They can recover deleted data, decode encrypted files, and restore corrupted files, as well as determine which Websites a person has visited to acquire information or make contacts. But they can also manipulate or plant information, with no one the wiser.

To become a forensic computer investigator, someone must know both computer operating systems and the law. In terms of evidence gathering, the role of the computer as a repository and organizer of information is both valuable and tricky. The major dangers include loss of information during an investigation and its potential alteration. Computer data must be well-handled to be admissible in court, with the gathering method invulnerable to challenge.

Computer operating systems use virtual memory for retrieval and speed, which means that information exists in fragile form. It can be erased or overwritten when a computer is switched on. Computer specialists in law enforcement rely on equipment that can duplicate whatever is on a computer's hard drive without having to turn the computer on. Thus, if they follow the right protocol and take total control over a machine, they can work on encrypted data without the risk of destroying it.

Courts have set forth a clear protocol: The tools used cannot affect the data during collection, they must be able to collect everything necessary, they must be accepted by the forensic informatics community, and they must be capable of producing replicable results. With chain of custody issues, the investigator will have to prove that the evidence is an accurate representation of what was on the computer—which is not necessarily easy to do, as we shall see shortly.

Criminals were quick to figure out ways to use computer technology to commit their crimes. During the early 1970s, people gained unauthorized access to computers. At first, they mostly stole online time that others had paid for, which alerted lawmakers to the need for laws to cover a whole new arena. Intrusions and fraud were the most common type of crime in those early days, and in 1978, Florida enacted the Florida Computer Crimes Act to deal with unauthorized access. Other states followed, as did other countries.

But criminals didn't stop there, and their diverse activities have challenged law enforcement to follow them into the digital maze, not only to track them but also to anticipate what they will do next. That means police officers must have at least some basic technical knowledge about computers and the World Wide Web. In recent years, many have specialized in this field. Courses are offered for law enforcement training, teaching officers how criminals keep and erase records, communicate with their networks or cells, and engage in illicit acts such as child pornography. The Internet has become an accessible arena to traffic in illegal items, and also to hack into the records of corporations and governments, sometimes to screw up their files and sometimes to change or steal important records.

By the 1990s, when millions of people around the world had access to the Internet, computer crimes extended to infringement of copyrights, the proliferation of illegal child pornography, identity theft, and violations of privacy. Law enforcement had to scramble to learn how to detect these crimes and punish offenders, and for a while, the criminals were way ahead. There are now regional centers for digital evidence processing, as well as local ones for those areas with greater demand, such as large cities. Investigators are more adept, with some acquiring expertise in collecting digital evidence, some processing it, and some analyzing it for its relevance to a case. But it's not quite as straightforward as it sounds. The handling of digital data requires specific protocols that are often not in place because people don't understand their importance. Let's turn to an expert to better learn the issues.

Steven W. Teppler is an inventor and attorney, as well as the chair and founder of TimeCertain, LLC. He has practiced law since 1980 and is admitted to the bars of New York and the District of Columbia. He is a litigator, a member of the Information Security Committee of the American Bar Association, and a founding member of the Information Assurance Consortium. He advises private and public sector clients about risk, liability, and compliance issues unique to electronic data generation, alteration, transmission, and archiving.

"My concern," Teppler says, "is the authenticity of digital data content, or lack thereof. Most information generated today is digital in format, not paper-and-ink-based. The ability to detect forgery is so much more evolved in the tangible, or nonelectronic, world than it is in the electronic world. People figure that if it comes out of a computer it's okay, because a computer made it; since it's electronic it has to be true. But just the opposite is true. Computer data was designed by scientists to be ephemeral and to be easy to manipulate so they could work with it. It's infinitely more alterable than ink and paper, or substances that will have some sort of aging characteristic that can be detected."

The problem, then, is largely one of how easy it is to alter the data. It's not like something written on paper, which can then be examined with various instruments or levels of expertise. With digital data, there's no hard copy.

"What we print out, view on a monitor, see in our file folders, or even put into custodial care as evidence," Teppler points out, "is not 'source' or original data. You can't look at this data under a microscope. Real source data is now nonhuman readable binary digits—those pesky zeroes and ones. And they have no age. They look now like they did yesterday and will look the same twenty years from now. But when you look at your original data, a forensic investigator will say, 'This is the data that came out of the hard drive.' What you don't know is whether the data was created at the time it says it was. Unless you can establish provenance for digital data, you're setting yourself up for nasty consequences.

"One cannot tell from any examination of zeroes and ones what that data says, when it was created, or if it has been altered since its creation. What we see is what we call a 'view' of a 'view'—at least two, and possibly three renderings by other processes or systems of those zeroes and ones until the binary data is humanly readable."

In other words, digital data has been processed several times, with no sense of *provenance* or chain of custody identified. "Until we know for sure that the zeroes and ones are what they say they are," he explains, "and they have not been changed since they were created, we won't know whether what we're examining is a legal memo or a recipe for dog biscuits. The problem here is that data generation systems are controlled by, and therefore subject to, easy manipulation by insiders. Enter Enron, RiteAid, NextCard, World-Com, Parmalat, AIG, Frank Quattrone, and Martha Stewart, among many others. What is not generally known is that they each engaged in electronic data backdating and manipulation. Data manipulation in the digital age has already climbed into the hundred-billion-dollar category.

"The nature of digital data is so ephemeral that a mere click of a mouse to backdate a system clock can recreate the binary information that comprises real source data. This time-based vulnerability exists in every current data-generating environment, from a small PC to a mainframe cluster in a server farm. My company (and others in our arena) are strong advocates of trusted data timestamping. We lock down the zeroes and ones at a time that can't be re-created. Put into nontechno-geek terms, we fingerprint digital data content in such a way as to ensure its long-term integrity, and we provide the ability to detect any alteration or manipulation."

In fact, it was the evidentiary implications of how easily this data can be manipulated that inspired Teppler to form his company's technology. It has not yet been tested in court, although he's well aware from personal experience that the courts need to wake up to what's at stake.

"The case that caused me to come up with the idea was a nasty case that we had settled as litigators. It was about seven years in duration and I was the designated timekeeper for three attorneys. We were entitled in accordance with the terms of the settlement to apply for attorneys' fees to the court, and then the defendant would pay the fees after the court made a determination. I'd never written timesheets on paper, the way it's been done for hundreds of years. Instead, I used a computer, because I'd been on the cutting edge of technology and I didn't want to keep track of paper. So I submitted a printout on the day that it was required of 150 pages, with 1,300-plus entries. The other side was entitled to, and did, vigorously object to it, claiming that the printout date was the night before—and that I'd therefore made it all up. We had approximately $800,000 in attorneys' fees that we were claiming over six years for three attorneys, and they took us to court. It cost us a quarter of a million dollars to get our money."

To Teppler's chagrin, the resisting argument was focused on the suggestion that his entries were all made at once, rather than at the time the transactions occurred, and he couldn't prove otherwise, other than by credible testimony. "The printout didn't help me; it was my swearing that I'd made the entries at other times. So I said to myself, Wouldn't it be nice if I could prove that my computer entries were created at the time that I said they were?"

When he tries to explain these issues to others, he relies on a simple story. There was a high school girl working in his family's business and she asked him about the technology. To make her understand, he asked her if she used a computer. She said she did. She also acknowledged that she was required to hand in some assignments on a disk. He asked if she had deadlines and she said yes. Then he asked, "Have you ever turned back the clock in your computer so you can make it look as if you completed your assignment on time but really didn't?" Her eyes widened as she realized the implications of his work: "You're going to stop *that*?" she asked.

"In the computer world," says Teppler, "you don't know what your source evidence is, so you have two problems. One, the generational issue, which is how you know that what you took off the drive is what it says it is. Second, because they're zeroes and ones, how can you be sure that the evidence in custody has not been changed? Without taking robust measures like timestamping to ensure content integrity, these are challengeable. Everything gets timestamped, but you can change it. You can edit anything."

In other words, you might realize you did not fully document a crime scene with a digital photograph, so you could turn back the camera's clock and return to the scene to make it appear as if you did the right thing. And nobody will know, because that's the only data available—the photographs with *that* timestamp.

"There's an apocryphal story, which I have not been able to locate, which at least illustrates the problem," Teppler states. "A man was arrested for dealing drugs, and an undercover policeman had taken a picture of him doing it. At the trial, his defense attorney introduced into evidence a picture of the same defendant dancing at a Rave party across town, with a clock in the back that had the exact same time, and a timestamp on the photo. The judge threw both photos out because he said the man could not be in two places at once and he found both to be untrustworthy."

Digital data can be used offensively or defensively, to create or escape liability, or to challenge real data with forged data, and no one will know the difference. "An *LA Times* reporter taking pictures in Iraq created a photo montage," Teppler added, "but he merged two digital photos to make it look as if a soldier with a gun was menacing a young child being carried by his father. The problem is, you don't know what's authentic. Gartner [a provider of global IT research and analysis information] calls it 'counterfeit reality.' And when it comes to legal activity, the basis for introducing such evidence is that if you've sworn to it and you can show that the process that created it was reliable and authenticable. But just swearing to it and showing how it works does not mean that you've authenticated it. The ability to dicker with underlying data is so easy that anyone can do it and it dilutes the evidentiary quality of what you're presenting. If you have control over time, you have control over history."

Some IT industries already realize that digital fraud is going to be an exponentially growing business, and investigators will have to master skills in its identification, analysis, and exposure. The sale and purchase of fake reality will become widespread. To this point, there has been no landmark case to alert people to the threat, but it's coming. A case decided in 2001 and appealed on technological grounds does indicate that the courts are now recognizing the need, at least, for stronger authentication standards.

In 1991, the body of Carla Terry was found in a bag on an abandoned road north of Hartford, Connecticut. She had been strangled, and bruises around both breasts were identified as human bite marks. Terry showed a lack of defensive wounds, which led police to believe that she knew her attacker. Two days into the investigation, a woman reported that Carla Terry had been in a bar, teasing a fortyish black male named Al.

Investigators tracked down Al Swinton and searched his home and car. They found a brown plastic bag the same color, size, and manufacturer as the one that had encased the dead woman and a black bra that Terry's family identified as hers. They got a warrant for Swinton's teeth impression, and a forensic odontologist compared it to the bruises found on Terry. He believed they were a match. Yet a judge ruled that the state must prove the marks were made at the time of Terry's death. He ordered Swinton released, and the investigation went cold.

Advances in forensic science brought the case back into the spotlight in 1998. While the original crime scene photos had not changed, the way detectives viewed them had. Lucis, image-processing software that could differentiate fine contrast variations, enabled them to see image detail that would otherwise be either difficult or impossible to see. Its pixel digital image contains 255 levels of contrast, far beyond the eye's thirty-two levels.

Forensic odontologist Gus Karazulas worked on the Carla Terry bite mark, scanning the photo into the computer with Adobe Photoshop software and adjusting the contrast levels. He made a transparent copy of Al Swinton's teeth from the plaster moldings made in 1991 and laid them over the enhanced picture. It was a perfect match. But that had already been done. They still needed to establish just when the bite had been made in relation to Terry's death.

Karazulas knew that when an individual's heart stops, the healing process stops, and from Terry's color, he could tell that between the time she had been murdered and the time she was found, no bodily changes had occurred. The bruise color represented a fixed point in time—the approximate time of Terry's death. Starting with that premise, Karazulas attempted to replicate the color of her bruises by taking the upper and lower plaster cast of Swinton's teeth and clamping them onto his own arm. Taking a constant stream of pictures to verify his work, he timed how long it took for the color in his arm to return to normal—for the arm, in effect, to heal itself. He observed that fifteen to twenty minutes after it had been made, the bite mark disappeared. From the color of the strangulation marks on the victim, the color of the bite marks on her breasts, and the color of the bite mark on his arm, the odontologist determined that Terry had been bitten about ten to fifteen minutes before she was strangled. He repeated this test more than fifty times with the same results. That finding effectively put Swinton with Terry at the approximate time she was strangled.

Swinton was rearrested, and in March 2001, he was convicted and sentenced to a prison term of sixty years. His attorney appealed, challenging the technology. He said that the state had failed to present foundation testimony on the adequacy of the computer programs and that the experts using them had only elementary knowledge. As a result, the court created a six-part admissibility test, with the following qualifications:

1. The computer equipment is accepted in the field as standard and competent.

2. Qualified operators were employed.

3. Proper procedures were followed with the input and output of data.

4. A reliable software program was utilized.

5. The equipment was programmed and operated correctly.

6. The exhibit is properly identified as the output in question.

The court found that the computer-enhanced photos of the first expert were properly admitted but the computer-generated overlays of the second expert were not, because the expert did not personally perform the operations but had instead watched it being done. That evidence was thrown out, but the conviction was upheld.

"But they still don't fully understand," says Teppler, referring to the courts. "They think that the issue is between something that's been computer-generated versus computer enhanced. But if it's computer-enhanced, it's still computer-generated. They haven't addressed that yet. But these early cases show that the courts recognize that there are some innate problems with digital data. Defendants can be set up or exonerated, as long as you put in enough bogus digital evidence for reasonable doubt or for someone to do the same for the prosecution's side. It's not sufficient to just claim that they don't manipulate the data on hard drives in their possession. It's a threat to both sides and to the orderly administration of justice. It's treacherous ground."

He recalled a case in Riverside, California, where two hackers changed the criminal records of five people, who would have then been released. They altered data to make it appear as if the charges had been dismissed, including weapons and drug charges against one of them. They were caught after court officials noticed changes in several ongoing cases and a bail bond company inquired about a closed case as if it were still open. Upon investigating further, officials noticed that computer files had been altered. The Computer and Technology Crime High-Tech Response Team (CATCH) monitored the system and identified the guilty parties via the past association of one man with law enforcement. He had stolen a password and had accessed the court databases more than seventy times. The hackers pled guilty, and were sentenced to nine years in prison.

"They could only have changed it [the computer file] by backdating it," Teppler explains. "When you re-create history, you must backdate. And if the change was done on the date when it looks like it should have been done, it's accepted. If you have control over the data-generating system that creates it, you have no forensic methods to determine the provenance of that data. If the data are timestamped and fingerprinted, you have the ability to verify the data from then on."

SIMULATION AND ENHANCEMENT

Computer simulation programs provide ways to construct possible scenarios for an incident, based on raw data input and its facility for manipulation. For example, a reconstruction expert might measure the distance a person fell from a window, add in his weight, the prevailing wind conditions, clothing factors, how the person went out the window (falling versus running), and watch the action via computer to determine if the calculations match the way the person actually landed. Or investigators might track a bullet trajectory to determine a shooter's position, as they did on the episode "Officer Blue," on *CSI-NY*. First they used a Scanosphere laser 3-D program to acquire a 360-degree view of the park where the incident occurred, and then put in coordinates, based on where the officer and his horse were hit and the bullets' trajectories.

The program is an interpreter, and different data will yield different results, but the point is to enter the data accurately. An arson program may show the way the fire would burn in a specific type of building by entering a point of origin and other data about the fire (whether an accelerant was used, for example). If that doesn't match the scene, another point of origin can be considered. Nick Stokes had to reenter data several times in "Bad Words" to get the point of origin that seemed most accurate.

An interesting type of software allows investigators to use virtual reality to look at a reconstructed crime scene from different angles, or to pan in and out to get different perspectives or study details. First, the investigators must take photos of the scene with a digital camera and fish-eye lens, and using a Pano head on a tripod, they can rotate the camera in a steady and continuous manner. The photographs are "stitched," or imported into the virtual tour via instructions in the program, and they can now see a 360-degree, three-dimensional scan of the scene. It allows investigators to "walk" through the scene again and consider different angles that they might not have noticed when actually there. They can zoom in for a better look at something, interact with it, lift a detail and enhance or enlarge it, or view separate aspects of a scene side-by-side. They can also lay out a diagram and use the program to move pieces around or re-create the crime, step-by-step.

Yet simulations can offer simple results as well. On "Ashes to Ashes," when the team in Miami examined the amount of blood a murdered priest had lost, given the type of bullet that had hit him, and the part of the body it had entered, they were able to calculate how long he had lain there before he was removed, which gave them an idea of when he'd been shot.

A computer animation, on the other hand, is simply a way to turn data from an expert's report into a visual for the jury, similar to a graph or chart. It's a simple reconstruction that does not manipulate the data or interpret it. Like a chart or graph, it provides juries with a visual sense of the crime or crime scene.

In Scranton, Pennsylvania, Michael Serge, a retired police detective, was standing trial for the murder of his wife, Jennifer. The prosecution relied on a seventy-two-second computer animation of the crime to show how he had shot her in the living room of their home. The figures of Serge and his wife were digital figures. In the simulation, Serge appears, armed with a gun, and fires three shots at Jennifer. Colored lines extend from the gun to the victim or the wall or wherever a bullet seemed to have gone. The jurors were able to see just how the shots would have entered the body, as described by the pathologist who did the autopsy, and the state trooper who drew a diagram of the room. The prosecutor did not have to say much of anything: The pictures spoke for themselves.

The first computer animation to appear in a courtroom was in the Bronx in 1984, to re-create an automobile accident for a civil trial. In 1992, animation was used in a criminal trial for the first time. Not only does this technique provide a strong visual re-creation that improves jury comprehension but it also speeds up the litigation process. Animators use data from the crime scene and from reports, photographs, and specific information from relevant areas such as ballistics or pathology. With all of this, they create a cartoonlike scenario. Yet for all its glitzy images, computer animation is not science but art, and juries must be warned that it's merely an interpretation.

And not all animations are admissible. In one case in Idaho, the defense was barred from showing theirs to the jury because the judge decided that the simulation did not resemble the actual event.

The attorneys for Sarah Johnson, on trial for shooting her parents when she was sixteen, had videotaped a simulation of a mannequin firing a .264 caliber round at a coconut as a way to demonstrate how the blood would spatter from the impact of the bullet. The coconut was supposed to represent Johnson's mother's head, shot point-blank to the back of the skull. (Her father had been found next to the bed, shot in the chest.) The video showed a frame covered by a blue sheet. The coconut, lying on a pillow, was filled with half-and-half and topped with a wig. A mannequin with a Winchester Magnum rifle, stood next to it. The attorneys wanted to demonstrate what would happen to a liquid-filled vessel from the impact of a high-powered firearm. Their reasoning was that they would simulate the scene in such a way as to prove that a comforter had not been wrapped around the victim's head, as contended by police witnesses who'd found the bodies.

However, the judge ruled that the dissimilarity between the items in the video and the actual crime scene were problematic, as was their approach. They were attempting to show a result and work backwards to then create a scenario. In addition, the prosecutor complained that a coconut is not the same as a human head. That made the video misleading and the claims from it unreliable. Sarah Johnson was convicted of first-degree murder in the deaths of both her parents.

AMBUSH AND APPREHENSION

Pedophiles may pose in chat rooms as teenage boys or girls to lure children to meet them. As a result, some kids have been molested and even abducted. At first it seemed like an overwhelming task to attempt to go in and out of chatrooms to find these offenders, but then investigators came up with a way to turn the MO back on the predators. They, too, posed as teenagers to lure the pedophiles to meet them at a specified location, where they would be waiting with an arrest warrant. (At times, they've alerted the media so they can catch these people on camera and humiliate them as well.) Some police departments assign such officers to full-time computer policing. In fact, the largest international pedophile ring, known as the Wonderland Club, was cracked by police from twelve counties in a coordinated effort to arrest more than one hundred people. Yet it's a growing concern, and determined addicts keep finding ways to victimize.

IDENTITY THEFT

On *CSI-M*, in the episode "Identity," the investigators were confused about which of two women was lying about the other having stolen her identity. Both had apparently genuine credentials and both had all the requisite documents certifying that they were victims of fraud. Both acted sincere, so more specific methods of identification became necessary: a bone scan and comparison to medical charts finally differentiated between the victim and the thief.

Identify theft is a fast-rising crime that thrives on the pervasive availability in the computer age of people's personal information, from bank accounts, to Social Security numbers, to home addresses gained via computerized databases. There's also an old-fashioned method of simply going through people's trash for credit card statements or stealing bills from mailboxes. Thieves may also buy information from others, or sell it. There's been concern lately, for example, that methamphetamine addicts, who can stay up for days, are turning in increasing numbers to the Internet to support their habits with computer crimes. They move stolen goods on auction sites, use e-mail scams to "phish" for victims, and break into company computers to steal credit card information. They're often employed by non-drug users because they can complete menial tasks, such as testing credit card validity, for many hours.

In 1992, Trans Union Corporation, a credit bureau, recorded less than 3,000 inquires a month regarding identity theft. Five years later, it had increased by 1200 percent. An identity theft hotline for the Federal Trade Commission (FTC) reported a fourfold increase in complaints between the end of 1999 and the spring of 2001, and Image Data, a protection service, put out a report that found that one out of every five Americans had been or were related to someone who had been a victim. The figures continue to climb, although as the media makes people aware of their vulnerability, more people are taking steps to thwart this type of crime.

Once thieves access even a little information, they can use it to get more. They may call a credit card company with an unsuspecting person's number and change the address, then run up bills and leave before anyone can catch them. Or they'll open a new account with someone else's information. They may take out mortgages and fail to pay them, or purchase cars, porn, expensive gifts, or weapons. They may open a bank account and write bad checks. Their crimes are accomplished anonymously, with a devastating impact on the victim, who may spend years trying to rectify the situation and restore his or her credit status.

Crimes like this have a high probability of going cold, in part because the criminals can be difficult to catch and in part because institutions that become victims are reluctant to report it. Identity theft is the primary way that terrorist groups that have targeted the United States have managed to get professional training, driver's licenses, bank accounts, and access to sensitive information.

Anyone can be a victim, even a dead person. Investigating an identity theft crime takes a lot more effort than committing it, because with Internet capabilities the criminal can be in so many places at once, and can cost the victim much more than he or she will ever be able to recover.

The Department of Education uses a DVD featuring an interview with a man who used more than fifty aliases via Web-based application processes to siphon over $300,000 from federal student grants and loans. He was caught and agreed to do the interview to tell people how he did it, so as to make them aware of how to protect themselves against such scamming. He had stolen identities from inmates in the Arizona prisons, contacting them under the auspices of assisting them with their cases. He then used the IDs they'd provided to access the online loan process. The Department of Education distributed the video to colleges and universities to combat this form of fraud.

While the Internet has made cybercrime possible and necessitated the discipline of cyber-investigation, computers have also enhanced the ability to find missing persons and identify deceased John and Jane Does. That's the realm of computer art.

CHAPTER TWO

Face-to-Face

Forensic art, facial approximation, and the use of computer art have become more prominent for investigators on *C.S.I.* While they initially called in experts when the program first began, it's more often the case now that one of the team will do the work, as Aiden did in "American Dreamers" on *CSI-NY* when she prepared a skull for facial sculpture and did it herself. *CSI-LV*'s Sara painted the face onto a mold made from a victim, in "Nesting Dolls." The investigators also utilize the techniques of age progression, the computer enhancement of surveillance photos, art forgery identification, and other procedures that rely on interpretive art. They usually employ computer programs that assist forensic artists with non-contact surface measurements such as laser scanning and topographical systems, and may use simpler devices that put artistic tools in nonartistic hands. For example, Catherine Willows from *CSI-LV* used a "painting" program like Photoshop to work on a suspect drawing.

As with computers, there's some argument over whether this aspect of forensic methodology can be considered a science, particularly since the recognition rate of unknown persons via forensic art is generally low, but it's improving and more artists are looking to scientific and medical technologies to refine their approach. So let's review the procedures and add some enhancements, compliments of the computer age.

THE COMPUTER AND THE SCULPTOR

There's no doubt that identification of an unknown victim is paramount to solving a crime that involved that person. Even without a crime, a person's identity is important for bringing closure to an ambiguous case. Forensically, to know about them is potentially to discover how they crossed paths with whoever may have been involved in their deaths. Often there's no means of identification on a discovered body, and it might be decomposed to the point where identification procedures must involve sophisticated artwork. This is usually done after all other methods of identification have been exhausted: fingerprints, DNA, odontology, and even radiology. If no other approach produces results, forensic art may come into play.

The various types of forensic art include composite images; drawn or computer-generated portraits; image modification, such as age progression; and postmortem reconstruction from remains, often just a skull. This latter may involve clay sculpture, 3-D computer imaging, or some other type of artwork that uses the skull as a basis for facial replication.

To produce the replication, artists study various parts of the skull, such as the teeth or cheek structure, to determine how a person looked before death. The point is to get an accurate rendering of the arrangement of the features and their relationship to one another. Some parts of a face are more difficult to guess about than others. Thus, measurements of the skull and its various angles are an important first step. Repairs may also have to be made if the skull has damage or significant deterioration. That's where a computer can be quite helpful.

In the case of bone fragments, as they had when a skull was crushed in "Nesting Dolls," reconstruction involves several steps: The fragments are digitized with a special program that measures from surfaces in true-to-scale 3-D copies. Then the digitized images are "assembled," putting them together on the basis of the fractures and relevant anatomical features. After that, the distance between the fracture of the two fragments is measured and the pieces are morphed together on the screen until a skull is digitally present. An artist can build or draw something from there.

One technique begins with a two-dimensional blueprint for a guide. Either the skull or a cast of it becomes the base, and wooden pegs are placed in specific spots to assist with adding skin and muscle depth with clay. The muscles and features are carefully built up along the bony structure and then a thin layer of plastic or clay goes over the skull. The sculptor must interpret certain things, such as hair color and style, skin textures, and the width of the mouth. Then a wig and prosthetic eyes are added, and the eyelids are formed and perhaps makeup applied. Once the sculpture is finished, photographs and/or drawings are made for newspaper articles, television programs, or posters. Research has shown that the final rendition does not have to be perfect to evoke recognition; it has only to capture some aspect of the individual's characteristic appearance that will stimulate an associate's memory.

The critical task, say many artists, is to maintain the "look" of the person, particularly in the area of the eyes. Also, most people tend to maintain a certain recognizable manner of expression throughout their lives. The squint of former President John F. Kennedy is a good example. One advantage of using computer-generated alterations from photographs is that the baseline expression remains the same throughout the alteration process.

Before computers, the facial reconstruction process was originally done in a painstaking manner. Eventually computerized imaging systems were introduced, which involved image processing and image editing units to compose facial components. In other words, once the approximation is done in one medium, it can be projected onto a computer via scanning or photography and refined. Image processing software such as Adobe Photoshop can sharpen or apply features. Others such as Illustrator will allow someone to draw directly onto the image, and to change things, as required, if someone wants to see a face with some features added, removed, or altered.

There's a computer database that contains component parts, such as different types of eyes, noses, lips, and cheek contours. Once the skull is complete, the image processor generates a representation of it and selects from the database sets of facial components that seem appropriate. Different components are pasted onto the image, as specified by the anatomical criteria. A provisional reconstruction is created, and then the artist chooses a hairstyle and retouches skin tones with an electronic painting program. It's quite a bit faster than the more traditional drawing or clay sculpture, although some artists think that certain qualities are sacrificed.

Another technique that relies on computer algorithms sets a skull on a turntable and subjects it to computerized tomography. As it turns, information is scanned into a computer via laser beams and mirrors. It's assembled into a likeness, based on information from other faces with similar measurements and racial origins. A program calculates everything required to make a face and offers a digital image of the skull. Then, using CT scans from the living, flesh is "wrapped" onto the skull image to form a face that matches the skull's topography. Eyes, facial coloring, and hair are added digitally, using interpretive estimations. The resulting image is three-dimensional and can be rotated for a sideways angle—an improvement on drawings.

The accuracy of these sculptures relies on how closely the features of the person resemble features commonly associated with the person's identified ancestry, and whether or not he or she may have been overweight, worn glasses, had facial hair, or possibly had a hairstyle quite different from the typical style at their estimated time of death. It's not always easy to guess, so the more information that can be gained about the person, the better.

The remains of a murdered woman found in Wisconsin in 1999 were quite difficult to work with for identification, because she had been dismembered and the skin methodically stripped off her face. The police wanted to deflesh the skull so that an anthropologist could create a sculpture, but they were afraid that by doing so they might destroy evidence. A year later they heard about a computerized technique they believed might work for them.

The Milwaukee School of Engineering's Rapid Protoyping Center offered a way to develop a facial image without damaging the remains. The technicians were able to produce just what the police needed. First, they did a CT scan of the head, using thousands of thin layers of paper to make a 3-D prototype of the skull—what it would look like if they'd defleshed it. The forensic artist then glued pegs onto the prototype and built a face in the usual way. With this, the police made and distributed posters in the hope that someone would recognize her. Soon she was identified as the missing Mwevano Kupaza, and her husband was arrested, charged, and convicted in her murder.

There are other computer programs as well, such as FaceGen Modeller, and with the hope of improving both speed and accuracy, they are getting better. The right program will provide a great deal of flexibility and gradient texturing. In any of them, skull models become digitized, and some turn it into a mesh ready for editing. That provides grids on which markers can be "placed" and values for skin and muscle depth calculated. Since it's not as painstaking as applying the erasers or rods by hand, many more landmarks can be utilized. (It takes time initially to set up and calculate, but in subsequent renderings, the time involved is greatly reduced.) With the right tools, computer-generated approximations are better for giving texture to the face than is sculpture.

There's also a method that uses photographic facial templates, morphing "donor faces" onto a computer-generated skull, and then manipulating the software features until the face "fits" the skull. But that has its own set of problems, notably to make the subject's face too similar to the donor face.

AGE PROGRESSION

Computer-generated or hand-drawn age progressions are utilized in most cases of reported missing children who have been gone for a considerable period of time. They also help to assist in the capture of fugitives who have been on the run long enough to have changed physically, or who have a reputation for altering their identities via facial hair, weight gain or loss, disguise, and hair dye. The artist faced with this task takes into account the way most humans age, with reference to specific family characteristics such as weight and wrinkle formation. If a photo isn't available, a sketch can serve the same purpose.

When doing an age progression with a computer program, the features to be added can be painted directly into the computer image.

The techniques for fugitives who are already adults are somewhat different from those for missing children. For a child, the artist needs a photograph after the age of two, and it's helpful to also have photos of siblings or of the parents at different ages, especially the age at which the child currently would be. If there are any potentially disfiguring or aging medical conditions, that's important information as well. All of this is combined with standard information about quantifiable growth data common to most children of a specific culture and race.

The photos are then scanned into a computer set up with the age-progression software. The software helps to predict the structural changes that the face would undergo during specific ages, and as the artist manipulates it, the program morphs the photo until it offers images of those changes. A child's face would broaden and lengthen, because faces grow downward and forward. Secondary teeth grow in larger than the baby teeth, and the bridge of the nose typically rises. The cranium expands and the eyes become less rounded. The mouth widens to make room for more teeth and the nose lengthens. Light-colored hair tends to darken, and different styles reflect different cultural fashions. By age twelve, the face is looking mature, with the chin forming. Eventually the cheekbones become more prominent and eyebrows fill in. To make changes most accurately, the digital image is placed side-by-side with photos of the parent or grandparent that the child most resembles, and the artist can then shift the image to take on a similar appearance.

Fugitive age progression involves something a little different. With aging patterns in adulthood, while they don't have the dramatic growth patterns that children growing into adults show, there will be issues such as weight gain, baldness, color changes, wrinkles, sagging jowls, and other featural shifts. There is also a possibility that the person will shave or grow facial hair, or will get cosmetic surgery. It helps to have access to photos of family members around the target age, as well as information about that individual's personal habits, such as smoking or eating, exercise, and degree of vanity. Their personalities affect the type and depth of facial tension lines, and a medical condition may also influence how they look.

To cover several possibilities, the artist may develop multiple appearances, especially with different hairstyles, and with or without glasses. General anatomical guidelines of how faces age through the decades, such as a sagging jaw line, hair loss, and thinning lips, provide the most important clues.

Robert Nauss, a former leader of the Warlocks motorcycle gang, had been convicted of the 1977 murder of his twenty-one-year-old girlfriend. She'd disappeared, but a witness claimed that Nauss had displayed her body in his garage. In 1989, Nauss escaped from Philadelphia's Graterford Prison with drug dealer Hans Vorhauer, by hiding inside an armoire he'd built in the prison shop.

When it became clear that the fugitives had likely changed their appearance, the task force asked Philadelphia-based forensic artist Frank Bender for assistance. The U.S. Marshals gave him Nauss's Warlock pictures from before the time of his incarceration, along with his prison intake photo, but they were all several years old. He was faced with having to make some decisions.

Bender thought that because Nauss had been raised in upper-middle-class status and would adopt what he'd once known that he'd be clean-shaven, short-haired, and living in suburbia. The task force was skeptical: This guy had been a hard-core biker, after all. Still, they knew that Nauss realized he was the subject of a national manhunt. They decided to listen to the artist.

It turned out that Bender was correct. Nauss apparently went right to Michigan where he'd grown up, and when he was caught, he was clean-shaven, with short hair. He looked as Bender had drawn him.

Vorhauer was another matter. Reputed to be a genius, he was more elusive. Bender thought he'd dye his hair blond, because it would work with the color of his prison-pallor skin. The marshals had several fuzzy surveillance photos from where his girlfriend lived, but they believed that the people in them were different individuals. Bender showed them that they had the same person with different appearances. Vorhauer, too, was caught, despite his IQ.

ANALYSIS

It's important, throughout the stages of making a person look older, to retain his or her basic expression, so that each "look" is recognizable as that person via certain facial traits unique to them. While aging effects tend to occur in a predictable series, they do occur at variable rates for different individuals. So the forensic artist working on the renditions must be skilled in photo comparisons and alterations.

The forensic artist has become a facial identification specialist, and many are certified by the International Association for Identification. Photo modifications for the purpose of identification can be accomplished in a variety of ways and the artist must consider many factors before deciding which would be most advantageous.

The identification of a subject from one photo to another, also in use today, relies on a skillful observer and interpreter. While the comparison process has its limitations, positive comparisons can nevertheless assist in the identification of someone long missing. In that regard, computers can be most helpful.

For example, before making comparisons using images of poor quality, such as those available from in-store video cameras, the images may need to be digitally enhanced, and this is often done by an "imaging specialist" who might be either a photographer or an artist. Then the artist can make a drawing from the enhanced image to use as a basis of comparison, or if it's good enough on its own, the enhanced image can be compared on a point-by-point basis to a suspect photo.

In her book, *Forensic Art and Illustration*, Karen T. Taylor, a frequent consultant for these techniques to the *C.S.I.* shows (and whose hands were used on *CSI-NY*), provides guidelines for photo-to-photo comparisons. First, she states, it's important to gather as many photos as possible to assist in the comparison, and second, the imaging specialist must use the best-quality photos available. If the face is at an angle, the specialist will know that the facial shape or some of the features may be distorted. To guard against mistakes in perception, Taylor suggests that the identification process should "consider the base of the nose in relation to the ears." It may also help to turn photos upside down to view the features with greater objectivity. She points out that aging does not go backwards, so if one photo appears younger than the one to which it is being compared, either cosmetic surgery has been performed or it was taken at an earlier time.

In light of a 2003 videotape of terrorist Osama bin Laden walking in the mountains, questions arose as to whether it was an older videotape being passed off as recent to inspire his followers. Some sources said he seemed older than a photo taken of him two years earlier, while others claimed that he appeared younger. The footage was broadcast by Al-Jazeera television, claiming it had been produced only four months earlier. This led to speculation that bin Laden was hiding out in Pakistan. In an audiotape that accompanied the footage, a speaker who sounded like bin Laden honored the September 11 attackers, who brought down the World Trade Center in New York City in 2001 and crippled the Pentagon, and praised the damage done to "the enemy." He also called on Iraqi warriors to "bury" U.S. troops. Thus, the tape appeared to have been made aftor America invaded Iraq in the hope of running bin Laden to the ground and killing him.

In a chilling speech, Ayman al-Zawahri, bin Laden's chief deputy (or someone who sounded like him) warned, "The true epic has not begun." He also mentioned the second anniversary of the "raids" on New York and Washington. That comment indicated that the videotape was made close to the time when it was actually broadcast.

It was incumbent on the United States to learn whether the video had indeed been made recently, since there was every reason to believe that another attack could be in the works for that second anniversary, only days away. Thus, experts had to employ the latest computer methods to help make political decisions for the country's defense. That involved the use of age-progression technology. But in the end, there was no attack.

An important consideration for deciding on a computer program for facial clarification or alteration is the quality of the tools offered for image modification. A program should allow for fluid movement and the adjustment of features in all directions, and for change in coloration and scale. The artist should use a system that incorporates "draw" or "paint" functions, relying on a stylus on a pad to capture subtle nuances in small increments.

People tend to underestimate the difficulty of these processes, including writers for the shows. There is a general misconception that computers can miraculously perform transformations on a photograph from one age to another, or one look to another, but these changes actually result from the skill of an experienced and knowledgeable user. Then there are certain visual decisions to consider, such as with color and angle. If the only available photograph is black and white, it's wiser to work within that scheme than to speculate about color—unless color information is available from verbal descriptions and something like hair color is a distinctive trait. If the face is angled away from the camera, then only certain types of manipulations are possible.

Back to bin Laden. If he's out of sight for a significant period of time, the artist can use typical age-progression programs to help with identification. If it's suspected that he has changed his appearance to better avoid capture, the artist can alter his look in a number of ways. In any event, the alterations are still interpretations and may assist with identification but will not answer significant questions about terrorism.

NEW TYPE OF ART: THE DNAPRINT

A new technology was used in a cold case in Los Angeles in 2005 to learn what a perpetrator may have looked like. On March 9, 1994, Mildred Weiss, eighty-five, was attacked in an elevator, dragged to a laundry room, and left for dead. Rescue workers were unable to save her. There were no leads, aside from a witness report of a black man in white shorts hanging around the area, but investigators took evidence from blood spatter, a pair of white shorts, and a finger sliver rolled into a newspaper—possibly sliced from the killer in the heat of the assault. There was also blood on the victim's wallet. They developed a composite sketch from witness reports, but the murder went unsolved.

Eleven years later, a company in Sarasota, Florida, DNAPrint Genomics, offered a new approach. They had an expensive but ingenious test that could create a genetic sketch of someone from a DNA sample. They could determine what percentage of the person's makeup is from the major continental groups: East Asian, Sub-Sahara African, Native American, or Indo-European. If the police have a list of suspects, the test can compare them to a database of photographs of people who have voluntarily had their DNA screened.

This test assisted in the apprehension in 2003 of the Baton Rouge serial killer in Louisiana. Although most of the witnesses who came forward had given police descriptions of a white man, and investigators were convinced the crime was too messy to have been the work of black man, the test indicated that they were indeed looking for a medium- to light-skinned black man who would be 80 to 85 percent Sub-Sahara African and 15 percent Native American. In short order, regular DNA testing on Derrick Todd Lee in the context of an unrelated crime confirmed via comparison to specimens from the Baton Rouge murders that he was the killer, and the racial components were correct. After his capture, he was convicted of the five murders.

The sample from the Weiss murder indicated that the person they were looking for was a black male, which affirmed witness reports. Although the DNA profile pulled up no hits on databases of convicted felons, the police were able to narrow down the pool of possibilities to a homeless man seen in the area. As of this writing, the case is still unsolved.

The test case for utilizing genomics, according to the company's Website, was a murder in Mammoth Lakes, California. At a campground there, in May 2003, a set of disarticulated skeletal remains was discovered in a shallow grave, hidden for months under snow. The San Francisco medical examiner determined that the remains were of an Asian woman, between thirty and forty years old. A worker in the visitors' center recalled a woman who'd resembled the victim who had visited with a large male who she claimed was abusing her. Investigators looked into that possibility but came up empty.

Then a sheriff's deputy learned about a new technology based in Florida, and the remains were sent to DNAPrint Genomics, which indicated that the victim was Native American. In fact, with the assistance of other scientists, it was determined that she had been a Zapotec Indian from southern Mexico, probably Oaxaca. Other labs analyzed her diet via hair and teeth, placing her inland for a time in Oaxaca, with a period in southern California. That changed the thrust of the investigation. Using a new technique, they did a facial reconstruction over the skull and sketched what the woman may have looked like. It fit the memory of the worker, who'd believed the woman who visited the center was Asian. It seemed likely that she had been the victim of an abusive husband, who'd left her behind. While that did not net the murderer, it did give them an important part of the puzzle, which may one day help to solve the case.

A program, DNAWitness 2.0, can determine the likely genetic heritage from four distinct groups of DNA samples found and preserved from crime scenes, such as the blood and finger left at the Weiss murder. It goes beyond earlier DNA analyses that simply identified a source via matched specimens, requiring something from the suspect to make the match. DNAPrint technology utilizes ancestry information markers (AIM), or single nucleotide polymorphisms (SNP) from the human genome. They are mapped via admixture linkage disequilibrium, which relies on known statistical data about populations. With an update, DNAWitness 2.5, they can now determine the likely eye color, based on tests of thousands of subjects. According to ABC News, Tony Frudakis, head of the lab, calls this method SNIPS, based on SNP technology. Frudakis said in June 2005 that after more than three thousand blind tests there has not been a single error.

In Britain, the Forensic Science Service has also attempted to develop such tests for the "Celtic look" via a program called DNA Photofit, but drawing a direct connection between genes and facial appearance proved to be too complicated to achieve.

One issue that may crop up in this work is racial profiling and civil rights. In police work, minorities may get targeted as suspects as a rule, based on stereotyping, which can create tunnel vision for investigators, who may then fail to see or follow other leads. If this refinement of DNA analysis can yield sufficient information to generate police sketches, investigators will use it in a suspect search. If the technology is as accurate as they say, and if it continues to be improved, that scenario is not far into the future. The current standard of using fifteen DNA markers to make a match, as determined by the National DNA Advisory Board, does not include those markers that reference a suspect's race and ethnicity. They choose to avoid that issue, but some labs are moving forward in these areas and law enforcement sees an opportunity.

While they could not really narrow a sketch down to the actual person's appearance—could not, for example, consider disfiguring accidents after birth or cosmetic surgery—they can utilize the predominant features of a given ethnicity to assist with a general idea of who the suspect might be. At any rate, knowing that a suspect is white rather than black would provide a useful lead. But there is understandable concern that DNA work may attempt to identify future behaviors via genes, such as with sexual predators. But if we can predict from genes the trouble a person might get into, we may really have a problem. What would we then do with them? Scientists must ponder the ethics of their work as well as the technical possibilities.

In the meantime, "genetic witnesses" are being developed, whether we like it or not, and may one day prove to be indispensable to solving a crime. That might deter a few potential offenders.

ENHANCEMENT

In "Stalkerazzi" on *CSI-M*, a photo taken from the camera of a dead paparazzi reveals not just the celebrity scandal he was hoping to sell but also a murder. Yet the photo is blurry, so the lab must find a way to bring the background into sharper relief. They elect to turn the developed analog film into a digital rendition with gray scales, because they can achieve more variations in shading, and that allows for a clearer view on close-up.

More crimes than ever are caught on video surveillance systems, but many suffer from various forms of degradation. These could be from poor camera or film quality, poor transmission signals from the camera, or environmental factors. Poor lighting is among the most common factors, and for outside cameras, poor weather conditions, such as rain or fog.

Software that diagnoses and overcomes these problems can enhance a visual picture or eliminate background noises to better hear what a recording picked up. That way, investigators can filter and stabilize the tainted film to isolate details that might be critical in solving a crime or identifying someone, victim or perpetrator. Most of the programs now work on basic computer systems, for editing, enhancing, and clarifying the content.

Since the number of pixels in an image is finite, magnification can only enlarge the pixels, not make them clearer. The best procedure is to use a camera with good image resolution. The same goes for replacing tapes and keeping equipment clean.

ART FORGERY

Another issue in the specialized world of forensic art is the detection of a forgery. An episode of *CSI-NY*, "Tri-borough," involved the need to determine if a painting was a fraud in order to solve the murder of an art dealer.

Art forgery has been around ever since people have been willing to pay for artistic renderings, especially high-priced ones. Some experts estimate that as much as 15 percent of art sold today may be falsely passing as genuine (and commanding those prices) when it's not. Some renderings are that good.

Along with the art of forgery, methods for detecting it have been developed. Generally, authenticating a work of art is left to an art historian, an expert on a particular artist, or a museum curator. They examine such things as the strokes, pigment, signature, and qualities of the canvas and paint. In recent years, they've also employed X-ray analysis, but there's now another tool that even people unfamiliar with an artist can use: digital analysis.

Similar to the type of forensic analysis often used to examine a writing style, a digital program for forgery detection can classify an artist's works according to that person's unique style. This would help to determine if more than one person worked on the painting, as well as whether there are traits unique to the artist that a forger just cannot duplicate.

The way it works is to scan and compress the art produced by someone like Norwegian artist Edvard Munch, famous for *The Scream* and other works of human emotion, to remove redundancies. These then form a statistical base against which to compare all works by Munch, much like document examinations rely on exemplars for comparison purposes. Then when the authenticity of a work of art is questioned, it can be scanned, compressed, and compared against the statistical model. If there are a sufficient amount of consistencies between the questioned work and the model, it is deemed more likely to be authentic. Too many inconsistencies make it questionable. Generally imitators, while getting the appearance right, cannot achieve the same fluency of stroke that the original artist employed, and thus their work will fail the statistical test.

An experiment with the software program used thirteen drawings, eight of which had been done by Flemish artist Pieter Bruegel the Elder and five of which were imitations. The technology accurately separated them.

Whether the technology is foolproof is still a question in the minds of authenticators. More research and testing must be done before it becomes widely accepted as a way to complement their more painstaking work. However, it's thought to be a contribution to the art of separating imitators during artists' lifetimes from those works done by an artist, as well as those paintings done by more than one person—a practice by prominent artists who used apprentices. Those parts that are statistically similar can be identified and differentiated from those that aren't.

VIRTUAL AUTOPSY

Not everyone who dies gets an autopsy, but for those who do, there may be a procedure for some cases that will eliminate the need for a scalpel. This is good news for people of religious persuasions who don't want an autopsy performed on themselves or their loved ones, and for parents of babies or young children. Horatio Caine faced this on *CSI-M*, in "Money Plane." When parents resisted the autopsy of their daughter, he arranged to fund a Virtopsy.

Virtual imaging can produce a 3-D image without cutting the body open. A combination of CT scans for an overview of the body and magnetic resonance imagining (MRI) can detect many ailments in the organs and muscles. MRIs detect heart failure, for example, and with imaging, pathologists can go right to the problem without having to slice up the rest of the body. Radiologists in Sweden have performed virtual autopsies on numerous crime victims, which has helped to clarify the cause of death. This procedure has not only assisted the trial process but also medical education via unusual cases.

Interpretation requires a radiologist trained in forensic procedure. In some places, the technique is already practiced and will likely spread as its benefits become known, the time it takes is reduced, and its costs decline. It's also easier on juries to see computer images than actual autopsy photographs, and there's no chance of destroying forensic evidence, such as a bullet trajectory path, as there is with an actual autopsy. In addition, the digitized images can easily be stored or sent to other pathologists for consultations. Those who have done both on the same body, to check for quality, have found that the virtual autopsy is as accurate as an actual one.

In addition, there's a new method that may become useful. Phase-contrast X-ray imaging shows promise, because it yields vivid pictures of soft organs. However, in the past it has required a synchrotron, a particle accelerator that is rather large and expensive. A team in Switzerland has created a new way to achieve the same results with a normal X-ray machine, which is a vast improvement. To understand this, let's look at how the method works. Phase-contrast X-rays rely on the ray's trajectory being deflected by various bones and organs and precisely measured to produce images. This team offers an analyzer for refracted X-rays that utilizes a pair of gratings that generate an interference pattern. From this pattern, an image arises. That means that the technique, which involves weaker beams than do many X-rays now in use, can be applied via this device in a clinical setting to help physicians spot tumors and weak arteries. It might also assist with noninvasive autopsies, another boon to forensic investigation. But it's a long way off.

Now let's jump from one of the most recent innovations in forensics—computers—to the oldest of the forensic sciences, toxicology. While computer analysis is used for tox screenings these days, that wasn't always the case. But the most innovative scientists found ways to detect and measure poisons in the body and to present their findings in court.

CHAPTER THREE

Pick Your Poison

In the *CSI-M* episode "Identity," a woman is attacked and crushed to death by a boa constrictor that crawled out of a hotel room. The snake was tracked and found dead, so the pathologist performed an autopsy to determine the cause. It turned out that when the snake crushed the victim, it broke a vial inside its stomach containing drugs. The reptile had been utilized as a "mule" for dope dealers, and to find out what kind of drug was used, they employed toxicology tests. The tox section is standard to any crime lab, since so many victims have drugs or poisons in their system or have been exposed to environmental hazards, and many of the shows involve substance detection. It may occur with an accident victim, such as in "Ashes to Ashes" when the Miami-based team looked for substance ingestion to explain a single-vehicle crash, or with a murder victim, as investigated in "Burked" on *CSI-LV*.

The Insidious Weapon

Toxicology, or the detection of substances in human tissue that can have a noxious effect, was the first science to be utilized in a courtroom. Thanks to the increasing popularity of poison as a murder weapon across many centuries, forensic toxicology has acquired a fascinating history. Examples of poisons that have been commonly used to kill include aconitine, atropine, strychnine, thallium, antimony, arsenic, and cyanide.

Jane Toppan seemed to be a sensitive woman who was indispensable to well-to-do families in Boston, Massachusetts, during the 1890s. She ingratiated herself as an "angel of mercy," got hired as a private nurse, and went to work on her own secret passion—watching people die. Caught in 1901 after four members of the Alden Davis family had died in quick succession, Toppan was exposed. An autopsy indicated lethal doses of morphine and atropine in one of the victims. Investigators looked into Toppan's past, discovering a history of mental instability in her family and a long list of patients who had died. She admitted to her attorney that she had killed thirty-one people, though writers who repeat the 1938 *New York Times* report of her dark legacy have quoted a victim count up as high as one hundred. Her MO was to drug people with lethal doses, crawl into bed with them, and hold them as they expired. Reportedly, this gave her an erotic thrill.

Toxicology analysis covers not only poisons but also other foreign substances in the body, such as alcohol, industrial chemicals, poisonous gas, illegal drugs, or drug overdoses. Sometimes a procedure involves analyzing a blood, hair, or urine sample; other times it requires a full autopsy in which tissue samples are removed from various organs. A living person may be tested for a suspected substance with a basic kit, such as a breathalyzer for detecting alcohol levels, and if that registers a positive result or if symptoms show something different, a more sophisticated analysis may be required. When it's not, that can cause problems, as it did in the following case.

Richard Alfredo, sixty-one, died in 1990 after eating Jell-O. The manner of his death was recorded as a heart attack until suspicious activities spotlighted his live-in companion, Christina Martin, and her daughter. The body was exhumed and tested with Radio Immunoassay (RIA), in which the samples were liquefied and radio waves were sent through them to detect quantities of proteins. It was a test used for screening: if something turned up, more sophisticated tests would be ordered. But in this case, only the RIA was used. The analysts claim to have found massive amounts of LSD in Alfredo's system and Martin was convicted of overdosing Alfredo on LSD injected into the Jell-O. On appeal a forensic toxicologist criticized the initial analysis and insisted that no one had ever been killed with LSD. Indeed, embalming fluid could give off the same postmortem readings, and a better test did not find LSD. In addition, Alfredo had a history of heart disease. The first-degree murder conviction was overturned. But Martin pleaded to manslaughter, avoiding another trial, and was sentenced to time already served. So while the manner of death remains unclear, the use of a basic screening test for a toxic substance in a murder case was proven inadequate.

Almost any natural substance in the right dose can be a poison, and many poisons mimic common diseases, so some physicians quickly conclude that a victim died of natural causes. Toxicology is important not just for an investigation in which foul play is suspected. It is equally essential for the determination of accidental deaths and suicides—and even for substance abuse while on the job.

Currently the American Chemistry Society indicates that there are around twenty-one million registered compounds. But there are lab screening tests for only several thousand. Some people realize that, so they try using poisons that would not be commonly recognized. But that doesn't mean they won't get caught.

In 1993, Maurice Glenn Turner, a police officer in Cobb County, Georgia, named Julia Lynn Womack the beneficiary on his life insurance policies and retirement account. Three months later, she became Mrs. Glenn Turner, but within the year, she started an affair with Randy Thompson, apparently leading him to believe that she was divorced.

On March 2, 1995, Glenn Turner went to the emergency room for extreme flulike symptoms. He was treated there and went home. The next day, he was dead. No one could understand how an apparently healthy young man had just suddenly collapsed. The attending medical examiner, Dr. Brian Frist, decided that he'd died from a complication related to an enlarged heart. Julia Lynn Turner collected $153,000 in death benefits.

Within days, she leased an apartment for herself and Randy Thompson, a sheriff's deputy for Forsyth County. By the end of 1995, Thompson had started proceedings to designate Turner as his insurance beneficiary. A year later, they had a daughter, and in 1998, a son. Thompson doubled his insurance coverage to $200,000.

The relationship hit the rocks and Thompson moved out but continued to see Turner, who was deep in debt from her spending. One evening early in 2001, after he had dinner with her, Thompson reported to the emergency room with a stomachache and constant vomiting. He was treated and released. Turner made him some Jell-O. By the next day, he was dead. The cause of death was listed as an irregular heartbeat, due to clogged arteries. Turner received $36,000.

But the family of Glenn Turner knew that something was wrong. Glenn's mother saw the newspaper articles about Thompson and sent a letter to Randy's mother to discuss the similarities. They contacted Dr. Mark Koponen, deputy chief medical examiner of the Georgia Bureau of Investigation. He looked over the reports. Noticing calcium oxylate crystals in Thompson's kidneys during the autopsy, Koponen, who had seen this symptom before, sent blood and urine samples to the crime lab. Yet toxicologist Chris Tilson found nothing amiss. Koponen then sent samples to National Medical Services (NMS), an independent testing lab in Pennsylvania.

Their results proved that Randy Thompson had high levels of ethylene glycol, the principle component of antifreeze, in his tissues and blood. Ingested, it produces slurred speech and a tipsy sensation before causing severe headaches, nausea, delusions, dizziness, and a feeling of breathlessness. Death occurs from kidney failure or heart attack. That substance would not naturally be found in the human body, which meant that Thompson had been exposed to it in large doses. His cause of death was changed to antifreeze poisoning. He was exhumed for reexamination, and the results were confirmed. A re-autopsy on Glenn Turner, run by NMS, was the same.

These deaths were the only two in Georgia ever attributed to antifreeze ingestion. Julia Lynn Turner was charged with the murder of Glenn Turner. Between plenty of circumstantial evidence and the autopsy findings, along with facts about Thompson's death that offered a "criminal signature" linking the two, the defendant was in trouble.

Her attorney insisted that the readings were the result of embalming, but chemists at the companies that had supplied embalming fluids to the funeral home that embalmed Turner said their companies did not use substances containing ethylene glycol.

Cobb County medical examiner Brian Frist, who had ordered Turner to be exhumed, described experiments he performed in which he put antifreeze into various food substances such as Jell-O and Gatorade. In his opinion, the antifreeze could have been introduced without changing the texture, behavior, or color of the food, so the victim could have consumed it without suspicion.

On the evening of May 14, 2004, after five hours of deliberation, the jury found Turner, thirty-five, guilty of "malice murder" in the death of her husband, Glenn Turner. She received a life sentence. In October, she was indicted for the murder of Randy Thompson, and as of this writing that case outcome is pending.

GETTING INTO COURT

The documented history of poisons started around 2500 B.C. with the Sumerians, who worshipped a goddess of poisons. The Egyptians understood the uses of venom, and the Hebrews had poisoned arrows for warfare. In India, around five hundred years before Christ, physicians had written directions for the detection via personality traits of poisoners, while the physician Nicander of Colophon compiled the earliest known list of poison remedies.

The concept of poisoning is related to the Greek word *toxicon*, which referred to poisoned arrows, and it is the root of "intoxicated," which to the Greeks, meant being sickened by poisoned arrows.

In the eighth century, an Arab chemist turned arsenic into an odorless, tasteless powder that was impossible to trace in the body until centuries later, enhancing its use as an undetectable murder weapon, especially among those standing to inherit from aging relatives. It was used for centuries thereafter.

During the Renaissance, poisoning became an art form, inspiring subtle ways to dispense with people via such items as poison rings, swords, knives, letters, and even lipstick. Poisoning societies developed, as did family businesses that relied on poison-for-hire as their trade. Notorious poisoners came out of Italy and France at this time.

The history of toxicological analysis for investigative purposes goes back about two hundred years. The first person to suggest a chemical method for the detection of poisons was Dr. Hermann Boerhaave. It consisted of placing substances suspected of containing poison on red-hot coals and then testing the odors. He focused on arsenic, since it was the most common poison during that era.

One such case that went to trial in England in 1751 illustrated some odd methods for making a forensic examination, and was the first murder trial to actually feature toxicological testimony from medical experts. Mary Blandy had agreed to marry Captain William Cranstoun, a man of supposed wealth and position, but he already had a wife. He also did not have any money, so Mary's father asked him to leave. Instead, Cranstoun persuaded Mary to put a white powder into her father's food. She was in love, so she did as he asked.

Arsenic is absorbed from the bowel into the bloodstream and organs. The liver, which takes up toxins, gets the brunt of its effect, but when delivered in one large dose, quickly hits the brain, causing damage there and in the spinal cord. When delivered to someone in small doses over a period of time, the poison affects the peripheral nerves, stripping their insulating sheaths and causing damage. The person will feel a prickly heat and the skin may blister. Next come severe headaches, nausea, numbness, and general weakness.

Mr. Blandy grew ill with gastric distress, so his servant examined the food. She found the white powder and showed it to an apothecary. He wasn't sure, but the servant told Blandy of her suspicion that Mary was poisoning him. Mary tried to destroy the powder by throwing it into a fire, but the servant rescued it. Despite the warning, Blandy allowed his daughter to continue to feed him, and he soon died.

Cranstoun fled, but Mary was arrested. At her trial, four doctors who had observed Blandy's internal organs at autopsy stated in court that the "preserved quality" of these remains suggested arsenic poisoning. One doctor had applied a hot iron to the powder that the servant had rescued and analyzed it by smell. It was most likely the servant's testimony that convinced the jury, and Mary was convicted and hanged, but the medical testimony set a precedent.

One of the most important events in the history of forensic toxicology was the discovery of the "arsenic mirror" as a method for detecting the poison. In 1787, Johann Daniel Metzger discovered that when arsenious oxide was heated with charcoal, it formed a black mirrorlike deposit on a cold plate held over the coals. That substance was arsenic. Then in 1806, Valentine Rose showed how to detect arsenic in human organs. He used nitric acid, potassium carbonate, and lime, evaporating that mixture into powder and treating it with coals to get the mirror substance.

Around the same time, in 1813, Mathieu Joseph Bonaventure Orfila published *Treatise of General Toxicology*, a classification of the known poisons and a treatise on the unreliability of the tests. Assuming that toxicology could become a real science, he refined Rose's method for improved accuracy. With animal testing, he also proved that after ingestion, arsenic gets distributed throughout the body. His work won him a position at Paris University, where he was invited to consult on criminal cases. Orfila was further assisted by the work of the next prominent scientist James Marsh.

In the 1830s, Marsh analyzed the coffee of a supposed victim of poisoning, but was unable to clarify for a jury how he had detected the arsenic, so he decided to make his methods more demonstrative. In a closed bottle, he treated suspected poisoned material with sulphuric acid and zinc. From this bottle emerged a narrow U-shaped glass tube, with one end tapered, through which arsine gas emerged to hit zinc and escaped. The escaping gas could be ignited to make it form the expected black mirror substance. The Marsh Test, as it was called, was sufficiently exact to test minute amounts of arsenic and sufficiently vivid to make a jury better grasp it.

And there was one more significant forensic contribution: Orfila used the Marsh Test to analyze cemetery soil so that exhumed bodies that had absorbed arsenic in the grave would not help to falsely convict anyone. It turned out that cemetery soil quite often did contain levels of arsenic, which made defense attorneys happy: They now had a tool to combat potential convictions.

The case that established the "science of poisons" in the courtroom was the prosecution in France in 1840 of Marie LaFarge for the murder of her husband, Charles. He managed a rat-infested forge, and she had purchased a large amount of arsenic, allegedly to exterminate the vermin. When her husband became violently ill, servants claimed that Marie had stirred white powder into his food. A local pharmacist tested the food and found arsenic. The circumstances were clearly against her.

However, the experts could not determine with the Marsh Test that the contents of LaFarge's stomach contained arsenic, so they requested that the body be exhumed to test the organ tissues. That was done, and still the tests were negative. The experts were stumped, so Mathieu Orfila was invited into the case. He performed the same test, proving that it was not the method but its practitioners that were at fault. He detected the presence of arsenic in LaFarge's body and proved it had not originated in the soil surrounding the coffin. Marie was convicted.

Doctors and pathologists were thus the first forensic scientists, and certain procedures were formalized in terms of what must be proven in court for a conviction based on poisoning. Arsenic is still used, but often it's subtle, as in the chronic arsenic poisoning in *CSI-*

LV's "Crow's Feet" of victims of a fraudulent spa practice in helping women to look younger.

THE TOX COLLECTOR

John H. Trestrail III, an expert on poisons, knows this history well. He writes poetry about poison, collects ancient manuscripts on the subject, grabs vacation time to seek out Orfila's grave, and is the go-to guy for many crime programs, including *C.S.I.* His office contains such items as poisoned darts, pickled snakes, and exotic concoctions meant to dispatch someone, but unlike many of those he studies, he uses his gifts for good. He's the managing director of the DeVos Children's Hospital Regional Poison Center, responsible for answering questions about poisonings across the state of Michigan. Yet his real occupation—or preoccupation—is the passion he has for poison.

He's collected as many stories as he could find about the world's poisoners, and his database now numbers over one thousand cases, with new ones reported to him daily. In 2000, he published *Criminal Poisoning*, a guide for law enforcement, attorneys, and anyone else interested in the subject of how people throughout history have used poison to commit murder. Trestrail also discusses how poisons kill, along with the characteristics of the poisons that criminals view as the ideal weapon. In addition, he offers a list of misconceptions people have about poisoners and describes the classical symptoms of a poisoning. As a result of his expertise, for many years he often lectured at the FBI's National Academy at Quantico.

It all began when he was a boy. After purchasing a snake head from a museum shop, he started doing research. Unlike the way most kids explore a passing interest and then move on, his passion never diminished. As he grew up, he wanted to do a bit of cultural anthropology—or, rather, to become the Indiana Jones of toxicology. He wished to go into the field to hear about poison substances straight from the mouths of medicine men. He did enter the Peace Corps, learning what he could in the Philippines, and he even spent his honeymoon at a conference on poison control. (His wife's still with him.) It's likely that no one in the world is as obsessed with this subject as he is.

Trestrail understands that he's considered eccentric, but few people have the satisfaction of making their passion their life's work—and also developing an expertise that assists victims around the world. As a result, he's traveled widely to speak at conventions and hospitals about toxic substances, and along the way he's collected a wide array of samples: toxic mushrooms, voodoo necklaces, spiders, and poisoned arrowheads. Yet he's most interested in crystallizing the psychological traits of those murderers who make poison their weapon of choice. An obvious question to Trestrail, then, is just how one traces the use of a poison in a murder case.

"It all begins," he says, "with the proof that the poisonous substance is in the victim. The victim tends to be the center of the evidence. A pathologist who's doing an autopsy with a toxicology screen may say, 'We've identified substance X and that shouldn't be in the normal individual in that amount.' So then, the question becomes, 'Let's try to explain how substance X is in this individual.' Now, it could be there by accident; or it could be there by intentional ingestion, as in a suicide; it could also be from the environment; or it could be related to the food chain. You have to rule out all of those possible causes, and when you've done that, if it's not accidental or intentional by the person, you can say that someone else gave it to them. That becomes a homicidal poisoning."

The next step is a victimology, which means learning everything that can be discovered about the victim, especially in the days and hours before death. "You want to see who would have something to gain by this individual's death. Then you take the substance and ask, of those who would have something to gain, who would have access to that substance? And you begin to put these pieces together. It's difficult to investigate, because it's all invisible. When I teach homicide detectives, I say, 'What does a negative screen mean? It does not mean there's no poison. It means they can't find what they're looking for, but maybe the substance is something that they didn't look for.' If I turned to the dark side and became a sophisticated poisoner, I'd go for something they don't look for."

Among the cases that most fascinate Trestrail is that of a physician and patent salesman who was executed. In 1910 in London, Hawley Harvey Crippen was said to have killed his wife, Cora, in part to escape her domineering, alcoholic ways and in part because he was in love with his young secretary, Ethel Le Neve. One night, so the story goes, he poisoned Cora, dismembered her, and buried some of her parts in his cellar. Ethel began to live with him and even to wear Cora's jewelry, while Crippen told friends that Cora had died while visiting friends in America. Questioned by an investigator from Scotland Yard, Crippen said that the embarrassing truth was the Cora had run off to be with a lover. Under a pseudonym, Crippen then boarded a ship, with Ethel disguised as a boy, to head for Quebec, which raised the inspector's suspicions. He returned to Crippen's house to do a thorough search. Cora's dismembered and decomposing torso, *sans* some organs, bones, and the genitals, was found buried in the coal cellar. It was determined that she had a lethal dose of hydrobromide of hyoscine in her system. In a first for radio technology, a telegram was sent to the ship regarding the fugitives and Crippen was caught as he arrived in Canada. He was returned to England, where he was tried. A chemist testified that he had sold the fatal drug to Crippen five days before Cora disappeared. The jury took twenty-seven minutes to convict him and he was hanged. (Ethel Le Neve was acquitted of any involvement and she sold her story to the press.)

Trestrail believes that this case may have involved a miscarriage of justice. "What brings me back to this case over and over again," he says, "is the dismemberment, because it goes against the intent of the poisoner, which is to take down a victim in order to reach a goal, such as love or money. The removal of the victim allows access to the goal. That's the motive. As a poisoner, I would want the elimination to appear natural, because I want a 'natural death' certificate issued so I can walk away with my goal, and no one's the wiser. In Crippen's home the remains of a body were found that had been dismembered. The court proved to the jury beyond a reasonable doubt that those were the remains of his missing wife, and he was hanged. Yet there are things about the case that indicate that something's wrong. For one thing, I have speculated after pondering it for years that if that was in fact his wife, he never intended to kill her. I believe it was an accident and he panicked. He hadn't thought it out. If that's so, then it was manslaughter, which is not a hanging offense. Dismemberment doesn't go with a premeditated murder. If you've thought a murder through, you're going to think it through to the conclusion. I believe he should not have been hanged."

Trestrail is looking into identifying the remains via mitochondrial DNA analysis and possibly reopening the case. Along these lines, he's interested in the mind of a murderer who decides on poison as a weapon.

"We're going to use a version of the Psychopathy Checklist that we can apply to written documents to look at the cases in my database. We have newspaper accounts, books, and things like that, and we hope to find statistically significant evidence of this personality disorder among poisoners. I believe that there are commonalities in the persona of male poisoners and female poisoners. I have speculations and I want to be able to prove or disprove them. I also want to contribute something of value to homicide investigators and attorneys. After we analyze the database, we'd then interview convicted imprisoned poisoners."

Has he found that there is a difference between male and female poisoners? "If you look at the male poisoners," Trestrail explains, "they're effeminate in the way they deal with confrontation. For women, that's their style. It's more natural to them. As a gender, in general, they're not confrontational. They also have the opportunity to use poison because they provide the food and take care of the sick. They can put stuff on the food chain to do the job. The psychology of male poisoners is that they're not physical kind of guys."

Presumably, then, if personality traits can be scientifically isolated in poisoners, then along with a victim's symptoms and toxicology screenings, it may be possible to make a stronger case for specific investigative routes, probable cause for a search, and prosecution.

REFINEMENTS

Detecting metal-based poisons was only one concern for toxicology during its history. Once that was accomplished, these professionals had to make their readings more precise. In addition, they had to look for other types of toxins as well. As killers learned that arsenic was so easily detected and prosecuted, they turned to other substances to achieve their goals. It wasn't difficult to find them, and for scientists that meant new tests had to be developed for law enforcement. So let's look first at the quantification issue.

Just because arsenic could be found did not necessarily point to murder. Since there were other sources for a person's exposure, toxicologists were pressured by defense attorneys to prove that the substance existed in a body in sufficient amounts to say definitively that someone had deliberately poisoned the victim. In a British murder case in 1911, Dr. William Willcox developed the first method for measuring the amount of arsenic used to poison someone. In the incident, Frederick Henry Seddon was arrested for killing Elizabeth Bar-row, and Willcox ran hundreds of weight tests for arsenic. He developed a method to figure out how much arsenic was in each of the poisoned woman's internal organs by calculating the amount via body weight in milligrams. His method was refined over the years to detect the presence of arsenic down to the microgram in soil and bodies. But arsenic was not the only poison to turn up in murder cases, so other substance detection methods became necessary as well.

Another major story in the history of forensic toxicology was the development of methods during the nineteenth century for detecting the presence of vegetable alkaloids, such as caffeine, quinine, morphine, strychnine, atropine, and opium. These poisons affect the victim's central nervous system. Plant alkaloids leave no demonstrable traces in the human body, thus requiring relatively complicated methods of extraction during the early days before an analysis could be performed. The Miami team can be grateful for the development of these detection tests, as they were able to prove that a victim had been poisoned with nicotine in "Breathless."

In a murder trial in 1850, the male victim showed clear chemical burns in his mouth, tongue, and throat. Toxicologist Jean Servois Stas searched for three months for the agent and managed to isolate nicotine from the body tissues. Using ether as a solvent, which he evaporated to isolate the drug, he found the potent substance. The man's killer had extracted it from tobacco and force-fed it to the victim. Stas was the first person to develop a method to extract the material containing the plant alkaloids from the organic material of the human body.

Madame de Pauw had fallen ill and quickly died. Her alleged murderer was Couty de la Pommerais, her lover. De la Pommerais was in financial trouble and de Pauw had a large life insurance policy. An anonymous note alerted the police to foul play.

The forensic pathologist, Professor Ambroise Tardieu, suspected
from the victim's symptoms—especially her racing heart—that de la Pommerais had used the drug digitalin. To demonstrate its presence in de
Pauw's body, Tardieu injected several frogs with the extract he had obtained using the Stas method, as well as with a standard solution of digitalin. The reactions were exactly the same, proving that the drug was
present, and on June 9, 1864, de la Pommerais was convicted of murder.

Yet it soon became clear to some scientists that there was a problem
with these tests: At times, an alkaloid might develop in the body after
death that mimicked the reactions of the qualitative color tests for the
vegetable alkaloids and produce false positives. These substances are
known as "cadaveric alkaloids." In order for the toxicologists to be
certain they were identifying a poison correctly, they needed a
method that was specific only to that vegetable alkaloid.

Toxicologists soon realized the need to look for new methods of
demonstrating the presence of alkaloids. Dr. William Willcox was the
first to propagate the idea of using the melting point and crystalliza-
tion patterns of the alkaloid as an identifier. However, even this
method had its problems, as some alkaloids had similar melting
points. More and better tests were developed, and by 1955, there
were thirty tests for morphine alone.

A significant concern for modern toxicologists was the production of synthetic alkaloids, developed with the growth of pharmaceu-
tical chemistry, which required entirely new methods of separation
and identification. One scientist proposed the use of column, or paper, chromatography as a means of separation based on molecular
size or polarity. It makes colorless alkaloids visible and easily separated onto filter paper.

This was a good thing, because with industrialization, poisons of all types were becoming available to millions in the form of cleansers, medicines, and pesticides, with endless variations. People could use ordinary house cleaners to poison someone, so toxicologists had to keep up with tests that could detect any and all of them.

CONTEMPORARY ANALYSIS

For both alcohol and drugs, the analysis these days will involve spectrometry and some form of chromatography. Toxicologists dissolve tissues for analysis in an acidic or alkaline solution and then use high-pressure liquid or gas chromatography with the mass spectrometer (LC/MS, GC/MS). Most things encountered at a crime scene are complex mixtures and this method can separate them into their purest components.

A small amount of the suspect substance or unknown material is dissolved in a solvent and then injected by needle into a hollow tube. A flow of inert gas (helium or nitrogen) propels the heated mixture through the coiled glass tube, where a highly sensitive, computerized detector identifies the separate elements at the other end. Since each element moves at its own speed, as it crosses the "finish" line it can be identified. The amount of pure substance in the mixture is measured as well, producing a chart that offers a composite profile (via travel time measured). Comparison—or control—substances are also put through the GC/MS. This helps to identify suspicious substances, such as an accelerant on a piece of charred wood. GC can be used to identify many things, from poisons to drugs to explosives, and even blood alcohol evaluations.

The mass spectrometer bombards the sample with electrons produced by a heated cathode, breaking it into electrically charged fragments. These fragments pass through the spectrometer, accelerated by an electric field. A magnetic field deflects them onto a circular path, the radius of which varies according to the mass of the fragment. As the magnetic field is increased, a detector linked to a computer records the energy spectrums. The position of each fragment on the spectrum measures its mass, and its intensity indicates its proportion in the sample. This comes through as a printed readout. In other words, no matter how the samples are divided according to molecular weight, the spectrometer can identify the smallest traces of individual chemicals. Thin-layer chromatography is also used, where a sample is placed in a vertical gel film and subjected to a liquid solvent that identifies its constituent parts.

The four basic types of situations that require toxicological analysis are when:

- the cause of death is known but drug findings are needed to clarify the circumstances

- drugs or poison are the suspected cause of death

- negative results permit the pathologist to rule out drugs or poison and concentrate on disease

- the unexplained death of someone with no obvious trauma and no medical history or trouble.

Sometimes a toxic substance poses a risk to the investigating professionals, such as appeared to have occurred in the following case. On February 19, 1994, thirty-one-year-old Gloria Ramirez was taken to the emergency room of Riverside General Hospital in California. She passed out there. A nurse took a blood sample, and in moments, she fainted. Dr. Julie Gorchynski, assisting her, smelled ammonia and looked at the syringe. The blood appeared to contain strange crystals. Then *she* fainted and experienced convulsions. Another doctor also saw the white crystals. Other medical personnel were vomiting or passing out, so the ER was evacuated. In all, six people had severe reactions, a few more had slight reactions, yet two others in the ER and the paramedics from the ambulance had been unaffected.

Ramirez died and an autopsy was performed, rather carefully, by people in decontamination suits. (The odor also came from the body bag that encased her.) They performed a number of toxicology screenings but came up empty. Ramirez had experienced kidney failure and a urinary blockage due to cancer of the cervix, diagnosed six weeks earlier, but this condition failed to explain the effects on the ER staff. The county decontamination unit came in, but there seemed to be nothing amiss in the building or the air. Tests they performed came back negative. Yet Dr. Gorchynski came down with hepatitis and other medical conditions that put her in the hospital for two weeks and resulted in a rare bone disorder. Officials were stymied.

Several explanations have been offered through the years, including organophosphates used in nerve gas and pesticides, mass hysteria among the staff, and the possibility that the hospital harbored a secret methamphetamine lab and someone had inadvertently grabbed an IV bag that contained meth crystals.

A team of scientists at the Forensic Science Center at Livermore National Laboratory believed that a chemical found in Ramirez's blood, dimethyl sulfone, was responsible. It was likely from a home remedy for cancer, but may have built up sufficiently to convert to dimethyl sulfate, a poison gas used in warfare that produces many of the symptoms suffered by those who were near Ramirez. However, they could not figure out what had caused the actual conversion process. And the gas itself evaporates, so it could not be detected later. Yet the victim's family insisted that she had taken no home remedies.

Not everyone accepted dimethyl sulfone as the causal agent since it couldn't be proven, so a satisfactory medical description of what actually occurred has not yet been offered. Other such cases have been reported, including the illness of staff members at another hospital who treated some of the affected workers from the incident. And in Bakersfield, California, a week after the incident, in an unrelated facility, a woman struggling to breathe emitted gaseous fumes after a breathing tube was inserted. Many of the attending health-care workers experienced burning eyes and nausea.

But many cases do get explained, thanks to sophisticated techniques. With the right analytical methods, hair samples can help to trace the history of a poisoning. In a *CSI-LV* episode, strands of a dead woman's hair offered a way to map her use of drugs, and this analysis also detected other substances in her system. The technicians managed to pinpoint within days how close to her death she had suffered a traumatic event that had resulted in a stronger antidepressant, which implied the possibility that she had committed suicide. In an actual case, investigators were able to track and document a murder.

Robert Curley, thirty-two, grew ill in August 1991 and soon died in a hospital in Wilkes-Barre, Pennsylvania. His symptoms had included burning skin, numbness, weakness, repeated vomiting, and rapid hair loss, and heavy metal tests showed that he'd had elevated levels of thallium in his system—once a common ingredient in rat poison. But there was no thallium at his work site, and only a trace of it in the thermos he carried to work. His widow, Joann, was a good suspect, but there was no evidence against her.

Dr. Frederic Rieders of the National Medical Services was hired to test samples from Curley's exhumed body. He focused on the hair shafts, conducting a segmental analysis on the hair shafts to devise a timeline of thallium exposure. The strands from Curley's head were sufficiently long to "read" more than three hundred days of his life prior to his death. Thallium levels were recorded in the hair shafts at different times using atomic absorption spectrophotometry: a chemical was used to break down each segment of hair into individual atoms and then the specimens were stimulated to the point where they absorbed energy, which allowed the measurement of thallium.

Concentrations were found in the hair over the course of nine months, with spikes and drops that suggested a systematic ingestion. There was also a massive spike just a few days before his death, which suggested intentional poisoning.

This timeline was compared to events in Curley's life: When he was away from home or in the hospital, his thallium levels dropped—except for the few days prior to his death. At that time, his wife had brought food and was alone with him. Under pressure from these discoveries, Joann Curley confessed to murdering her husband with rat poison in order to enrich herself on life insurance. She received a sentence of ten to twenty years in prison.

This was a good case in which an individual's exposure could be accurately measured, but sometimes, even when the toxin and its origin are known, the killer cannot be found.

POTENTIAL FOR HARM

In "Last Laugh" on *CSI-LV*, two water bottles were found to be tainted with a substance that resulted in death. Among the most worrisome situations in toxicology is the anonymous person who attempts to poison a supply of food, medicine, or water—in other words, the terrorist who uses lethal substances to hold communities hostage. In the United States, the first such case involved product tampering.

In the Chicago area in 1982, people suddenly began to die in a mysterious manner. There were seven victims in all, and one of them had lingered in agony for two days before finally succumbing. The police eventually discovered a frightening connection: the victims had all purchased bottles of Extra-Strength Tylenol and had consumed capsules that had been laced with cyanide. Apparently a sociopath had opened the Tylenol capsules and inserted the substance.

Tylenol's manufacturer, Johnson & Johnson, immediately recalled all packages of their product around the country, at great cost to them. U.S. residents witnessed a form of terrorism—someone, somewhere, could contaminate almost anything they bought and innocently consumed and they could die. People wanted this perpetrator found. Yet the underlying concern was that even if the incident was successfully investigated, a new idea for such crimes had been introduced, and others would copy it.

The problem was the random nature of the product tampering. No specific person or store had been targeted, and there appeared to be no motive. No one was using it to blackmail a company into paying a ransom. It was a crime involving psychological distance, which made it difficult to even generate leads.

Despite all efforts, the identity of the Tylenol Killer was never revealed. To this day he (or she) remains unidentified. Yet as suddenly as they had begun, the cyanide poisonings stopped (though other cases of product tampering occurred in other places). This case changed forever the manner in which over-the-counter drugs were sold in this country. Now we have tamper-proof seals and warnings of all kinds not to take drugs in which the seals have been broken.

Since toxicology was the first science to get into court, let's look more closely at the judicial procedures that affect the way evidence must be identified, gathered, and handled. The C.S.I.s have to keep these guidelines and rules in mind at all times, or they risk having a case thrown out or conviction overturned.

CHAPTER FOUR

Nothing but the Truth

A crime is an act forbidden by law, and criminal laws control the behavior of people who live in the countries that make them. Principally, laws exist to protect people, but perpetrators have rights as well and in the United States, they are not guilty until proven so. Legal protocol in arrest procedures and evidence handling is qualified by those rights, so evidence handlers must be aware of behaviors to avoid when investigating crimes.

In several *C.S.I.* stories, members of the team have testified in court and have bumped up against admissibility issues. For example, in "Compulsion," an episode of *CSI-LV*, a detective used a voice stress analyzer (VSA) to get a confession from a boy about killing his brother. Nick protested that it would not be allowed in court, but when evidence supported the boy's story, it no longer mattered (unless he were to recant). Yet such procedures raise the issue of how investigators may use devices like the VSA, when the evidence found with it may be barred or dismissed. What is the difference between actual science and pseudoscience, and when does the court accept it? These are the issues that forensic scientists and technicians grapple with on a daily basis. When procedure deviates, or when mistakes are made, evidence is faked, or professionals misrepresent themselves, it can have a deleterious effect on what happens in court.

CRIMINAL PROCEDURES

A barking dog in Brentwood, California, alerted a neighbor on the evening of June 12, 1994, to something amiss. The neighbor followed the dog back to a condominium, saw the horrendous bloodshed, and urged his wife to phone 911. Police arrived and found Nicole Brown Simpson, former wife of former football celebrity O. J. Simpson, lying on her side in a pool of blood just inside the front gate of her home. Nearby was the blood-covered body of Ronald Goldman, twenty-five.

The police went to Simpson's home to talk with him and noted a bloodstain on the door of his white Ford Bronco, parked in the driveway. A trail of blood also led up to the house, but Simpson was not there. He had just flown to Chicago.

When contacted, he returned to Los Angeles and agreed to answer questions. Investigators then noticed a cut on a finger of his left hand, and he told several conflicting stories about how he had gotten it. In addition, more evidence made him into the best, then only, suspect.

Several droplets of blood at the scene failed to show a match with either of the victim's blood types. Then Simpson's blood was drawn for testing, and comparison between his DNA and that of the blood from the crime scene was a match. The tests indicated that only one person in 57 billion could produce an equivalent match. In addition, the blood was found near footprints made by a rare and expensive type of shoe—footwear that O. J. wore and that proved to be his size.

Next to the bodies was a bloodstained black leather glove, which bore traces of fiber from Goldman's jeans. The glove's mate, stained with Simpson's blood, was found on his property. There were also traces of the blood of both victims lifted from inside Simpson's car and house, along with blood that contained his DNA. In fact, his blood and Goldman's were found together on the car's console.

Then other evidence emerged, such as the testimony of the limousine driver who came to pick Simpson up for the ride to the airport: He saw a black man cross the driveway and go into the house. Then Simpson claimed that the driver had been unable to get him on the intercom because he had "overslept." There were also photos of Nicole and diary entries that attested to Simpson's abusive and stalking behavior. In addition, when Simpson was notified that he would be arrested for murder, he fled with his friend Al Cowlings, and hinted in a note that he might kill himself. With him were a passport, fake beard, and thousands of dollars in cash. Nevertheless, he pled not guilty and hired a team of celebrity lawyers.

Three different crime labs performed the analysis. All three determined that the DNA in the drops of blood at the scene matched Simpson's. It was a one in 170 million match, using one type of analysis known as restricted fragment length polymorphism (RFLP), and a one in 240 million match using the polymerase chain reaction (PCR) test.

Nevertheless, noted criminalist Dr. Henry Lee testified that there appeared to be something wrong with the way the blood was packaged, leading the defense to propose that the multiple samples had been switched. They also claimed that the blood had been severely degraded by being stored in a lab truck, but the prosecution's DNA expert, Harlan Levy, said that the degradation would not have been sufficient to prevent accurate DNA analysis. He also pointed out that control samples were used that would have shown any such contamination, but Barry Scheck suggested that the control samples had been mishandled by *all* of the labs. Defense attorneys then intimated that Detective Mark Fuhrman, who had gone to O. J.'s home the night of the murder, was a racist who had planted evidence.

Deliberating less than four hours, the jury freed Simpson with a "not guilty" verdict.

How do we get from crime to conviction?

When a crime has been committed and a suspect identified, there's an arrest. That involves booking, fingerprinting, taking a mug shot, doing a criminal records check, and in some contexts, collecting samples for blood and DNA analysis. The person is advised of his or her rights to remain silent and engage an attorney (which they may or may not waive), placed in a holding cell, and allowed to call someone, which is usually an attorney. If the right to an attorney is waived, there may be an interrogation and search of the person. In some places, there are several additional steps, such as two separate arraignments. At some point, the suspect enters a plea, and in this case, Simpson declared that he was not guilty of the crime of which he was accused.

Certain types of homicide are capital crimes, meaning they could be punished with a death sentence. But the definition can differ from one jurisdiction to another. In over twenty states that have death penalty statutes, if a crime is considered particularly "heinous," "vile," "depraved" or "atrocious," the defendant can be considered for execution. Yet Manhattan-based psychiatrist Michael Welner contends that there is no guidance for juries to determine just what these terms really mean. When it comes to "aggravating factors" in certain acts, there is no clear standard by which to define them. That encourages juries to make emotion-based judgments, which may precipitate unfair sentences.

From his experience consulting for both prosecutors and defense attorneys, Welner has seen the terms haphazardly handled. To correct this situation, he devised the "Depravity Scale," which involves a standardized set of criteria, based on facts and evidence. He examined over one hundred court cases in which findings of "depraved" or "heinous" were upheld or reversed, culling an inventory of examples of actions and attitudes that were regularly upheld as examples of evil in crimes. This initial research yielded the first items for closer study to potentially comprise the scale.

With emphasis on the capacity of the offender to make a deliberate choice, he asks professionals to rate these factors in terms of degree of depravity, such as whether it's depraved to intend emotional trauma or physical disfigurement, or to carry on a prolonged attack. He then controls for variables such as religious persuasion, geographical location, and experience with the court. With enough participants, he believes he will achieve a validated scale that reflects a consensus about typically vague terms. In that way, he hopes to scientifically establish standards that courts nationwide can all utilize.

But that's for the most extreme crimes. Many others are of much lesser degree, with sentences far less than execution.

As the prosecution team examines evidence to decide about an indictment (which may occur before an arrest), the defendant's attorney tries to anticipate the case and decide what motions they might be able to make concerning the evidence. A grand jury may be convened for indictment in federal felonies and other complex cases, as it was in the Simpson case, and a preliminary hearing is arranged to consider probable cause (or it may be waived). Or there may be an arraignment (a preliminary or probable cause hearing before a judge). In a grand jury hearing, the prosecution presents its evidence in a closed session; in an arraignment, the evidence is shared with the defense. Thus, defense attorneys can make plans for having certain pieces of evidence dismissed during pretrial hearings. They may challenge methods used in the police search or interrogation procedures at this point, or they may propose bail or an assessment of competency. In "Invisible Evidence" on *CSI-LV*, a defense attorney succeeded in having evidence thrown out because the search for it had been improperly handled.

Once pretrial motions are heard and resolved, there may be an attempt at a plea bargain. If not, then the case moves toward court—coming before either a judge or a jury, or both.

In some cases where mental illness, youth, mental retardation, or other factors are involved, there may be hearings to determine such things as the person's competency to waive their rights, to confess, and to stand trial. Then the case moves into pretrial discovery. That means that the two sides start to collect their evidence and witnesses. The defense attorney may make plans for pretrial hearings on evidence or a change of venue (trial location).

Both sides devise a theory about what they believe happened, and why. At this stage, there may be attempts at a plea bargain. If the case keeps moving toward trial, then witnesses are prepared and strategies planned. While these procedures are not explicitly addressed on the *C.S.I.* shows, they're always in the background, because the stronger the evidence, the stronger the case.

In the Simpson case, both sides relied on jury consultants to advise them, based on questionnaires from the potential jury pool, who their ideal juror would be. The consultant may be either a single person or an entire organization. Depending on the resources available and the perceived stakes, psychological experts may become part of a legal team. Introduced in the 1970s as a scientific approach to jury selection, sometimes consulting is done by individual freelancers and sometimes by a team from larger firms. It's criticized for having no basis in sound psychological principles, yet attorneys continue to employ them. Such consultants have several functions, most specifically, that of evaluating the various people going through voir dire to become members of a jury.

The goal is to help attorneys assemble a group of people who will listen with an open mind to their client's story, so they prepare a "juror profile." This is a list of the attributes of the kind of person who will view the specific case favorably. In other words, jury analysts examine such things as racial bias, whether a prospective juror has ever experienced police brutality or gender discrimination, and how conservative their values are. The consultants examine what people wear, what their body language expresses, and those aspects of behavior that reveal "predictive traits"—characteristics most likely to affect a person's beliefs that are relevant to the case. Research indicates that juries make decisions based more firmly on their values, beliefs, and experiences than on the case facts. Some cases, such as those involving the death penalty, require particular care in looking out for authoritarian attitudes, a political agenda, or an urge to punish. And attorneys should take into account what people are like in general.

As the Simpson trial heated up, the defense team debated over the evidence. Each lawyer wondered how the jury would process complicated information like blood analysis, but it was DNA expert Barry Scheck who had an idea that shifted the strategy. Based on what he said, O. J.'s lead lawyer, Johnnie Cochran, quickly constructed a case that resulted in one of the most controversial verdicts in legal history—and gained his client's freedom. Essentially, Scheck offered one simple finding from psychological research: People transform testimony into a story that makes sense to them. They build a narrative and absorb all subsequent information into it, so the key to winning a case is to tell a compelling story.

As part of the process, jury analysts might conduct a mock jury trial in the target community, do a telephone survey, or run a focus group to try to determine the types of responses they can expect in a given area. A focus group composed of people who are likely to represent the typical juror can help them to offer advice on developing arguments, opening and closing speeches, the effectiveness of visual aids, questions for voir dire, notes for jury instruction, and aspects of the case that might not have been obvious.

The consultants ask each person who participates in these surveys or groups a list of questions that will yield clues about what the relevant population might think of a case. The consultants then record age, sex, race, employment history, hobbies, experiences growing up, marital status, socioeconomic background, evidence of compassion, and life attitudes. That provides a database from which to develop a preferred profile.

THE TRIAL

"Mea Culpa" on *CSI-LV* features Grissom on the witness stand discussing evidence for the prosecution. In a criminal trial, the prosecutor goes first, and also closes first. Once the jury is seated (which can take a few hours or several weeks), the prosecutor presents an opening statement, which generally specifies a theory of the crime. Then the defense does the same, although some defense attorneys may withhold their theory at this time so as not to reveal their strategy too soon. Each side puts on a case, using witnesses and evidence, which are open to cross-examination and objections from the other side. There's a rebuttal, wherein both attorneys revisit testimony and are allowed more witnesses if they need them, and finally both deliver their opening arguments; the prosecutor gets the last word with a closing argument. The judge then instructs the jury, going over the charges, and important legal points, and the potential verdicts they are allowed to bring back. They then retire for deliberations. (In the event of a bench trial, the judge is the fact-finder, rather than a jury, and the judge then decides the verdict.) "Eleven Angry Jurors" on *CSI-LV* took viewers behind the scenes to investigate the death of a member of the jury while they were in deliberations on a case.

In bifurcated trials, in the event of a guilty verdict, there is then a phase prior to sentencing in which both sides can deliver arguments and factors that assist the fact-finders in deciding among possible sentences.

Potential experts must first qualify as such with the court, so they generally get questioned by both attorneys and even by the judge. This is known as part of the voir dire, and is usually conducted while the jury is present. Qualified experts may then offer testimony, including expert opinions. The voir dire establishes the boundaries of their expertise. Crime scene investigators, by virtue of their position and significance in the presentation of evidence, are not subjected to the same type of procedure as an outside expert, such as a psychologist or meteorologist. Some labs offer moot court training so the technicians will be prepared to testify and endure cross-examination.

If the witness is impressive, the opposing side may stipulate to their qualifications—in other words, not ask many questions. Basically, the questioning elicits a history of the witness's education, certifications, publications, and experience. There may also be questions about prior court experience and fees.

Any experts hired should have a pretrial conference with the attorney to ensure that their testimony is consistent with the attorney's strategy. The attorney may also be able to describe characteristics of the judge and the opposing counsel, anticipate the types of questions in cross-examination, and fill in any final details.

ADMISSIBILITY STANDARDS

In 1923, the District of Columbia Court of Appeals issued an opinion that became the first guideline for the admissibility of scientific evidence. In a case known as *Frye v. United States*, the defense counsel tried to enter evidence about a device that measured blood pressure during deception. The court decided that the thing from which the testimony is deduced must be "sufficiently established to have gained general acceptance in the particular field in which it belongs." In addition, the information offered had to be beyond the general knowledge of the jury. This *Frye* standard became general practice in most courts for many years.

However, over the decades critics claimed that it excluded theories that were unusual but well-supported. Several attempts were made in the courts to rephrase the *Frye* standard, but each generally had problems of its own.

In some jurisdictions now, the *Frye* standard has been replaced by a standard cited in 1993 in the Supreme Court's decision in *Daubert v. Merrell Dow Pharmaceuticals, Inc.,* which emphasizes the trial judge's responsibility as a gatekeeper. The court decided that "scientific" means grounded in the methods and procedures of science, and "knowledge" is more reliable than subjective belief. The judge's evaluation has only to focus on the methodology, not on the conclusion, and also on whether the scientific evidence applies to the facts of the case. In other words, when scientific testimony is presented, judges have to determine whether:

- the theory can be tested

- the potential error rate is known

- it was reviewed by peers and has attracted widespread acceptance within a relevant scientific community

- the opinion is relevant to the issue in dispute.

Many attorneys look to these guidelines to try to separate junk
science from work performed with controls, scientific methodology,
and appropriate precautions. This applies to all areas of science, including the behavioral sciences.

But some guidelines are slippery, particularly when it comes to
examining a suspect's state of mind. There is some question as to how
objective psychological evaluation is, but a number of standard examinations have been put through extensive reliability and validity
studies. As long as the practitioner is experienced and unbiased, the
results should be trustworthy. While some issues, such as insanity, are
quite specific to experts in psychology or psychiatry, and will be discussed elsewhere, the issue of competency involves an assessment of
legal comprehension.

COMPETENCY

Whether a defendant is mentally competent is a frequent issue in a
trial and can occur at different stages. There are many types of com-
petencies. In the criminal arena, there is the competency to waive the
right to silence and legal counsel, agree to search and seizure, confess,
stand trial, testify, plead guilty, conduct one's own defense, refuse the
insanity defense, be criminally responsible, serve a sentence, and be
executed. In the civil arena, the issues involve competency to consent
to treatment, be a guardian, and take care of a child.

Those that require formal evaluation most often involve standing trial, waiving rights, and criminal responsibility. At any time the defendant is thought to be unable to perceive the situation realistically or participate ably in the process, he or she may be tested for competence.

On July 31, 2001, a Houston grand jury indicted Andrea Yates for the murder of three of her children: Noah, John, and Mary. (Five children were drowned, but prosecutors withheld two of the murders for a potential trial at a later time.) She was eligible for the death penalty.

On August 8, Yates's attorneys entered an insanity defense. A rudimentary psychological report done for the court indicated that she was competent to stand trial, but her attorneys wanted a jury to say so, since their own psychiatrists had concluded that she could not participate in her own defense. The judge granted their request.

Dr. Gerald Harris, a clinical psychologist, had interviewed Yates in prison, where she had shown signs of severe psychosis. She said she had "seen" Satan in her cell, asked to have her hair cut into a crown, and believed the number of the Antichrist (666) was imprinted on her scalp. By the end of August, medication had restored normal awareness, but she still had delusions about Satan, and had difficulty remembering things.

Dr. Lauren Marangell, an expert on depression, testified about changes in the brain during different psychological states. She also provided a map of Yates's psychotic episodes since 1999. She concluded that Yates would be competent in the foreseeable future, with continued treatment.

The prosecutors took their witnesses—mostly prison staff—over the thirteen points involved in assessing competency. Then they questioned Dr. Steve Rubenzer, who had spent over ten hours with the defendant and who had administered a competency examination on several successive occasions—the assessments in dispute because they were done without a defense attorney present. It was his opinion that the defendant's compre-

hension had improved over time and that she passed the state's competency stipulations. However, he believed that Yates had a serious mental
illness and he thought her psychotic features were only in partial remis-
sion. Under cross-examination, he admitted that she believed that Satan
inhabited her and that Governor Bush would destroy him—but Bush had
not been the governor of Texas at that time.

Two more mental health experts testified, and while they were divided on the competency issue, all recognized psychosis in Andrea's condition and no one thought she was malingering. Despite this, the jury
deemed Yates competent to stand trial, because despite her illness, she
seemed to know what was at stake for her in the proceedings.

If people are judged incompetent, they're given treatment toward the
goal of restoring them to competence. That means they could be
locked up indefinitely, or that civil matters such as business decisions
that need attention must be put into the hands of a guardian. Resolving these issues in some manner allows the court to move forward. Yet
in criminal proceedings, once a person is judged competent, an even
more challenging evaluation may remain ahead: the mental state at
the time of the person's offense.

We'll discuss that in chapter Five, but one more competency issue
has been raised on *C.S.I.* that is largely concerned with legal comprehension, so we'll examine that here. In "Pro-per," an episode of *CSI-
M*, a defendant chose to defend himself, meaning that he would be
questioning the witnesses. While that's annoying for professionals,
and it was for Calleigh Duquesne, it has its own set of problems for the
defendant, as seen in a number of actual cases of self-representation.

When his capital murder trial started in the fall of 2003, Beltway Sniper
suspect John Allen Muhammad, part of a team that terrorized Virginia,

Maryland, and Washington, D.C., the year before, opted to defend himself. Presiding Judge Leroy F. Millette, Jr., decided that Muhammad was competent to do so, although many legal experts doubted it.

Muhammad, forty-two, was accused in the slaying of Dean Harold Meyers, fifty-three, the seventh victim in the three-week shooting spree in which ten people died and three were wounded. The manhunt ended when Muhammad was found in his car, apparently modified for sniper activity, with seventeen-year-old John Lee Malvo. Since he could not afford an attorney, Peter Greenspan and Jonathan Shapiro were appointed to represent him. At first he seemed satisfied, but then he demoted them to stand-by counsel.

In his rambling opening statement, Muhammad insisted that he was not involved in the string of shootings that claimed so many victims, and during his case presentation he urged witnesses to admit that even if they spotted him at a crime scene they did not see him shoot anyone. Nor did they see him with a gun. He seemed to believe these admissions made his innocence obvious. Yet prosecutors set out to prove that the case was much more complicated than the conclusions of eyewitnesses.

It wasn't long before Muhammad apparently agreed with them and invited his legal team back into the picture. Nevertheless, with his brusque questioning of witnesses whom he may have shot or shot at, it was possible that he did his case some damage. Jury alienation can be a factor in such decisions and they could not have been pleased with his badgering of witnesses—especially not in an area where so many people were terrorized. Muhammad was convicted as the mastermind of the sniper murders and sentenced to die. Many legal experts said that Muhammad had set himself up for a fall.

The legal doctrine of competence originated in English common law at a time centuries ago when defendants argued their own cases. People are declared competent when they have voluntarily waived their rights and currently have no mental disease or defect prohibiting them from understanding the proceedings, the parties involved, and the consequences. Being judged competent is about having a "good understanding." It does not imply normal mental functioning. Yet given the increased sophistication of the legal process since the time when competency was first made an issue, it would seem that allowing people to defend themselves based on mere comprehension rather than on a higher level of knowledge or ability may at times be against the defendant's best interest.

But a federal ruling declared that "the Sixth Amendment as made applicable to the States by the Fourteenth Amendment guarantees that a defendant in a state criminal trial has an independent constitutional right of self-representation and that he may proceed to defend himself without counsel when he voluntarily and intelligently elects to do so."

This conclusion was reached after an in-depth analysis of the history of self-representation in America and England. The Bill of Rights was based not only on rights provided in English common law but also on several apparently unjust events in England, one of which was the 1603 trial of Sir Walter Raleigh.

On trial for treason against King James, Raleigh received no advance knowledge of the charges. Indeed, they were read to him on the morning of his trial. He was not allowed to question any witnesses, including a key witness against him, Lord Cobham, with whom he was accused of planning to overthrow the king. The authors of the U.S. Constitution noted all of this with deep concern, and carefully outlined a way to preserve the rights of anyone accused of a crime.

He or she will be asked questions to determine their level of education, understanding of and ability to speak English, and understanding of how a trial works. The judge cannot determine at this point just how well someone may perform in court, only that he or she understands the proceedings and consequences.

In addition, *State v. Crisafi* in 1992 spelled out the appropriate areas of inquiry, including the disadvantages of self-representation, knowledge about the charges and punishment for them, the risk of an unsuccessful defense, and knowledge of the rules of evidence procedures.

In cases where these conditions are met and the judge still refuses to grant the defendant's request, such as in *State v. Thomas* in New Jersey, in which Thomas proved his knowledge of the laws and his ability in a prior case to win an acquittal, then a conviction may be vacated. If the judge cannot show that a defendant would create a disorderly proceeding and the defendant conforms to the requirements of competence, the judge may not deny his request to represent himself.

DNA: A LEGAL BLOCKBUSTER

DNA analysis, one of law enforcement's greatest technological advances, has solved "hopeless" cold cases and supported many convictions. It also has embarrassed the legal system. DNA testing has exposed an unacceptably high number of wrongful convictions, often confirmed by faulty eyewitness testimony (an issue addressed in "Bloodlines" on *CSI-LV*). After the first success with DNA typing in two related rape-murder cases in England, a company called Lifecodes developed the technology in the United States. In 1987, Florida's Assistant State's Attorney, Tim Berry, contacted forensic director Michael Baird about a serial rape case that was going to court. He wondered about the possibility of bringing in DNA identification as evidence. This was to be the first U.S. case to admit DNA testimony into the trial.

The case had begun in May 1986 when a man entered the Orlando apartment of Nancy Hodge and raped her at knifepoint. Grabbing her purse, he left. During the succeeding months, he raped more women, taking care to keep them from seeing him, and on his way out he always took something that belonged to them. In six months, he had raped more than twenty-three women, and he proved to be maddeningly elusive. However, he had made one mistake: He left behind two fingerprints on a window screen. When another woman eventually called him in as a prowler, his prints were matched to those from the window screen and they had their man: Tommie Lee Andrews.

Although his blood group matched semen samples taken from several of the victims, and the single victim who had caught a glimpse of him had made a positive identification, proving him to be a serial rapist would be difficult. There was too much potential in each of the other cases for reasonable doubt.

Blood samples from Andrews and semen samples from the rapist were sent to Lifecodes. Within two months the results were confirmed: the bar codes were too highly consistent for the semen in the rapes to be from anyone other than Andrews.

Nevertheless, DNA testing had not yet been accepted into court and before it could be used, it had to go through a pretrial hearing. Any time new scientific technology is introduced as testimony, it must pass certain tests of acceptability in the scientific community. That way, the courts can avoid admitting evidence based on whim or junk science. DNA analysis had to be proven scientifically sound in method, theory, and interpretation, and positively reviewed by peers. The hearing was long and complex, but finally the judge allowed the evidence into the case. However, the prosecutor made a misstep by stating impressive odds that he could not substantiate, and the jury was hung. Andrews was then tried on a second rape charge and convicted. Months later, the first rape charge was retried and the DNA evidence was brought in with more clarity and power. After that trial, Andrews's prison sentence stretched from his initial twenty-two years for rape to 115 years for serial rape.

From there, DNA gained increasing acceptance in the courts, although challenges were aimed at the way samples were interpreted or at shoddy handling of specimen evidence, such as happened in the Simpson trial. Because many different things can occur between the collection of a sample and the final interpretation, to ensure high standards, DNA testimony was reviewed on a case-by-case basis.

When first introduced, DNA faced only a few challenges from attorneys or the courts. But then a decision in a New York case put on the brakes. This 1989 decision by the New York Supreme Court was based on a pretrial hearing that lasted three months. Joseph Castro was accused of murdering his neighbor and her two-year-old daughter, and a bloodstain on his watch was analyzed for DNA codes. The court looked closely at both the DNA theory and the identification procedures, and held that they were generally accepted by the relevant scientific community. In essence, the testing could be used to show that the blood on the watch was not Castro's (exclusion), but could not be used to claim that the blood was from one of the victims (inclusion). The prosecutor indicated that it was not Castro's and offered astronomical odds to support his statement. The defense expert challenged these odds and the match criteria used. The trial court then excluded the DNA evidence, although Castro later pled guilty and got a lesser sentence.

By this time, there had been press reports around the world about the miracle tool for crime-solving. As eager as prosecutors were to use it, defense attorneys matched their zeal with spirited resistance. There followed several years of hearings that finally culminated in acceptance of the original protocols.

But then there was another issue.

When Illinois Governor George Ryan learned that thirteen men on death row had been exonerated by DNA testing, he placed a moratorium on the death penalty in his state. He was shocked that innocent men might have been executed, and everyone wondered how many might already have been. Thirty-seven other states allow the death penalty and it is no secret that the court proceedings are not always about justice. Even when they are, many convictions rely on eyewitness testimony, which has proven to be notoriously corruptible and unreliable. Lack of funding and prosecutorial zeal also top the list of reasons why someone might be falsely convicted. Whatever the reason, DNA testing can provide a way out—but it is not always accepted without a fight.

EYEWITNESS ISSUES

In CSI-M's "10-7," Calleigh feels a gun placed to her head and hears the click of a bullet entering the chamber. As a weapons expert, she believes she can listen to the click of each type of gun and narrow down exactly which weapon was used. She's more likely to have her memory reshaped by the clicks of other guns as post-event information than to be able to identify what she actually heard. While most testimony is about visual evidence, this is acoustic evidence and would probably not be accepted into court. Moreover, a click heard under stressful conditions could corrupt her memory. Another episode, "And Then There Were None" on CSI-LV, eyewitnesses to a robbery all have conflicting stories, which indicates just how problematic eyewitness testimony can be. It's not difficult to understand how innocent people can sometimes be arrested and even convicted.

On August 1, 2005, Thomas Doswell, forty-six, was released from prison in Pennsylvania. Nineteen years earlier, he'd been convicted of rape and assault. He claimed he was innocent, and post-conviction DNA tests proved he was. But the victim had identified him. An example of police procedures indicates why.

The police had shown the victim a photo spread of eight men, but one of them—Doswell—was marked suggestively with an "R" because he'd earlier been charged with rape but had been acquitted. Not surprisingly, the victim picked out Doswell, as did a coworker who had seen the attacker. Blood-typing was unhelpful, so the entire case rested on their identification. Doswell did not, as they had described, have a beard or marks from being scratched during the attack. Still, he went to prison.

The Innocence Project, a legal resource for post-conviction DNA testing, investigated the case and tested biological specimens from the rape kit. Doswell became one of 180 men exonerated thus far, many of whom had spent years in prison. More than three-quarters of them had ended up there, says Innocence Project co-founder Barry Scheck, in part from eyewitness misidentification—which occurs even under the best circumstances.

Number 161 was Luis Diaz, sixty-seven, who served twenty-six years for crimes he did not commit. In August 1979, Miami-Dade County police arrested him for a series of rapes over the previous two years attributed to the "Bird Road Rapist." One victim, who identified him as the killer even though he looked dramatically different from her original description, had given police his license plate number after she spotted him at a gas station. Seven other victims looked at a photo spread that featured him and agreed, despite similar inconsistencies among their descriptions (two later recanted).

In 1980, Diaz was convicted of seven rapes and attempted rapes. Only two semen samples were recovered, but that was sufficient for later DNA analysis. They matched each other, but not Diaz. He was cleared.

These men fell victim to a legal system that fails to grasp how fragile and impressionable eyewitness testimony is. Since the early 1900s, research psychologists have attempted to educate the police and courts on this point, but they've often been ignored. Yet experiments indicate that showing a witness a photo of a person similar to the attacker can subtly shift the witness's memory toward that person, especially when photos of several suspects are shown together. Witnesses often select the one who looks most like the remembered assailant, because perception homes in on familiar features.

Also, case investigators who handle the identification process can inadvertently cue witnesses, who want to please, about whom they should select. In other words, eyewitness memory is susceptible to influence and vulnerable to distortion. Thus, treating memory more carefully, guided by insights from research, can only assist the process of justice.

The accuracy of eyewitness reports relies on the quality of three different perceptual processes: encoding (converting information for storage), storage (retaining information for short-term use or long-term recall), and retrieval (finding and providing the stored information for use). The quality of each of these processes depends on how many interfering factors are present.

Factors that can affect memory encoding include:

- how much the information is rehearsed

- whether it's rearranged into meaningful units or patterns

- whether a person was traumatized or stressed

- whether it has personal associations

- whether someone else made suggestions or used pressure to remember an item or incident a certain way

- how divided the person's attention was.

There are many different types of interference factors. Sometimes simply trying to memorize something can interfere with what one already knows, while at other times, what one already knows hinders the ability to memorize a new item.

Being exposed to new information between storage and retrieval can also affect what is recalled, even if that information contains errors about the original experience. In an experiment, subjects were exposed to a film of a murder in a crowd. They then received written information about it, but half were misled about certain details, such as describing a critical blue car as white. Those who had been exposed to the wrong information tended to report *that* rather than offering what they had actually seen, with error rates as high as 40 percent. In similar studies, people have reported nonexistent broken glass, a clean-shaven man having a mustache, straight hair as curly, Stop signs as Yield signs, and a barn in a pastoral scene that contained no buildings at all.

Exposure to misinformation after an event can lead people to erroneous reports of said information. It's called the Misinformation Effect. A person sees the theft of a hammer, but another witness tells him she saw the thief take a screwdriver, so when he responds to questioning, he says that a screwdriver was taken. The errors result from the means of acquiring, retaining, and retrieving the information. The acceptance of suggested information affects how new memories get formed. In other words, misleading or new information can interfere with how we may remember an event and can supplant our own memory with information that is not our memory at all. This effect was strongest when the original memory had eroded with the passage of time. It was weak in the face of a strong original memory.

This has been confirmed by numerous experiments in several countries. Subjects who reported erroneous information from the Misinformation Effect retrieved the "memory" as quickly as they did an actual memory and felt confident that they had had the experience that they "remembered."

When we encode an event or information, we tend to select some aspects and ignore others. We accept those things that fit our schemas or make sense to us. We also reconstruct memory to work for us. Leading or suggestive comments tend to influence this process and reform the memory, especially if we find them acceptable. So do preexisting expectations.

Then there are memory schemas, or mental shortcuts by means of which memory is organized via a cluster of related facts and experiences that guide how things are encoded. What we expect to occur influences how we remember something. We all have mental "scripts," which are widely held beliefs about sequences of actions that typically occur in situations. In a struggle between a man and woman, for example, we expect the man to be more violent because we hold social ideas about males and females, and we have seen more stories about male violence in domestic situations—to the point where it's familiar and we develop expectations about the sequences of events. We are trained by our exposure to expect a certain situation and we rely on scripts to fill in gaps in our memory. In other words, we create material to make a story work. Memories can be distorted to be made consistent with our schemas and we may ignore memories that contradict them.

Confidence in one's memory, contrary to what juries have long believed, is unrelated to the accuracy of a memory, in part because confidence levels can be manipulated with encouragement. Research indicates that memory is malleable, and many influences can cause memories to change.

Jennifer Thomason, twenty-two, was raped by a man she was able to see from several different angles. She managed to escape and she gave police details for a composite drawing. It was circulated and people called in with names of men it resembled. Ronald Cotton heard that his name had been mentioned, so he went to the police station to set them straight about his innocence, and instead, he was arrested and placed in a lineup. Jennifer identified him as the man from the lineup and from a photo spread. She was strongly encouraged by police when she made her choice, increasing her confidence. Cotton went to trial and was convicted, but DNA evidence a decade later exonerated him and implicated someone else—a man in prison for another rape. He admitted he had done it. He did not look like Cotton. While Jennifer had to admit that she had been wrong and she now knew what the real perpetrator looked like, she continued to have a persisting memory of Ronald Cotton as her rapist.

It's estimated that each year, 4,500 wrongful convictions are based on mistaken eyewitness identification, which generally grows out of faulty memory encoding. It is the most common cause of wrongful convictions—around 65 percent.

In an experiment in 1992 by Victoria Holst and Kathy Pezdek on juries and scripts, they questioned subjects to determine popular beliefs about common scenarios, such as a convenience store robbery. The "scripts," or common beliefs, proved to be widely shared among the subjects about how a criminal cases a store, acts inside the store, uses a gun to demand money, and drives away in a getaway vehicle. The second stage of the research was to expose the same subjects to a mock trial of such a robbery. Most of the aspects of a typical script were played out, but some key elements were missing. The robber did not case the store, use a gun, or take money. Nevertheless, when asked to describe the trial afterward, the subjects "remembered" these very elements. The implication is that prior ideas and beliefs do get mixed into actual events when a person is making sense of familiar situations for recall.

In short, memory recall involves a construction of memory, which can be rebuilt from both the original experience and from information to which the person was exposed afterward.

But mistakes made by witnesses, while alarming, are generally not malicious. The worst issues involved in criminal prosecution are the attempts by experts to introduce junk science into the proceedings and experts who are simply dishonest enough to lie or to fake the data results.

SCIENCE: GOOD, BAD, AND UNDECIDED

Many different organizations keep an eye on forensic fraud in an effort to keep the legal system honest. The Innocence Project, Professor James Starr's *Scientific Sleuthing Review*, and truthinjustice.org are examples. The legal system itself should do its own policing, and on *CSI-NY*, Mac Taylor does exactly that in "The Closer" when he reexamines the case of a man claiming to be innocent and finds the evidence, which he'd initially interpreted one way, to actually affirm the man's story.

According to information that the Innocence Project offers, in twenty-five of the first eighty-two cases of exoneration of innocent people via DNA analysis, experts, and prosecutors presented tainted or just plain poor evidence to the jury. Examples of such procedures include experts who did not conduct the tests to which they testified, falsified results, falsified credentials, statistical exaggeration, and suppression of facts about the improper handling of evidence. In *CSI-NY*'s "Summer in the City," Aiden is so determined to get evidence on a man she firmly believes committed a rape that she contemplates planting evidence.

Ethically speaking, professionals in any field who serve as consultants or experts must resist pressure to offer opinions on subjects, or aspects of subjects, over which they fail to have expertise. They shouldn't oversell their expertise or overstate their degree of certainty if research does not support it. Within their range, they should advance the highest level of competence possible, which means knowing the results of the latest research in their field.

However, there have been several cases in which an expert lied or falsified evidence, damaging the trust factor that girds the legal system and tightening procedures for evaluating experts.

- Fred Zain, a West Virginia state trooper in charge of serology, testified in hundreds of trials in twelve different states. He was accused of faking his results and committing perjury, and was tried in 2001. The investigation of his procedures began with the case of Glen Dale Woodall, a grave digger in West Virginia, who was convicted of two abduction rapes. DNA evidence proved he was innocent, and it was Zain who had testified erroneously against him. The subsequent investigation turned up evidence that Zain had been "dry-labbing." In other words, he either did not do a test he claimed he did or he overstated inconclusive results.

- Jeffrey Pierce spent fifteen years in prison for a rape he did not commit. The testimony of Joyce Gilchrist, the Oklahoma-based criminalist who identified him via supposed matched samples of hair from the crime scene, was proven to be false, and all of her cases had to be reexamined. A quick review of eight cases indicated a botched analysis in five. This finding forced a review of nearly 1,700 convictions on which she had worked.

▪ Rolando Cruz and Alejandro Hernandez were wrongfully convicted for a 1983 murder in Illinois, and Cruz went to death row. After the real killer confessed, prosecutors refused to release the two men. The Illinois Supreme Court reversed the convictions and they were retried but convicted again, based largely on testimony from police officers. DNA testing finally exonerated them in 1994, but prosecutors went forward with a third trial after the convictions were once again reversed on appeal. A cop finally admitted that he'd lied under oath when he'd stated that Cruz had offered details specific to the murder. The judge directed a verdict of not guilty for Cruz and charges were dropped against Hernandez. Cruz also received a pardon based on innocence.

Then there's a question of whether certain procedures are based in scientific methods. Experts disagree on the following devices, both of which have been used on some episodes of *CSI-LV*. The first one was questioned by an investigator on "Compulsion," because it is not admissible in court, and the second was utilized on "Sounds of Silence" as if there were no doubts, but it was part of an investigation rather than a method that might be presented in the case. Still, it did quickly dismiss a potential suspect who perhaps should have been further investigated.

▪ Computer Voice Stress Analyzer: Supposedly the voice reveals deception because it measures variations in emotional stress called "microtremors." When subjects lie, its inventors insist, their voices reach a higher pitch. The machine analyzes the sound of the voice and prints the results onto a graph. Technicians say that the VSA can detect differences in the voice not available to the human ear. However, the American Polygraph Association did a study and concluded that for deception detection the voice stress analysis is no better than chance. They also pointed out that, while the Department of Defense uses polygraphs, it does not employ voice stress analysis in any investigative context. Twenty-five other studies have been run, with roughly the same results. Yet many police departments nationwide use the stress analyzer for interrogations and thousands of officers have been trained on it. In San Diego, confessions were coerced from two teenagers using the device, but charges were later dropped when they used legal channels to complain.

▪ Brain-fingerprinting, developed by psychiatrist Lawrence Farwell, is supposedly 99.9 percent accurate. Since the brain is central to all human activities, Farwell has said, it records all experiences. Like other experiences, a crime and crime scene should be neurologically stored and a "brainprint" would offer measurable evidence. The suspect's electrical activity is monitored with sensors while the subject is exposed to "prod" words or images, some of which are relevant to the event and some irrelevant. If his brain activity shows recognition to the relevant stimuli—an electrical spike called a memory and encoding related multifaceted electroencephalographic response (MER-MER) occurs, which indicates that the subject has a record of it stored in his brain. Innocent people, the scientist claimed, will display no such response.

One flaw, also true with fingerprints, was that if the person was at the crime scene but did not commit the crime, there is no way to make that distinction. They may also recognize some part of the scene, or the victim. The best prods will trigger the memory of someone with very specific knowledge about a crime.

There are also genuine problems with some types of analyses:

- The Illinois state police canceled its contract with a certain lab that had long performed DNA analyses for investigations, because a check on back cases determined that technicians there had failed to find semen evidence in 22. That meant that more than one thousand cases had to be retested, at considerable cost. Not only that, in cases where negative findings were in error, it's also possible that criminals had been allowed to go free. Ten other states had contracted with this lab as well.

- DNA evidence that had helped to convict a teenager of rape in 1999 also exonerated him. After an independent investigation proved he did not commit the crime, it was found that the Houston crime lab had mishandled or overstated DNA findings to support the prosecution. An examination of several of their cases indicated real problems with the handling of DNA evidence, and the serology lab was shut down, pending further investigation. They had failed to run controls, adequately document their work, and take precautions against evidence corruption. In court, they'd overstated conclusions from the results.

- In 2005, an FBI fingerprint computer analysis erroneously freed a sex-crime fugitive, Jeremy Bryan Jones, and he may have gone on to commit several murders (investigations are still pending). Jones had been wanted on a sexual assault charge, but after a break-in that resulted in putting his fingerprints from the scene into the FBI's AFIS database, they failed to match his own prints already in the system. This same system had also falsely implicated an attorney from Oregon in the Madrid train bombings. FBI spokespeople said that the system, which contains over 45 million sets of prints, is 95 percent accurate. The issue may be that prints are now taken as digital images, and sometimes they can be of poor quality. But should they then serve as evidence?

Junk science, deceptive experts, and dubious devices occupy the ambiguous corners of the legal system, and these same issues come into play where the human mind is at stake. We've mentioned competency already, and there are many more psychological angles that can affect court cases, from insanity to profiling to corrections. Let's turn now to the discipline that directly addresses them.

CHAPTER FIVE

Psycho-logic

The three *C.S.I.* programs have delved into psychological areas such as interrogation strategies ("Compulsion"), profiling ("Blink"), and assessing disorders such as multiple personality ("Face-Lift"), automatism ("Night, Mother"), and psychopathy ("Grave Danger"). In this chapter, we'll deal with how psychology is used specifically in the legal process; in the next chapter, we'll tackle abnormal psychology, including the phenomenon of serial murder. While the programs rarely utilize a psychiatric consultant, the teams do the work of such consultants, so it's a good idea to see how the process actually works.

Psychologists and psychiatrists have several different types of functions in the legal arena, both behind the scenes and in the courtroom. Wherever the legal system and psychology interact, you have forensic psychology.

THE PSYCHOLOGIST AND THE COURTS

Psychologists and psychiatrists use their expertise with human behavior, motivation, and psychopathology to provide psychological services for the courts, and may also consult in criminal investigations. They appraise behaviors such as malingering (faking the symptoms of an illness), post-traumatic stress, or acting suicidal. "Committed" on *CSI-LV* mentioned some of these as Grissom and Sara investigated a murder in a psychiatric forensic hospital. While most such practitioners are clinical psychologists with a specialization in forensic issues, this applied discipline also involves those who engage in research relevant to legal issues. They may assess a degree of threat, determine the fitness of a guardian, or test the conditions influencing the accuracy of an eyewitness. They might also assist a forensic artist to develop an appearance based on personality traits or a coroner to resolve ambiguous death determinations. Some forensic psychologists work for police departments to screen for fitness for duty or provide trauma counseling. Many work in prisons or psychiatric hospitals.

To be effective, they must be familiar with the way law enforcement and the criminal justice system work. Whether it's to evaluate a killer's state of mind during a crime or assess whether a juvenile should be waived to adult court, psychologists are an integral part of those teams devoted to learning the truth, protecting others, and serving justice. Despite all these roles, they're most commonly perceived to be the experts in court who address whether or not a defendant was insane when he or she committed a crime. So let's turn to that issue first, going back to the case that has affected clinical and legal assessments for well over a century.

INSANITY

During the 1840s, Daniel M'Naghten believed that Britain's Prime Minister Robert Peele was going to harm him. In a delusional frame of mind, he went to shoot the man but mistakenly killed Peele's private secretary instead. M'Naghten was arrested and taken to trial. His defense counsel argued that while he knew what he was doing, given his paranoid ideas, he'd been unable to control himself. The court agreed and acquitted M'Naghten, but the public reacted badly to this decision, unwilling to accept that someone could be freed from moral responsibility for such an act. Thus, a royal commission was appointed to study the issue, and they found that the decision was just. From it, they devised the M'Naghten Rule. For future such cases, the House of Lords required that to establish a defense on the grounds of insanity, it had to be proven that "at the time of the committing of the act, the party accused was laboring under such a defect of reason, from disease of the mind, as not to know the nature and quality of the act he was doing; or if he did know it, that he did not know he was doing what was wrong." This wording has been at the heart of most insanity cases in the United States.

Insanity is a legal definition, although it's often used incorrectly to refer to someone who is psychotic, or even just eccentric. Sometimes it even refers to predators, just because they deviate from social norms. It means a lack of responsibility for one's actions due to a mental disease or defect, which reduces criminal intent. The law recognizes that responsibility for committing a crime depends on two things: *actus reus*, which is evidence that the accused engaged in the act, and *mens rea*, the mental state required to have intended to commit the act or foreseen its consequences. The legal system assumes that people are generally rational and that they can freely make decisions for which they are morally responsible. Mental health professionals may undermine this notion in certain cases by describing psychological factors that mitigate culpability. Thus, triers of fact must consider excusing the behavior of those without *mens rea*, because the acts of deranged people cannot be judged in the same way as the acts of rational people. We also don't wish to punish them if they did not really know what they were doing.

Insanity standards have a long history in English common law, which has been adopted by the United States. Yet from one state to another, there is currently no uniform standard for determining insanity, and a person found sane in one jurisdiction might be considered insane in another: A woman in Texas who kills her child because demons possessed it can be sent to prison but for mental health treatment in Minnesota—or even in another area of Texas. Federal and state courts use a variety of standards, generally grounded in knowledge of right and wrong but sometimes also including the ability to conform one's actions to the requirements of the law.

John Wayne Gacy was arrested in 1978 and charged with the murders of thirty-three young men, most of whom he had buried in the crawl space beneath his home. He'd lived that way for several years. After his arrest, he pretended to have an alter personality who was responsible for the crimes, so his attorneys offered a defense of insanity based on a compulsion to kill. A number of psychologists and psychiatrists put Gacy through a battery of assessment instruments and came up with a variety of diagnoses. The overriding claim was that he had experienced an "irresistible impulse" when he killed each young man and thanks to alcohol, had either blacked out or lost his inhibitions to such an extent that he was unable to control himself. This was in keeping with a phrasing of the insanity defense at the time in Illinois, which allowed that a person might realize that what he was doing was wrong but was nevertheless unable to stop himself. The jury rejected the defense, largely because the prosecutor was able to show that Gacy had planned several of the murders and his team's psychologist insisted that an irresistible impulse cannot be planned in advance. He also exhibited a good memory for the crimes and where he had placed each young man's body—an indication that he had not blacked out.

The key issue in a mens rea determination is the defendant's state of mind, specifically at the time of the offense. In other words, even if they are proven to have a severe mental illness, such as schizophrenia, the illness must be related in a meaningful way to the crime, such that the crime issued from it. For example, a man suffering from paranoid delusions might attack someone based on panic or hallucinated commands to do so.

In sum, a legal defense of "not guilty by reason of insanity" presents the idea that defendants have committed crimes but by reason of "disease or defect" are not responsible for their actions. Thus, they ought not to be held criminally accountable for something they could not help. The job of a forensic mental health professional is to make an evaluation about the relationship of their illness to their crime, and if there is good reason to believe that the defendant did not appreciate what he or she was doing, or that it was wrong, the jury must acquit. This is no easy job, and its determination differs from one practitioner to another, especially if one has a pet theory to promote.

This defense is not used nearly as often as the public believes, and it succeeds even less often, but certain sensational cases have put media focus on it—especially when someone who has been evaluated, treated, and released offends again (as was addressed with the registered sex offender-turned-porn distributor in *CSI-M*'s "Innocent"). The job of making this "MSO" determination is complex, since it's specific to a time and experience to which the professional was not a witness.

Forensic psychologists must know the procedures and expectations of the court. As expert witnesses, they must be credible, competent, and prepared. They should also understand that the court prefers jargon-free assessments and objective information that directly addresses the issues at hand—and only those issues. In fact, the legal system's approach may clash with the general attitude of psychology as a science, so those professionals who accept such cases must be prepared for some tension. For example, as stated above, the court expects that people have free will and are therefore responsible for their criminal choices; psychologists view choices in a context of other causal factors. The court seeks certainty; psychologists work within probability. The court seeks brief statements; psychologists may seek to offer complex explanations.

In any event, mental health experts have a specific role in legal proceedings, directed by whoever hires them, and the most effective witnesses know what the attorneys do in an adversarial arena and how best to address the fact-finders, whether judges or jury members.

REPRESSED MEMORIES

This subject is not specifically utilized on *C.S.I.*, perhaps because it so clearly requires a specialist to diagnose, but it's been influential in the legal system for over a decade, so it's important to address it—especially because many defendants attempt to use this condition as a way to escape responsibility.

Arthur Shawcross faced trial for the murders of eleven women in Rochester, New York, in 1989. He and his lawyers decided to mount a defense of Not Guilty by Reason of Insanity (NGRI). The defense hired Dr. Dorothy Lewis, a psychiatric expert on organic disorders and violence from New York City's Bellevue Hospital. She had more than twenty-five years of experience among criminals, illustrating that brain damage, abuse, and certain organic disorders play strong roles. She believed that Shawcross had been severely traumatized as a child and suffered from incomplete temporal lobe seizures, which blocked his memory. She was of the opinion that those seizures only occurred during certain situations, such as when he was alone with prostitutes at night.

Yet Shawcross had confessed to each murder and provided details that only the killer would know, including leading investigators to the bodies of two of his victims. Thus, the prosecution's psychiatrist, Dr. Park Dietz, said that while Shawcross suffered from antisocial personality disorder, that did not necessarily hinder his awareness of what he was doing. Shawcross had tried to avoid detection and apprehension, which clearly indicated his appreciation for the wrongfulness of his behavior.

After five weeks of trial, the jury took less than two hours to find him both sane and guilty of murder in the second degree on ten counts. Shawcross was sentenced to twenty-five years to life on each of the counts.

The idea that subliminal memories of real events could be recovered derives from Sigmund Freud's ideas about trauma and repression. Add to that the notion that people may deal with overwhelming childhood trauma (or disturbing thoughts) by fragmenting into "alter" personalities, which was popularized by such cases as "Eve" during the 1950s and "Sybil" in the 1970s. By the 1980s, even more cases of multiple personality disorder (MPD) were being diagnosed, and recovered memories were the central feature.

Often those who suffer from MPD, say advocates, do not even realize it. The condition is usually diagnosed through recovered memory therapy, in which the patient is found to have repressed trauma. Experts on this personality disturbance say that a hidden memory may emerge in depression, numbness, hypersensitivity, and overreactions to certain environmental triggers. Sufferers may also experience vague flashbacks, or the memory might recur spontaneously years after the incident. These people may "trance out," feel out of touch with reality, and experience sudden panic attacks. They may also have eating disorders, be abusive, or acquire serious addictions.

A mental health practitioner trying to determine whether this disorder is present would begin with a clinical interview to check if there are memories of childhood abuse or stretches of time that the subject cannot recall. The questions include ways to assess the types of symptoms present and to utilize a structured diagnostic test or way to get corroborating information. While other personalities can be elicited through hypnosis, it's also possible to hypnotically affect a suggestible person in such a way that they will act as if they have different personalities—especially if they have something to gain. In fact, some critics insist that alter personalities are nothing more then social constructs, suggested by a therapist to a vulnerable patient and supported by the social milieu. In short, there is no clear consensus among professionals on the disorder.

In 1990, a case that went to court had a significant effect in dividing professionals on the issue of just how reliable these techniques and their products were. Based on only a recovered memory, Eileen Franklin accused her father, George Franklin, of raping and murdering her best friend when they were both only children, some two decades earlier. She was absolutely certain that it had occurred and her friend had indeed been found murdered. Psychologist Elizabeth Loftus testified on the father's behalf that there were serious flaws in memory processes, and that as vivid as it may have seemed to Eileen, she could be mistaken. Memory, Loftus said, is a reconstructive process in which the mind easily blends fact with fiction. Even if Eileen believed she "saw" the rock as her father lifted it to pummel the other child, she could have added that image through the recovery process or from reading newspaper accounts. The mind likes to fill in gaps and is susceptible to suggestion; thus a "memory" can be a distortion of actual experience. The jury didn't accept it, and they convicted George Franklin. (Later, when Eileen admitted to having relied on hypnosis, an appeals court vacated the conviction.)

Loftus went on to try to prove that the techniques of recovered memory therapy could actually plant false memories or at least add details that were not true. She became the premier researcher in the country to show just how unreliable memory can be—including and especially "recovered" memories—no matter how confident the person is who reports it. She did experiments with situations in which 25 percent of the participants included fictional images of events in their recall repertoire, and other researchers corroborated these findings. But they could not ethically induce actual trauma, so recovered memory professionals claimed that their results weren't generalizable to the abused population.

During that era, nevertheless, recovered memory therapy was popular and patients were told that symptoms like forgetfulness, daydreaming, and inner arguments were subtle indicators of repressed memories of abuse. Many male relatives were subsequently accused and some convicted. "Traumatologists" went to court as expert witnesses, and increasingly more people sought their help.

But then during the early to mid-1990s, there was a backlash. One accused father and his wife read about the false memory experiments and they formed an organization for falsely accused relatives. This organization was instrumental in overturning some convictions and urging courts to reconsider memory alone as evidence of criminal conduct. Then as the media turned against the recovered memory movement, many patients retracted their claims or were proven to have made false allegations.

Among mental health professionals, the diagnosis of dissociative identity disorder (DID) is now the name given for what used to be called multiple personality disorder. Opinions on the disorder range from those who insist there is no such phenomenon to those who believe every reported case is genuine. Perhaps the most important issue for the legal system is to adopt an attitude of balanced skepticism that neither accepts professional opinion on this issue at face value nor denies outright a defendant's self-report. In that case, corroborating evidence would become key to the proceedings—a family's reluctance to comply notwithstanding. In the case of accusations against aggressors, genuine evidence should prevail, as required in other types of criminal cases. In the case of those who are defending themselves with the diagnosis, claiming lack of awareness or responsibility, then a psychiatric history or testimony from those familiar with the person before his or her crime should be found and utilized—with stronger evidence than mere episodes of forgetfulness.

STANDARD TESTS

Most forensic health professionals work in either a correctional setting or a psychiatric hospital. They usually perform the role of assessment and treatment, or therapeutic intervention, and they have a substantial background in abnormal and social psychology, along with considerable experience in psychometric testing. For the most part, their job is to determine competency (present functioning and understanding) or the defendant's mental state at the time of the offence.

While the *C.S.I.* episodes don't show much that happens in preparation for a case going to court, in fact, psychologists can often be involved. Each professional involved in a civil or criminal case runs a standard battery of assessment instruments, such as an IQ test, projective tests, and self-report inventories. The most common battery includes the Wechsler Adult Intelligence Scales, the Minnesota Multiphasic Personality Inventory-2, the Rorschach, possibly the Thematic Apperception Test, and when organic damage is suspected, the Bender-Gestalt and the Halstead-Reitan neuropsychological battery of assessments. Each mental health expert acquires proficiency with, and preference for, a certain selection of assessment examinations. Due to admissibility issues and the subjective nature of interpretations, some assessments are more easily used for court purposes than others. The practitioner then determines a diagnosis from the results.

Assessments can be done for the court (civil or criminal), the government, insurance companies, or any other decision-making factfinders involved in legal issues. A forensic behavior specialist may serve as an expert witness for the defense or prosecution, or may simply present findings as ordered by the court. They should remain impartial, but try as they might to avoid it, they may be brought into a case as a "hired gun"—a professional who says what he's paid to say. Such experts are all too readily available, although this practice is considered unethical and their reputation among their peers usually suffers.

Prior to starting a clinical interview, the psychologist informs the client that anything said or written down is for the court and may be entered into the legal process. For any type of assessment, the psychologist's first task is to collect information. They have the attorney's resources at their disposal, so they provide a list of what they need, such as school and hospital records, work appraisals, crime scene photos, autopsy reports, and witness statements. They also gain information from their clinical interviews and mental status examinations of the defendant. They will avoid information illegally acquired because it will jeopardize the admissibility of the entire report, and they will decide on the best ways to acquire details specific to their expertise.

One important consideration when testing a defendant for a diminished mental capacity or insanity plea is to check for malingering—the faking of symptoms. Several tests include scales that indicate lying, exaggeration, faking bad, and faking good. Those people with something to gain, such as avoiding a trial or the death penalty, may have learned about exceptions for mental illness. However, the tests may catch them faking because their ideas about the symptoms are often based on popular misconceptions.

Some psychologists are so well-versed in behavioral disorders that they may end up consulting for the police. Even so, the realm of profiling, while psychological in nature, is most commonly associated with a law enforcement agency, such as the F.B.I.

PROFILING

The first season of *CSI-LV* brought in an FBI agent to assist with a serial killer in the "The Strip Strangler," but the crime scene investigators generally take over that responsibility now. In *CSI-NY*'s "Blink," for example, they analyzed similar lividity marks on two victims to determine that a serial killer was responsible, and when Caine found the home of a child murderer and ordered the yard dug up in "Broken," the ME estimated how far apart the murders had been to describe the escalation in killing behavior. No matter who's doing it, the process calls on a dual expertise in criminal psychology and crime investigation. It's no easy task to determine that crimes are linked, as it often appears in retrospect. However, some killers leave clues or the evidence of certain types of behaviors that stand out—

known as a "signature"   as the clever Paul Milander did on several episodes of *CSI-LV*. In real life, other killers give themselves away by repeating their crimes in a similar manner.

A couple of teenage boys walking during the early evening in a field near I-75, southeast of Tampa, Florida, in May 1984 noticed a bad smell in the air. They went closer to investigate the area from which it emanated and realized that the blackened thing in the weeds they were looking at was the mangled remains of a nude woman. That same month a construction worker came across another female body in a lover's lane near I-4. Officials realized that this crime scene was oddly familiar. After a third victim whose murder bore similarities to the first two, they called the FBI's Behavioral Science Unit (now called the Behavioral Analysis Unit).

The agents thought the factors from both cases that were most important to their analysis were that the victims had to depend on others for transportation, they were nude when found, they had been similarly bound, they had been left near interstate highways in rural areas, and they were all discovered at quite a distance from where they were last seen. Carpet fibers on the bodies and tire impressions confirmed the relationship of the crimes and the fact that the victims had been transported.

It was clear that the killer was mobile and probably had or borrowed a vehicle. The ropes around the necks and brutal overkill showed deviance. The killer was believed to be a white male, in his mid-twenties, gregarious, extroverted, and manipulative. He would operate normally in society, but he would be argumentative, self-centered, selfish, and exhibit little or no emotion. He would also be impulsive, albeit not sufficiently so to risk being caught. At best, he'd have a high school education. If he'd even tried college, it was likely that he'd had trouble adjusting to the discipline and would have dropped out. He would have been intelligent but have issues with authority. He may have been truant and disruptive. In keeping with his self-image, he would probably take masculine jobs or a job where his manipulative skills would be useful.

His car of choice would be flashy, like a sports car. It was also likely that he would have a prison record, or some record of problems with the law. Prior to these murders, he may have committed neighborhood crimes, such as voyeurism or burglary.

More victims turned up in quick succession, but then seventeen-year-old Lisa McVey escaped from a man who had raped and tortured her in his home. She led the police back to the house, where they arrested Bobby Joe Long. He confessed not only to nine murders but added a series of rapes. By the time Florida was done with Bobby Joe Long, he had received two death sentences and thirty-four life sentences. The profile turned out to be largely correct.

Within the past two decades, there has been increased use of profiling, although it remains a controversial tool. Not everyone believes that devising a hypothetical portrait of a suspect contributes to solving crimes, but some have been surprisingly accurate. The problem is that it's difficult to know when the profile is a good one until the suspect is caught and compared against it.

Profiling has been developed in the FBI's Behavioral Science Unit by such people as John Douglas, Robert Ressler, and Roger DePue. However, it is also used by police departments all over the country—especially those with officers trained at the FBI's National Academy—as a tool in their crime-fighting arsenal. The basic idea for a profile is to gather a body of data yielding common patterns so that investigators can develop a general description of an unknown suspect (UNSUB). Profiling involves the psychology-trained expert using his or her knowledge in human behavior, motivation, and patterns of pathology to create a multidimensional report.

A profile is based on the idea that people tend to be guided by their individual psychology and will inevitably leave idiosyncratic clues. Are they male or female? Geographically stable or transient? Impulsive or compulsive? From a crime scene, a profiler can assess whether the person is an organized predator as opposed to having committed an impulsive crime of opportunity. They may also observe if the offender used a vehicle, exhibits criminal sophistication, or is addicted to a sexual fantasy.

Developing a profile works best off evidence of psychopathology, such as sadistic torture, postmortem mutilation, or pedophilia. Those conditions leave a better behavioral signature in terms of a personality quirk, such as staging the corpse for the most humiliating exposure, removing the eyes, or tying ligatures with a complicated bow. This helps to link crime scenes with one another and to alert law enforcement officers of the presence of a serial rapist, bomber, arsonist, or murderer. It may also help, if a pattern is detected, to predict future possible attacks, likely pickup or dump sites, and victim type.

Profiling is not just a personality assessment, but includes other types of data. Coming up with estimates about an offender's age, race, sex, occupation, educational level, social support system, MO, type of employment, and other sociological factors are just as important as evidence of a personality disorder. Generally, though, profilers employ psychological theories that provide ways to analyze mental deficiency such as delusions, personality characteristics like hostility, criminal thought patterns, and character defects. It's also important to include a geo-forensic analysis of the kind of place a killer might choose as a body dump site, such as Ted Bundy's preference for heavily wooded mountains.

The best profilers have gained their knowledge from experience with criminals and have developed an intuitive sense about certain types of crime. They also must know about actuarial data such as the age range into which offenders generally fall and how important an unstable family history is to criminality. This database often changes with new information, and that in turn influences how a profile may be developed. With increasingly more representatives from different racial groups and more women becoming serial offenders, the predictions about the UNSUB will shift to accommodate this data.

The Behavioral Science Unit, which got its start during the 1970s, was once part of the FBI's Training Division. In 1994, the Critical Incident Response Group (CIRG) integrated the FBI's crisis management, behavioral, and tactical resources within one entity. By that time the unit had become the Investigative Support Unit. At the same time, the Director of the FBI created the Child Abduction and Serial Killer Unit. Then the whole thing evolved into the Behavioral Analysis Unit, East and West. Based on the Protection of Children from Sexual Predators Act of 1998, the FBI received mandates related to crimes against children and serial murder, and one of them was the creation of the Child Abduction and Serial Murder Investigative Resource Center (CASMIRC). After the terrorist attacks of September 11, 2001, they trained agents in more counterterrorism responsibilities, and then the unit broke up into the Behavioral Analysis Unit 1 (counterterrorism and threat assessment), Behavioral Analysis Unit 2 (crimes against adults), Behavioral Analysis Unit 3 (crimes against children), and the VICAP Unit. The Training Division then recreated a new type of Behavioral Science Unit, not to be confused with the original profiling unit. They are involved in research and training at the National Academy, and are not operationally involved in cases.

Once agents are selected into one of the behavioral analysis units, they go through a sixteen-week classroom-based program, taught by both agents and outside professionals. They receive a foundation in psychology, and then specialize in criminal psychology, forensic science, Criminal Investigative Analysis, death investigation, threat assessment, and child abduction and homicide.

As always, those trained as profilers insist that there is no single answer or formula that fits every case of serial murder, or personality template that fits every serial killer. They address serial killer investigations in a multidisciplinary way, with input from law enforcement and academic and mental health professionals.

After offenders are caught and convicted, though, psychology plays a different role.

WHAT TO DO ABOUT CRIME

Some crimes are so heinous that the only response seems to be execution. In those states that have capital punishment, there's often a sentencing phase to a trial, in which the defendant can present mitigating factors to attempt to persuade a judge or jury not to deliver this ultimate punishment. Psychologists may be of assistance to them in this bid for mercy.

On October 7, 1998, Matthew Shepard, twenty-one, was found badly bludgeoned and tied to a split-rail fence east of Laramie, Wyoming. Despite emergency care, he died five days later and two young men were arrested for his assault and murder: Aaron McKinney, twenty-two, and Russell Henderson, twenty-one. Henderson accepted two life sentences for his testimony against McKinney. He admitted that they had picked up Shepard with the intent to rob him, but McKinney had beaten him savagely and ordered Henderson to help tie him up. McKinney's attorneys wanted to develop a case based on past traumatic homosexual episodes that had triggered rage against Shepard, but the court did not allow it. McKinney was convicted of felony murder, i.e., murder that occurs in conjunction with another felony crime such as kidnapping or armed robbery. He was eligible for the death penalty, and the prosecution was eager to press for that. But during the sentencing phase, psychiatric testimony helped to persuade all of those involved not to pressure for the death penalty, including Shepard's parents.

In the legal process, mental health professionals can often make a difference before a sentence is imposed. The purpose of a sentence involves one (or more) of four things: retribution, deterrence, community protection, and rehabilitation. But just how to decide what sentence an individual should get is not always easy.

The federal government, along with a number of states, has adopted determinate sentencing schemes to punish offenders equally, although this practice has come into question. These courts rely on sentencing guidelines that offer a range of time periods for given crimes, e.g., from ten to twenty years. In non–death penalty cases in most jurisdictions, the judge determines the sentence, but the probation department prepares a presentencing report with recommendations. They use all relevant information from the prosecutor, defendant, victims, defendant's family and employer. The defendant's attorney may suggest an appropriate sentence.

During this process, psychologists can make treatment suggestions, especially as they address the defendant's degree of culpability. They may also offer predictions about the future risk of reoffending. When there is little latitude in the sentencing, the clinician's role is restricted, but they can still discuss issues involving mental impairment or duress.

Death penalty cases are divided into a guilt phase and sentencing, or the penalty phase. During the latter, evidence is offered for aggravating or mitigating factors. A defense attorney may request a psychiatric assessment for the defendant, but a prosecutor may also do so as a way to strengthen the case against him or her. Aggravating factors might include such behaviors as a long criminal history or evidence of torture during the commission of a crime. Mitigating factors include childhood abuse, mental and neurological disorders, and distorted perception of danger. A jury considers the evidence and makes a decision.

In 1983, the Supreme Court upheld the constitutionality of permitting the death sentence based on predictions of future violence. In *Barefoot v. Estelle* such clinical testimony was allowed. Thomas Barefoot had burned down a barn and then shot and killed a police officer. He was convicted and subjected to a hearing for the death penalty. The decision was to be partly based on whether the defendant posed a threat of future dangerousness, and the state had to prove it beyond a reasonable doubt. The prosecution relied on the testimony of two psychiatrists who were given hypothetical situations similar to the case to consider and asked if the individual in the situation would probably commit future violent acts. Both said yes.

Professional organizations protested the reliability of such testimony, as well as of risk assessment in general based on such criteria, but the court cited precedents, and Barefoot's death sentence stood.

Since then, risk assessment has improved, and the predictions now utilize both clinical judgment and statistical data. The best predictions, however, are for short-term threat assessment, qualified by the context and its potential for change.

After someone has been sentenced to prison, psychologists may then see them in a different setting.

PRISON WORK

In a prison environment, clinicians generally classify prisoners for treatment programs, assess the presence of a mental illness, and consult on programs design, especially if it's about rehabilitation. They may also intervene in a crisis situation. How convicted offenders get classified is determined by psychological assessment tests, clinical interviews, and information about how well any given treatment works. Some offenders get singled out from the general population for special treatment, including repeat offenders, the mentally ill, sexual offenders, and youthful offenders.

Inmates are psychologically processed as they come into a jail or prison, and based on the testing results, are assigned to a facility or unit. Those at risk of suicide are placed under a twenty-four-hour watch. In prisons, inmates usually go to a reception center for assessments. Their records are reviewed, and they are interviewed and screened for emotional issues. Depending on their needs and risk factors, treatment goals are set. They may require anger management, addiction counseling, education, or vocational training. They may also need medication.

Clinicians aim to manage high-risk individuals, identify factors that contributed to their crimes, and focus on pro-social skills development for future release. Prison itself will not correct the criminal tendencies. In fact, studies have shown that prisons tend to inspire inmates to repeat or get worse.

Those offenders who can be placed in alternative programs outside prisons, such as supervisory halfway houses, may have a better chance to readjust to normal life. They may be able to work, attend school, visit with family, and get job training. Some offenders remain in their own homes under house arrest, with an electronic monitoring device. All such programs involve continued counseling and program participation.

THE CIVIL ARENA

While most people associate forensic psychologists with criminal proceedings or profiling, they engage in quite a bit of work on the civil side of legal issues as well. Among the issues that mental health experts may handle in civil court or mediation are personal injury cases involving trauma or emotional pain and suffering. Post-traumatic stress disorder is a common condition for assessment in civil cases. Yet attempting to provide a standard definition for this condition has been difficult, as has been evaluating its long-term effects, especially in terms of monetary awards.

Another area of concern for psychology is the involuntary commitment of a person who may become violent toward others or himself. A psychiatrist may have to assess the possibility that he or she should be hospitalized, even if that person does not wish to be. Depending on the state, a finding of "dangerous" may range from imminent threat of violence to self-neglect that may lead to foreseeable deterioration.

And then there are issues with child custody. Mental health experts may be asked to assess a parent's abilities to care for a child, based on the child's best interests. At stake are issues of visitation privileges and possible treatment for a parent or family.

Workplace issues also come under the purview of forensic psychology. Mental health professionals have played important roles in labor law, including the evaluation of employee complaints that involve emotional injury. They cannot express an opinion about whether an environment is hostile or abusive, but they may assess long-range emotional distress, which in itself can be suggestive of hostility in the workplace.

While many of these concerns play out in the background stories on *C.S.I.*, the episodes have grown bolder in addressing deviant or abnormal psychology. But that subject deserves its own chapter.

CHAPTER SIX

Deviance

In an episode of *CSI-LV*, "Committed," viewers got inside a psychiatric hospital for dangerous offenders, drawing them into the strange world of abnormal criminal psychology. Several disorders were mentioned, including some that are not formally accepted by the professional community. Delving into the arena of mental illness adds dimension to criminality far beyond the stereotypes of paranoid schizophrenia and multiple personality disorders. To solve some crimes, the C.S.I.s must be familiar with certain behavioral aberrations.

THE DIAGNOSTIC BIBLE

For diagnosis, billing, and treatment, mental health practitioners in the United States rely primarily on the symptoms and codes found in

The Diagnostic and Statistical Manual of Mental Disorders (DSM-IV-TR), now in its fourth edition. It conveys information about mental illness to insurance and managed care organizations, and provides common reference points among professionals for referrals and professional articles. Containing a standard diagnostic system, it goes through changes as the profession evolves in its research and understanding of psychological disability. The coding and classification of these disabilities relies on three diagnostic axes and two that cover conditions other than defined clinical syndromes. Inside the pages are clinical issues, personality disorders, medical conditions, psychosocial and environmental problems, and problems with global functioning.

Not all of these are germane to the forensic arena. Among those disorders that affect a person's state at the time of an offense or while going through the legal system, some are rather surprising.

PSYCHOLOGICAL ODDITIES

Sleepwalking

An episode in New York, " 'Night, Mother," involved a woman found near a person stabbed to death, and she apparently had no memory of what she might or might not have done because she was sleeping the entire time. Viewers might find that incredible, but the disorder has actually entered the courts in several incidents involving murder.

In Arizona, Scott Falater stabbed his wife forty-four times and shoved her body into their swimming pool. He then went inside, washed off his hands, and stashed his bloody clothing into a plastic container in the trunk of his car. Arrested for it when a neighbor sent the police to his house, he claimed that he was sleepwalking and did not know what he was doing. Apparently he did have a history of sleepwalking, and the prosecutor could offer only a lame motive for murder. There had been no evidence of trouble between him and his wife, and his children argued on his behalf. In addition, sleep disorder experts testified about other cases where a person committed murder in his sleep. Nevertheless, at his 1999 trial, Falater was convicted of first-degree murder and received life in prison.

The condition is known as automatism, and it means that some part of the brain has shut down while other parts remain active enough to compel the sleeper to move around. The person lacks *mens rea* for whatever he does while asleep. Thus, his behavior is involuntary. This defense does not work if it can be shown that the defendant had this condition on previous occasions, especially committing violence, and did not take steps to remedy it. It is a rare and extraordinary defense, but it has nevertheless resulted in several acquittals.

In 1987 in Canada, Kenneth Parks, twenty-three, savagely beat to death his mother-in-law and father-in-law with a tire iron and then stabbed them with a knife. His father-in-law survived. Parks claimed that he was asleep during the entire episode. He got into his car, drove to the police, and said that he had killed two people. The medical experts agreed that on that night he did not have voluntary control over his actions. He was acquitted.

Amputee Wannabe

Another episode of *CSI-NY*, "Outside Man," involved a unique syndrome in which people want desperately to amputate some healthy body part with which they cannot bear to live. They become obsessed with removing it, to the point where they participate in dangerous surgeries (including self-surgery) or even kill themselves. One young man with a perfectly normal forehead could not accept that it wasn't too large, and so he finally committed suicide to escape the humiliation of his "deformity." The most common desire is to amputate the leg above the knee, but many people suffering from this disorder just go for the fingers or toes. Nevertheless, surgeons tend to dismiss or shy away from people who seek extreme voluntary disfigurement.

In some instances, a person will damage the offending limb to the point where a surgeon believes it must be removed to save his or her life. They've shot themselves, froze the limb, hacked it with a chainsaw, or burned it to achieve their goals. Once the limb is taken off, the person believes his troubles will disappear. Some professionals refer to this group as "amputee wannabes." They believe the limb they want removed hinders them from being fully themselves. They don't understand it; they just "know" it's true, as with people who undergo sex-reassignment surgery. In some cases, people have become obsessed with amputation because they viewed another amputee in an erotic context, and thus became attracted to the idea of becoming an amputee.

Some professionals view the condition as an offshoot of body dysmorphic disorder (a.k.a. body integrity identity disorder), which is a mistaken belief that a body part is ugly or abnormal, and others see it as "apotemnophilia," or a type of paraphilia or displaced sexual desire. Another suggestion for a diagnostic category has been factitious disability disorder, because some such people actually pretend to be amputees, the way people with Munchausen's Syndrome (a factitious disorder) pretend to be ill in order to get the attention of physicians and hospitals. This condition has been documented in professional articles and documentary films. No one has investigated a cure, apart from outright amputation, and there are doctors willing to perform it at the behest of treating clinicians.

Renfield's Syndrome

In "Committed" a passing reference is made to a strange vampiric disease in which blood has an erotic connotation. It does not appear in the DSM-IV, but it's nevertheless gained some backing, because there have been genuine cases in which people believe they need blood so badly to survive that they will kill other human beings to get it.

Psychologist Richard Noll, author of *Vampires, Werewolves and Demons*, coined the term Renfield's Syndrome for clinical vampirism, based on the lunatic in Bram Stoker's *Dracula* who eats spiders and drinks blood from birds. People suffering from this syndrome are primarily male, and when interviewed they indicate that blood acquires a mystical, even supernatural, quality. Noll describes the typical progression:

"Renfield's Syndrome is a psychiatric syndrome and the character of Renfield lived out in his own life the same stages of development that clinical vampires manifest. The first stage involves some event that happens before puberty where the child is excited in a sexual way by blood injury or the ingestion of blood. At puberty it becomes fused with sexual fantasies, and typically the person with Renfield's Syndrome begins with autovampirism. That is, they begin to drink their own blood and then move on to other living creatures. That's the zoophagous element that Dr. Seward talks about in *Dracula*.

"The novel was published in 1897, and at that time in both occultism and science, there was a great deal of belief in the idea of 'correspondences,' where two beings who shared some sort of essence would eventually find each other. That's an ancient scientific theory that goes back to the Greeks, and by the nineteenth century, it had become an occult belief. However, in biology, the theory of vitalism was to some degree a theory of correspondences. The term *gene* wasn't coined until 1909, and Mendel published his famous work in 1900, so before we really knew the mechanisms of heredity, it was thought that some vital force was passed down in a way that like would attract like. There was also a theory of degeneracy that was based on the idea that degenerates would attract one another. It takes one to know one."

Despite its historical associations, the syndrome has shown up around the world, sometimes coupled with cannibalism.

Fetal Snatchers

One case that the C.S.I.s in Vegas investigated in "Bad to the Bone" involved an unsolved cold case in which a pregnant woman was killed and her fetus was taken from her and raised by the killer's sister. In fact, this kind of crime has its own category, "fetal snatchers," and there have been a number of such murders. Quite often, however, the pregnant woman is targeted and stalked before being murdered.

On December 16, 2004, Bobbi Jo Stinnett, twenty-three and eight months pregnant with a baby girl, was killed in Missouri. The story quickly unfolded. She had met Lisa Montgomery on an Internet message board and had apparently arranged to meet her in person. Little did she know that Montgomery had targeted her because she was pregnant.

When Montgomery came to Stinnett's home, she allegedly strangled Stinnett and removed the female baby. Montgomery then allegedly took the child from Missouri to Kansas, where she told her husband she'd given birth while shopping and tried to pass the child off as her own. In the meantime, Stinnett was found lying in a pool of blood. Her mother discovered her and called the police. The medical examiner indicated during the autopsy that she had been cut open laterally to facilitate removal of the baby.

Detectives examined Stinnett's e-mail and located Montgomery. DNA

tests confirmed that the child was the Stinnetts' so Zeb Stinnett, the father, was allowed to take her home. Montgomery was arrested and
charged with kidnapping resulting in a death. As of the writing of this
book, Montgomery has not yet gone to trial.

This was the eighth incident of this nature recorded by the National
Center for Missing and Exploited Children over the past two decades.
Such crimes are generally committed by women using a confidence-
type scam. They usually have a history of deception and tend to develop a relationship with a "predetermined target." In 2002, a study
was published in the *Journal of Forensic Sciences* on kidnap by Ce-
sarean section, and it was found that those who committed such
crimes were self-centered, obsessed with babies, and lived in a fantasy
world but were not considered psychotic. They often fail to think
ahead to the questions they'll be asked or about practical matters
such as birth certificates. In one case, the woman actually cut the fetus out with a car key while the mother was still alive.

Folie à deux/Induced Psychotic Disorder

This is a contagious madness or a delusion shared by two people,
which can influence a crime or suicide pact. It's been in psychiatric
literature since the seventeenth century, and between 1877 and 1996,
there were nearly four hundred published cases. People have jumped
off cliffs together, put bags over their heads to catch a ride on a space
ship, and believed one or both of them are being persecuted by some
conspiracy. Usually a dominant person develops the delusion and in-
duces psychosis into another person, most often a spouse or family
member. Sometimes, entire families are affected. Typically, the secondary partner gains something from sharing in the delusion, such as
preserving a relationship.

In England, a man reported to the police that he had witnessed a murder. His sister-in-law, Myra Hindley, had a boyfriend, Ian Brady, who had smashed open a man's head with an axe. The police found the victim's body and arrested Brady and Hindley on the spot. They soon learned that these two had murdered two children and buried them on the moors. As the investigation developed, the police suspected them in several other disappearances of children in the area, but they refused to confess and it was impossible to search the entire moors.

Brady was a postmodern nihilist with a criminal record, who had enlisted eighteen-year-old Hindley in his plan to commit the perfect murder. Their first victim in 1963 had been a sixteen-year-old girl. Before meeting him, Hindley had been a simple girl, easily infatuated, who liked children and animals. According to her diary, Brady gradually convinced her that morality was relative and some people were "supermen," and above the law. She eventually expressed the same sentiments of hatred that he did. He proposed that they enrich themselves through a life of crime, to which she acceded. Participating in his delusions, she became a killer. In 1966, both were sentenced to life in prison.

Other Rare Disorders

Among the most unusual syndromes or disorders are the following, some of which have shown up or been mentioned on a *C.S.I.* episode:

- Capgras's Syndrome—the delusion that others (or one's own self) have been replaced by imposters; it's often reported in paranoid schizophrenia and organic brain disease, and can lead to violence against the supposed imposter, especially if there's fear that the imposter is trying to harm or take over the deluded individual.

■ *Pseudologia Fantastica*—constant lying without any discernable purpose that is created by an underlying pathology; a certain amount of this behavior occurs in factitious disorders, APD, and psychopathy. It has numerous implications in court, from assisting in one's defense to perjury.

■ Jocasta Complex—a mother's libidinous fixation on her son, which may lead her to seduce him and carry on a sexual relationship. She will also attempt to keep complete control over him, to his detriment.

■ Pica—the compulsion to eat nonfood items, such as dirt, coffee grounds, hair, paint chips, or plaster. It usually occurs in children suffering from some other disorder, and it's considered temporary, although it can result in malnutrition and poisoning.

More common psychological conditions, especially among criminals, are the psychotic syndromes and personality disorders. We'll deal with the latter first.

Personality Disorders

A character or personality disorder is an enduring, maladaptive pattern of perceiving and relating to the environment, hindering one's normal functioning. These disorders manifest in the way people think, feel, and control their impulses. They generally cause a significant amount of distress to the person and/or to others. (In a few of them, the person fails to see that the problems emerge from him or her.)

There are ten recognized categories, which are grouped into "clusters." In cluster A are the bizarre disorders: paranoid, schizoid, and schizotypal. Cluster B includes antisocial, narcissistic, borderline, and histrionic, while avoidant, dependent, and obsessive-compulsive comprise cluster C.

While symptoms of one may overlap with another (borderline and antisocial are often narcissistic), clinicians look for a combination of several items to make a formal diagnosis: the chief complaint, long-term symptoms, known childhood difficulties, medical conditions, psychosocial stressors, IQ, and current mental status. Those personality disorders that most often occupy forensic mental health specialists in criminal cases are found in cluster B, so let's look at those more closely.

Narcissistic personality disorder is characterized by a pattern of grandiosity and an excessive need for admiration. Such people can achieve great things because they think so highly of themselves, but often people around them suffer. They tend to have an exaggerated sense of being special such that they limit their associations only to others they deem worthy. They may freely exploit others to advance their own ambitions, fail to develop empathy, and view others as envious. Their sense of entitlement makes them insufferable and they often engage in arrogant behaviors. Sometimes they're so self-important they think they're above the law, and that's when they're vulnerable to committing crimes.

More volatile are people with borderline personality disorder. Their relationships are unstable, in part because they exhibit poor impulse control, volatile emotions, a self-image that fluctuates between empty despair and grandiosity, excessive behaviors, and sometimes self-mutilation. They're known to over-idealize the very people upon whom they might suddenly turn with terrible accusation. They're anxious about being abandoned, but also fear engulfment within a relationship, so they offer mixed signals that wear out those closest to them. They can also become intensely paranoid or experience transient psychosis or dissociation, and can display intense anger. While they make frequent threats of suicide, they rarely carry them out.

But then there's antisocial personality disorder. It's often confused with psychopathy or sociopathy, and may one day be redefined to accommodate those populations. People with antisocial personality disorder are defiant of social norms, deceptive and manipulative, have had juvenile records, and quite often break the law. But they don't necessarily share some of the more dangerous characteristics of a predatory psychopath, so let's turn to that category instead. It's not among the personality disorders listed in the *DSM-IV*, but it's used internationally to describe a specific type of person.

Among the most dangerous features of psychopathy are a callous disregard for the rights of others and a propensity for violating norms. Psychopaths feel no remorse. They might not necessarily become outright criminals, let alone killers, but the likelihood of exploitive and deceptive behavior is high. Without remorse, psychopaths charm and manipulate others for their own gain. They lack a sense of responsibility and they con others with no regard for anyone's feelings. In fact, they don't see others as human. Those with low inhibitions against violence may kill.

Psychopaths are not considered to be mentally ill, but from brain scan studies it appears that they fail to process the emotional content of situations, such as empathy, concern, or alarm. Those who commit crimes have proven more brutal than other criminals, more aggressive, and more diverse in their activities. It's likely that the offender who kidnapped Nick in *CSI-LV*'s "Grave Danger" would receive this diagnosis. They also represent a high percentage of repeat offenders. They're resistant to therapy and intolerant of frustration. It doesn't matter whom they hurt; what matters is getting what they can for themselves. Because they don't have what people need for living in social harmony, some psychologists refer to them as "unfinished souls."

Robert R. Hare, a renowned expert on the disorder and author of *Without Conscience,* says that while there is plenty of data about psychopaths in prison populations, we know little about how the disorder manifests in the public at large. Nevertheless, there are indications that the personality structure and propensity for unethical behavior is shared by both criminal and noncriminal psychopaths, and they may be as common as one in every hundred people.

For the most part, when they offend, their crimes are cold-blooded and there appears to be a strong tendency toward sadism. They find victims easily because they're glib, charming, and predatory, while their victims are generally naïve. So they may thrive among us with homes and families. They may attend church (although without struggles of conscience) and even be considered good neighbors; they know how to go through the motions. But they're interested only in their own purposes and they have no qualms, when the time is right, about taking advantage.

Dissociative Identity Disorder (Multiple Personality Disorder)

This disorder has been confused with schizophrenia as a split identity, but it's generally quite different. Two or more subpersonalities develop in a single human being, each with its own identity, and each takes turns controlling the personality and behavior. The "core" person generally experiences periods of memory loss and may even find himself or herself in a foreign place with no idea how they arrived there. This is called an amnesic barrier between identities. One "person" may have full access to the memory bank, while others get only partial access. In some cases, the subpersonalities know which one the controlling or core personality is.

The first description of this condition may have been by S. L. Mitchell in 1816. A young British woman became psychologically disturbed as a teenager. She'd fall asleep and wake up seemingly a changed person. She had no memory of things she'd experienced and would have to relearn

what she'd known; after a few months, she'd sleep deeply again and emerge with her prior memories intact but the things she had learned over the previous few months now gone. The physician who described her saw her make these changes over a period of four years, and apparently she was thus affected until her death.

It's commonly believed that people with DID often develop it from an early childhood trauma, such as sexual abuse or violent beatings. They learned to dissociate—to mentally remove themselves from full awareness of the situation—and this form of psychological flight became a survival mechanism. This then disturbs the normal integrative functions of identity and memory. Polyfragmented DID may involve several hundred different identities in a single body. Some practitioners say it's extremely rare, while others believe it's more common than we even know.

Psychotic Disorders

The most prevalent of the psychotic disorders, schizophrenia, is often misunderstood as a split personality (just mentioned above). Actually, schizophrenia is an illness marked by a confusion of thinking and speech that is at times chronic and often marked by intermittent attacks. It occurs equally in men and women, generally appears between the ages of fifteen and thirty-five, and affects about 1 percent of the population. There appears to be a genetic component, in that a person may inherit a tendency toward its occurrence.

Schizophrenia can cause the sufferer to withdraw from the world and retreat into delusions and fantasies. The person's perception and thinking about reality can be so impaired as to become dangerous. The research evidence suggests that the cause of schizophrenia is either a chemical or structural abnormality of the brain—perhaps a combination of both. Initial symptoms include a mild feeling of tension, sleep disturbances, and general disinterest. In its worst phases, people experience delusions, hallucinations, or disordered speech. Some sufferers develop violent tendencies, although there is a misperception that this condition is inherently violent.

Of the different types of schizophrenia, the one of most concern in criminal work is paranoid schizophrenia, because voices may command a person to kill or take his own life, damage property, stalk someone, or otherwise cause havoc. People with this illness are difficult to medicate because they suspect others of poisoning them.

This is a lifelong illness with no known cure as yet. Antipsychotic drugs may help to stabilize the brain chemistry but must be taken under close supervision. There are many criminal cases in which a person stopped taking his or her medication. For example, a fatal tragedy in New York involved Andrew Goldstein, who had been treated for schizophrenia but had stopped taking his medication. He walked up to a woman waiting for a subway train and as it approached, he pushed her into its path, killing her. He was tried and convicted of murder.

But schizophrenia is not the only psychotic illness. Bipolar affective or manic-depressive disorder is characterized by dramatic mood swings that border on delusional. Such people may have intense periods of high energy in which they seem superhuman. They go without rest for long periods, have grandiose ideas, and seem to accomplish an astonishing amount. However, they may then swing into serious depression, accompanied by dangerously low self-esteem. They may hear voices during either phase, but between phases they may stabilize.

There are also disorders that may be deemed to be conditions of temporary insanity, such as extreme emotional disturbance and some forms of impulsive disorder. Any of these are vulnerable to being faked, and some of the most clever and dangerous criminals have actually studied abnormal psychology to learn how to do it.

Let's turn now to an extreme form of psychological instability that can be highly unpredictable.

Stalkers

On "Weeping Willows," the *CSI-LV* team is deflected in the wrong direction, thanks to an obsessive stalker who followed his former girlfriend with a GPS, saw her with a man, and killed her to frame the man. To reinforce this, he killed another random victim and left evidence pointing to the same man. Such elaborate plans are part of the obsession of a stalker and to solve this case, the team had to understand the nature of this type of calculating obsession. What we know about stalkers comes from a few tragic cases and from the psychologists who have taken the time to amass data and examine just what goes into becoming a stalker.

Actress Rebecca Schaeffer, twenty-one, played a character on the popular 1980s television sitcom *My Sister Sam*. She received a lot of fan mail and she tried to respond to each letter personally. A nineteen-year-old man from Tucson, Arizona, Robert John Bardo, had written to her and she had sent him a signed photograph. He became fixated on her, so he tracked her down. At dawn on the morning of July 18, 1989, he went to Schaeffer's Hollywood apartment. After a courier had delivered scripts to someone in the building, he decided to just go ahead and ring the buzzer.

Schaeffer opened the door and had a short conversation with him. He was about to leave but then went back to see her. When she opened the door a second time, he produced a gun and shot her in the chest. Schaeffer fell to the ground and died. Earlier, he had penned a note: "I have an obsession with the unattainable. I have to eliminate what I cannot attain." His sister turned him in.

Something similar had happened to another actress in 1982. Arthur Jackson had seen Theresa Saldana in the movie *Deliverance* and found himself hopelessly attracted to her. He decided to kill her, get caught, and get the death penalty so he could join her in death. He found her address through a detective agency that similarly got the address from the California Department of Motor Vehicles. Jackson went to her home and when he saw her, he stabbed her ten times, but a deliveryman intervened. She survived and Jackson was convicted of attempted murder. Yet he continued to send her threatening letters.

These cases provoked the first anti-stalking legislation. Country-wide, stalking was taken more seriously and by 1993, all states, as well as Canada, put anti-stalking laws into effect. According to the legislation, a stalker is defined as "someone who willfully, maliciously, and repeatedly follows or harasses another victim and who makes a credible threat with the intent to place the victim or victim's immediate family in fear of their safety." There must be at least two incidents to constitute the crime and show a "continuity of purpose" or credible threat. Another name for it is psychological terrorism.

Plenty of celebrities get stalked, but by far the more common type of stalking occurs between people who once had been intimate. Generally the delusion becomes an obsession and even a form of harassment through phone calls, unwanted gifts, letters, and surveillance. It's the "if I can't have you, nobody will" approach. Sometimes it has fatal consequences for one or both parties, or even for a third party. The typical person suffering from this delusion is single, unable to sustain close relationships, has a history of obsessive attachments, attains "unattainable" objects through fantasy, and may become predatory.

Then there's erotomania, which is the stalker's belief that another person loves him or her. It follows a fairly predictable progression: After initial contact, the stalker develops feelings of infatuation and places the love object on a pedestal. He or she then begins to approach the target person. It might take a while, but once contact is made, the stalker's persistent and sometimes frightening behavior sets him up for rejection. Rejection triggers the delusion through which the stalker projects his own feelings onto the object. The stalker also develops intense anger to mask his shame, which fuels the obsessive pursuit of the object. He now wants to control through harassment or injury: The stalker must restore his narcissistic fantasy. Violence is most likely to occur when the love object is devalued, as through an imagined betrayal (such as Bardo believed about Schaeffer when she took a role that contradicted her "little sister" image).

While many stalkers only threaten harm, a small percentage of them do carry out their threats—including damage against property or harm to pets. With the rise in popularity of the Internet, cyber-stalking has become yet another avenue of danger. Many have a prior criminal record and show evidence of substance abuse, a mood disorder, a personality disorder, or even psychosis.

There's no easy way to predict who might become a stalker: It could be a former boyfriend, girlfriend, or spouse; a fellow employee who has spotted his target in some casual encounter; a hostile neighbor; a video store clerk; even a stranger who happens to have seen the victim on the street. Even people who were not abusive prior to their obsession can become so in the throes of it.

On "Weeping Willows," that stalker actually took his obsession and anger so far that he became a serial killer. So let's turn now to that phenomenon.

Serial Killers

A number of episodes of *C.S.I.* have featured serial killers, such as the "Blue Paint Killer" in Vegas, warranting an overview of what criminologists and psychologists know about this breed of offender. In "Whacked," (*CSI-M*), DNA evidence from the throat of a victim who was one of a series of ax murders indicated that the killer, about to be executed, had an accomplice. To properly investigate this crime involved not just the psychology of serial murder but also the interaction between two people acting in tandem to commit such crimes. That's rare, but it does happen.

On October 17, 1977, a woman was strangled and dumped near the entrance to Forest Lawn Hollywood Hills Cemetery in Los Angeles, California. Four more women and three girls were killed in quick succession and dumped by the roadside. Thousands of leads were called in and the media dubbed the killer the "Hillside Strangler." Yet police believed there had to be two men involved.

Another murdered prostitute was soon found naked on the side of a hill. She appeared to have been posed in a spread-eagle fashion as an insulting statement. This time, there were witnesses who had seen two males with her.

Suddenly, the murders stopped as quickly as they had begun. Police waited through the holidays with no new bodies. Then on February 17, 1978, a highway helicopter patrol spotted an orange compact car crashed off a highway, and locked inside the trunk was victim number ten. But again the murders stopped.

Almost a year after the last Los Angeles victim was discovered, in Bellingham, Washington, two female college roommates were reported missing. They had done a security job for Ken Bianchi, a good-looking man with a girlfriend and infant son who was a captain at the security company. Police questioned him, but he denied any knowledge of the girls. They found the address for where the girls were house-sitting and then found their car. Inside were the bodies of both.

Bianchi was linked via hair and fibers to these murders. The police then linked him through his California driver's license with the string of the Los Angeles murders from the year before, and it turned out he had jowelry in his home from two of those girls. It didn't take long to connect him with his cousin, Angelo Buono, who ran a car upholstery shop near many of the body dumpsites.

Bianchi tried to fake that he had multiple personality disorder but he was caught and accepted a plea deal to testify against his cousin in return for life in prison. In 1982, the trial commenced. With physical evidence and Bianchi's statements, Buono was convicted of nine of the ten murders and got nine life sentences. Bianchi, who had pleaded guilty to five, was given five life sentences on top of the two he had in Washington.

Criminalists differ somewhat on the definition of a serial killer, but the FBI's official manual indicates that to be thus classified, there must be at least three different murder events at three different locations, with a cooling-off period between events, while the National Institute of Justice (NIJ) allows for only two incidents and also includes the idea of team serial killers. The FBI emphasizes different locations, but some killers murder their victims in the same place at different times. The NIJ's definition indicates that the motive is often psychological and the behavior at the crime scene will suggest sexual overtones.

Despite the emphasis in some definitions and in the media on sexual homicides, serial killing might also be driven by greed, thrill, lust, or even revenge. In many cases, the killer is relieving pressure, either sexual or from some other type of need, and generally does not desire to be stopped or caught. Once done, the need subsides but then often awakens again to renew the cycle. In all likelihood, such killers cannot stop, although they may have a period of dormancy that can last years. Typically, they lead double lives, deflecting attention from themselves as violent individuals.

With the arrest of Dennis L. Rader, a family man and church member, for the series of murders in Wichita attributed to the "BTK" killer and Gary Ridgeway in Seattle for the long string of murders that pegged him as the Green River Killer, people wonder how such violent criminals can move among them without detection for so long. In part, it's due to the secretive nature of such offenders, but they're also assisted by the cultural attitude that monsters are obvious. In other words, a Cub Scout leader, church president, and seemingly responsible citizen can succeed in extreme deviant behavior by exploiting naïve cultural assumptions.

We've had clear cases of this: the good-looking and charming Ted Bundy worked a crisis hotline as he murdered young women; John Wayne Gacy, a successful businessman, buried boys beneath his house while he hobnobbed with politicians and entertained sick kids as a clown; and Spokane's prostitute killer Robert Yates, Jr., was a decorated ex-army pilot with five children. Many have had families and jobs. Serial Killer Jerome Brudos actually murdered young women and hung them up in his home workshop with his wife, mother, and two children only steps away.

Some serial killers blend in because they're the type of person who can go through the motions of ordinary living and yet act out against others without giving themselves away. In other words, they're not obviously deranged, and can hide behind a bland everyday manner. A few, like Bianchi, have even enlisted others in their crimes.

Eric W. Hickey, a criminologist who wrote about a study involving over three hundred serial killers, said in *Serial Murderers and Their Victims* that "for some multiple killers, murder must be simultaneously a participation and a spectator endeavor; power can be experienced by observing a fellow conspirator destroy human life, possibly as much as by performing the killing. The pathology of the relationship operates symbiotically." The killers each add something to the other's excitement. Perhaps what they could not do alone, they could do within the chemistry of the dangerous association.

According to the study, 74 percent of team killers are white; female killers participate with males around one-third of the time; and
the majority of cases involve only two offenders working together. Of
victims of serial murder, some 15 percent were murdered by team
killers and in the majority of cases, the victims were strangers. Sometimes the team leader or dominant partner sends the others out to do
what he wants, and sometimes he participates. At times they're related or married, and other times they're strangers who happened to
spark the right chemistry. When females are involved, it's generally
the male who masterminds the homicides, unless the female is dominant, such as in a mother-son team. There is almost always one person who maintains psychological control.

There may be an association between smell and confidence that makes
the difference between someone who fears a predator and someone who
feels comfortable enough to go along with him—even to the point of a
partnership. Smelling oxytocin can make someone unusually trusting in
another person, sufficiently to give him money for a business deal, get
into his car with him, or let him into the house. Thirteen men playing an in-
vestment game who inhaled a nasal spray spiked with the hormone gave
more money (in the form of tokens) to partners in risky investments, according to one study in economics at the University of Zurich, than the
same number of males who had inhaled a placebo nasal spray. In fact,
about half of them gave all of their tokens to their partners, in contrast to
only one of the placebo participants. Previous animal studies indicated
that oxytocin encourages long-term mating between pairs and nurturing
behavior in mothers, because it appears to foster trust necessary for
bonding. In social situations, it affects a person's willingness to take a
risk.

In other words, oxytocin's presence adds a measure of trust to a personal interaction. The question remains whether a confident psychopath, like a confident lover or businessman, might secrete that hormone in such a way as to inspire trust in his potential victim.

The majority of serial killers operate alone. Some are organized predators who study the ways of law enforcement in order to carry out their crimes for as long as possible, while others are more disorganized and generally make mistakes that makes apprehension easier and faster. Richard Trenton Chase, the 1978 "Vampire of Sacramento," would kill his victims in the middle of the day and walk out into the open with blood on his clothing—even walk up to people he knew. It was clear that whoever had murdered a woman in one place and a family in another did not have a car and probably lived in the neighborhood. Thanks to reports of his frightening behavior, Chase was soon arrested.

A signature, defined in chapter five, also facilitates solving a series of crimes. Many killers who move from one victim to another leave a personal imprint that links them to each incident (some are obvious, others are subtle.) Grissom discovered this in "What's Eating Gilbert Grissom?" when a taunting killer left a strand of hair behind, along with notes and gruesome artwork. Signatures in real life include the "Texas Eyeball Killer," who removed the eyes of his victims; Jack Unterweger, who covered them with leaves and used their underwear to strangle them; and "Gainesville Ripper" Danny Rolling, who cut them up and left them posed provocatively. He'd also shower afterward in their apartments. Some killers remove shoes or jewelry, and some communicate what they've done to the press or police. These rituals offer psychological satisfaction. Often the behavior is linked with something in that person's fantasy or it reveals a specific psychopathology.

When such linked events occur, there is always the risk that media coverage will inspire a copycat. This person either wants the notoriety or wants to kill someone but hopes to leave their victims in such a way that the police will include them in the series. Often the copycat fails to accomplish a good replication, and gets spotted for what he or she is. They've overlooked something, staged something too obviously, or forgotten a crucial detail (which may have been withheld from reports by the police for just such a purpose).

The more we learn about serial killers, the more it becomes clear that there are distinct subtypes. One such category, for example, depicts health-care serial killers—doctors and nurses who kill patients. Among the world's most notorious murderers with one of the highest victim tolls was a "kindly" British doctor, Harold Shipman. But thanks to him, an effective method of detection may be utilized.

Although he committed suicide in his cell in Wakefield Prison in 2004, a renewed inquiry into Shipman's practice ended with a startling announcement on January 27, 2005. He'd had an estimated 260 or more victims, killed mostly with lethal injections of diamorphine. It was initially believed that Shipman, a GP, who made house calls to the elderly (mostly women), had taken advantage of the easy pickings among such patients. But that idea has proven to be erroneous. While he certainly engaged in such behavior on a large scale, it seems that he preyed on other types of patients as well. The latest report confirmed that Shipman appeared to have killed at least twenty-two patients in hospitals before he began his practice as a GP. Shipman mocked his victims and used derogatory codes for them, such as WOW—Whining Old Woman, and FTPBI—Failed to Put Brain In. He clearly had no concern for their welfare.

Not long afterward, a study indicated that a statistical analysis could have pinpointed Shipman as a killer. The UK Medical Research Council's Biostatistics Unit in Cambridge applied a statistical method used to ensure quality of explosives during World War II and since then in various industry settings, to data about Shipman's victims to determine if his quiet rampage might have been detected earlier. Having a high percentage of deaths is not considered sufficient, since Shipman and many like him tend to work among patients expected to die. However, cross-referencing other facts with those deaths may have waved some red flags. For example, often the deaths associated with him in a hospital setting occurred just after he started his rounds. With this method, the data from multiple years can be simultaneously compared. It's currently being adapted from industry applications to a healthcare setting.

And deviance does not always issue in violence. Subcultures often form around unusual fetishes and behaviors. Mostly, they're benign, even those that involve what appear to be extreme or painful practices. Yet within these subcultures incidents do occur that require investigation, so those investigators who go in must be prepared.

CHAPTER SEVEN

Learning the Language

At times, the C.S.I.s are thrust into an unusual subculture to investigate a crime; more to the point, they may need to know something about that subculture to solve it. That gets them into an arena that only a select few researchers have studied. Yet insights for investigative purposes are available.

From Vegas to Miami to New York, C.S.I.s have talked with gang members, professional clowns, trapeze artists, "vampires," bondage-and-discipline aficionados, extreme sports fanatics, videogame programmers, and even people who don giant animal costumes for erotic gatherings. They've gone to elite dog shows and made their way through the exotic world of high fashion. They've also been drawn into the arena of celebrity murder, with its privilege and protocol, and had to deal with the "Dove Commission," a group of judges committed to exposing police department errors. When the solution to a crime requires knowing about the subculture, they have no choice but to adopt a tailored approach to arrest, interrogation, and crime reconstruction. In addition, they must operate with an open mind, because members of subcultures quickly retreat from judgment and condemnation.

Superstars

Celebrities sometimes accept their own publicity to such an extent that they believe they're above the law. They're buffered by money, people, and an aura that they're untouchable. Sadly, often they do manage to sidestep the consequences of their acts, which can frustrate investigators who've worked hard to bring them to justice. As former Los Angeles prosecutor Marcia Clark said in an issue of *Justice* magazine, "He who has the most popular, sympathetic client, wins." Given the results of a number of celebrity trials over the past decade, it's clear that the "aura" does have an effect.

Yet celebrities also claim that the abundant publicity about them prior to trial puts them at a disadvantage. As early as 1807, politician Aaron Burr declared that due to publicity he could not get a fair trial, and his complaints have been echoed throughout successive decades, especially in our age of the celebrity arrests. Many trial consultants have noted the "unique calculus" that attends these proceedings and some are poised to offer celebrities advice as to whether or not they should leverage their fame and rally their fans to drive the publicity to their advantage.

Still, there are ways to get past the glitter and bring these people back down to earth . . . hard. On "Stalkerazzi," an episode of *CSI-M*, a movie star is caught in a photograph shooting a woman who is later found dead. While he claims the culprit is his movie double and also his live-in manager, the truth emerges and a case is made against him. Yet the difficulties were obvious: All around him were paid protectors—managers, attorneys, and security guards—who attempted to thwart the investigation. That's a reflection of real life.

Michael Jackson has twice been publicly accused of molesting young boys. The first time, in 1993, he settled the case for a reported $15 to $20 million. Then in 2004, Santa Barbara County D.A. Tom Sneddon decided that this time Jackson would stand trial. The defense claimed that the accusing family was looking for money, while the prosecution said they had a legitimate case of child abuse. Despite Jackson's impressive entourage of bodyguards, spokespeople, flacks and personal assistants, the police did manage to get search warrants to go through his property, Neverland Ranch. Yet Jackson had been a substantial employer in the town in which he was tried, and potential jury members had a good chance of having some distant acquaintance with him. In addition, the mother of the boy making the accusation was not sympathetic. In fact, she'd sued for money before. Sneddon had adult magazines that included fingerprints of Jackson and his accuser, along with corroboration from the accuser's older brother that Jackson had been inappropriate. But too many prosecution witnesses had agendas against Jackson for other things, so Sneddon lost ground. In fact, Jackson, freshly arrived from the hospital in his pajamas, looked more like the victim in the proceedings. During his defense, many celebrities showed up to side with him, which padded the aura. In the end, he was acquitted. Whether justice was done remains controversial.

If investigators hope to make a case, going head to head with a celebrity's "people" is generally a bad idea. That shows their hand to the entourage, giving them a way to trump it. Sometimes the evidence is compelling enough and the celebrity must yield, but often their money will buy a slick attorney who can twist it sufficiently for reasonable doubt. It's better, if an investigator is sufficiently clever, to find a more indirect route and catch the suspect and his or her protectors by surprise. Even so, in court, it's generally an uphill battle with a jury. Ordinary people are often impressed by the exotic world of a celebrity defendant.

Still, celebrity culture is more or less a known entity. C.S.I.s find much more challenge when confronted with certain subcultures, and for insight about that, we'll turn to a famous experiment done in social psychology.

Undercover

Some investigators go undercover, a la Donnie Brasco, and live with the people they're hoping to arrest to learn the secrets and acquire a list of names. This generally carries risk from dangerous groups, such as drug-running motorcycle gangs, domestic terrorism groups, and various crime organizations. Field research by psychologists offers ideas about the effects, both positive and negative, of submerging into a culture that's foreign to the investigator. They provide a framework for better comprehension.

During the early 1970s, David Rosenhan proposed to test how well psychiatrists could tell the difference between a person who was functioning normally and one diagnosable as psychotic or mentally aberrant. In particular, in those days psychiatrists were given the power to hold people in an institution, whether they wanted it or not, and to decide a person's suitability to be a parent, ability to make life decisions, and propensity for yielding to criminal reform.

Rosenhan and eight of his friends (three of them psychologists and one a psychiatrist) faked their way into different psychiatric hospitals by claiming to hear voices. Rosenhan was diagnosed with paranoid schizophrenia (as were the others, with one being manic-depressive) and held for days (from seven to fifty-two), even though they acted normally on the inside and claimed that their sole reported symptom had disappeared. In therapy, whatever he and his confederates reported of their actual experiences, without symptoms, their narratives were interpreted as part of their pathology. From this sometimes harrowing experiment, they claimed that they'd learned how context-specific perceptions can be.

Before being summarily ousted, Rosenhan managed to document what it was like to be inside a mental institution. He watched people being treated as objects, beaten, or ignored, and after being "one of them," he developed a great deal of sympathy for mental patients that he might not otherwise have had. While psychiatrists were largely critical of the way the study was conducted and reported—and some of his conclusions were indeed biased toward the systemic flaws—social psychologists say that at the very least, it supports the notion that subcultures form their own truths and perceptions, and that those perceptions can actually affect the behaviors of the recipients of diagnoses. Those concepts have provided a foundation for the psychology of undercover work.

An undercover investigator who understands these principles will attempt to blend in by first learning the perceptions and rituals of the subculture and then behaving in a similar manner. But he or she must also beware of the insidious effect of being immersed for a long period of time. It can erode their sense of identity or their belief systems—especially if they see people growing wealthy off crime while they're paid little to put their lives at risk to combat it. Yet numerous investigations of this nature have paid off in stopping terrorism, arresting drug lords, and convicting murderers who might otherwise have kept up their criminal behavior for longer periods.

Besides investigating criminal ventures, investigators are also faced with crimes committed in ordinarily benign subcultures, and their ability to ask questions and acquire cooperation often depends on their approach.

Role-Players

In an episode of *CSI-LV*, "Who Shot Sherlock," a group of role-players finds one member dead and their hypotheses about the incident range from murder to accidental overdose to suicide. One player mentions that the victim had wanted a death that would challenge the "master"—Holmes—and he got one. That indicates just how far some role-players might go. Indeed, a few have turned to murder. To solve these crimes, investigators need to learn about the realm of Live Action Role Playing (LARP).

Interactive role-playing games grew out of the popularity of playing war games with toy soldiers during the 1960s, typically focusing on one of the world wars or the American Civil War. Soon, games were invented to accommodate people interested in medieval times and players controlled the actions of specific tokens. Then in 1974, Dungeons & Dragons (D&D) was born, a game that went from the board game played on a tabletop with dice to real settings outdoors, with people not just moving characters about but actually "becoming" them to play the game. It was sort of like the chess game described in *Alice in Wonderland*. The game was highly popular, especially among college students, and generated imitators. It also developed into more advanced versions that appealed to players who had mastered the basic levels. Conventions offered a place where players could meet and refine their identities and skills, as well as acquire ideas about outfits, weapons, and other role-enhancing items. The rule books grew more complicated and gamers more professional.

Some people drop out when the rules become too intricate or they move on to another type of game, but there have been times when participants were so obsessed that they actually enacted a murder "in character." Two boys in Bellevue, Washington, learned that murder is no game—but too late for the victims.

Alex Baranyi and David Anderson were avid players of Dungeons & Dragons and sometimes they took their aggressive, sword-wielding characters too seriously. On January 3, 1997, they lured Kim Wilson, twenty, to a local park around midnight. Apparently in their roles, one or both of them strangled her, stomped on her ribs, and left her there to die. Then they went to the home of her parents, who were asleep. Baranyi beat Mrs. Wilson to death with a baseball bat and stabbed Mr. Wilson and Kim's sister, Julia.

Baranyi took full responsibility, but the forensics lab implicated Anderson as well, and he was arrested. Both were tried for premeditated aggravated murder. From the evidence, it appears that the trigger might have been Kim asking Anderson for money that Anderson owed her.

For the defense, Dr. Karen Froming explained that Baranyi suffered from bipolar disorder and low self-esteem, such that he would form an extreme attachment to another boy. Together they had developed an elaborate fantasy life involving D&D, and she thought it would have been easy for Anderson to get Baranyi to do whatever he asked.

The rebuttal witness, Dr. Robert Wheeler, offered a diagnosis of antisocial personality disorder, which involved being aggressive and lacking in remorse. He said that Baranyi knew what he was doing and was not suffering from diminished capacity.

In the end, both boys were convicted of the homicides.

During the mid-1990s, the card game Magic: The Gathering, developed a strong following, as did White Wolf's *Vampire: The Masquer-*

ade, which inspired a short-lived television series. Created by Mark Rein-Hagen and published in 1991, *Vampire*'s initial incarnation was a tabletop card game. Word was passed along the Internet among the savviest players, and a community took shape. It was an improvement over D&D, which relied on players stating their intention and actions. *Vampire* emphasized storytelling and gained momentum via hand signals. The central narrative was influenced by various vampire mythologies, with vampires essentially descended from Cain, the "bad" son of Adam and Eve, who was cursed for murdering his brother. The "kindred," or vampires in human disguise, formed a society called the Camarilla, and each territory had its hierarchy, with plenty of dramatic intrigue.

With *Vampire*, LARPs became popular around the world, as people adopted supernatural characters and joined "clans" that catered to their personality types (artistic, rebellious, solemn, or a natural leader). People could immerse into their characters and travel the game circuit, which often meant going to several different cities over the course of several days. Then White Wolf introduced more occult versions that included sorcerers, changelings, wraiths, werewolves, and other creatures, expanding the original rule book into quite a few more. The idea was to allow players to enact their own fantasies within the framework of a distinct world but also to be able to interact with others who also enjoy the world via a set of rules. They could become powerful heroes, secretive warlocks, crafty vampires, or whatever they desired within the vision of a particular game system.

Vampires have been in fashion among some types of people for over a century, but most notably since the 1960s. Mostly these people kept to themselves or found some small coterie of like-minded individuals with whom to exchange blood. They kept their secrets and indulged in their fetishes. But the LARPs changed that practice during the 1990s. People began meeting in clubs, in one another's homes, and in Internet chat rooms to share their ideas and feelings about vampires. The subculture grew, bringing people together into an international community, as seen on *CSI-LV*'s "Suckers."

Among them have been a few dangerous people who were attracted to the vampire's edgy, predatory mystique, and they easily blended in with those who just wanted companionship in their reach for mysticism and a personal statement embroidered with dark threads. Several vampire-related murders came light:

- Roderick Ferrell, on Thanksgiving 1996, went to Florida and bludgeoned to death his former girlfriend's parents.

- Joshua Rudiger slit the throats of homeless men in San Francisco in the belief that he was a vampire.

- Allen Menzies bludgeoned his best friend to death in 2003 and drank some of his blood to please the character Akasha, from the Anne Rice novel *The Queen of the Damned*.

Others with lesser criminal intent have simply taken people hostage to drink their blood, such as in the following case.

In the Ukraine, police learned that Diana Semenuha, twenty-nine, had lured street children to her home, supposedly to take their blood for occult purposes, so they arrested her. Apparently she got the children inside with food and the promise of a place to sleep, and then made them sufficiently pliable with alcohol and glue fumes to take their blood. She sold some to occult practitioners in her network.

The police entered her apartment and found it painted black and lit

only with black candles. Inside were seven children, all drugged into a stu-
por and strapped into a bed. Semenuha admitted being a witch and that
she took blood for herself, but since she'd given the children something in
exchange, she insisted it hadn't been stolen from them. One child claimed
that he'd seen Semenuha remove blood from him with a syringe, empty
the syringe into a silver bowl, and drink it.

To investigate crimes within a subculture, a detective needs to know
what drives such people, as well as how to distinguish the ordinary
participants who have no malignant intent from those who are truly
dangerous. At times, they're psychotic, as was the case of "Vampire of
Sacramento" Richard Trenton Chase. Driven by delusions that his
blood was turning to powder, he killed animals, a woman, and a family. But more often, these people identify so closely with the elusive,
predatory Dracula that they elude the police and perhaps even achieve
such secrecy that even people who know them cannot spot the danger.

At any rate, the key skill for investigators to learn is to put aside
judgments so that people who have adopted this lifestyle are not of-
fended and thus unwilling to cooperate.

BONDAGE

Among the more interesting worlds that the *C.S.I.* investigators have
entered is the one that appeals to people who seek some form of unusual sexual expression. Gil Grissom found himself having to tiptoe
lightly around a dominatrix dressed in leather and lace, in both
"Slaves of Las Vegas" and "Lady Heather's Box." She was already attuned to crass assumptions about her lifestyle, and he was all too
aware that he was no match for her.

These practices are based in what mainstream America views as deviance, something to be shunned or diagnosed. In fact, certain sexual preferences are referred to in psychiatric circles as paraphilias, and they are primarily male disorders that begin in childhood or adolescence and persist into adulthood. They may become compulsive and include fantasies and behaviors that focus primarily on objects, activities, or situations for sexual arousal. On "Spring Break," for example, *CSI-M*'s Horatio Caine interrogated a man who had sexually violated a corpse. The most common paraphilias include:

- Exhibitionism—the desire to expose one's genitals to other people

- Fetishism—sexual urges inspired by nonhuman objects, such as shoes, underwear, candles, or ropes

- Frotteurism—touching or rubbing one's body surreptitiously against another person, usually a stranger in a public place

- Pedophilia—the focus of sexual attention involves children, either as pornography or as molestation or assault of actual victims

- Masochism—the acquisition of sexual pleasure from being hurt or humiliated, via verbal abuse, bondage, and even being beaten, whipped, or cut

- Necrophilia—gaining sexual arousal from handling or having intercourse with corpses

- Sadism—the acquisition of sexual pleasure from dominating, torturing, or abusing others via such activities as verbal abuse, whipping, burning, stabbing, raping, choking, and killing

- Transvestitism—cross-dressing by heterosexual males, from wearing one piece of female clothing to dressing entirely as a female, and even passing as one

■ Voyeurism—deriving sexual pleasure from watching others from a clandestine position, such as peeking in windows where someone may be undressing or sleeping

It's not clear if anyone would add the fetish for dressing up like giant animals to rub against one another to this list, as seen in "Fur and Loathing" on *CSI-LV*, or the penchant for "cuddle parties" that the New York team comes across in "Grand Murder at Central Station." At any rate, it's unlikely that psychologists have seen everything, so their list of paraphilias cannot be considered exhaustive.

In fact, not on the official list but often utilizing items from it is the arena of bondage and discipline (B&D), in which participants typically take the role of master/mistress or slave/captive. It's based in dominance and submission (D&S), and there are masochistic elements to it, but the practice of B&D does not necessarily involve the infliction of pain (S&M). Yet even when it does, the point is not the pain but how the discomfort serves to heighten sexual arousal.

Many people not used to this arena—including investigators and attorneys—apply a superficial analysis to the B&D dynamics; they assume the dominant person is always in control and the submissive one may be at least partly excused, because he or she is more pliable and vulnerable. But that's naïve, and the notion that the dominant partner has a greater degree of control and responsibility has inspired misleading analyses of serious team crimes—and allowed some people (so-called helpless accomplices) to get lighter sentences than they deserve.

But that's a different issue. Let's stick with the subculture. Some investigators erroneously assume that B&D, D&S, or S&M scenarios are about violence. However, B&D is a much more complicated experience, and only practitioners understand the full impact of it. A few professionals who have made in-depth analyses via interviews and observations of the practices have discovered surprising paradoxes.

Thus, for law enforcement, a more sophisticated assessment of the activities that utilizes these insights means that whoever deals with the practitioners will be less vulnerable to faulty assumptions that can leave investigators open to mistakes or manipulation.

In truth, both partners in these B&D or D&S arrangements have strengths and weaknesses, and both variously exploit and complement the other. To make the dance work, they need each other. Thus, before anything begins, they agree on the terms: what each desires and what each needs in order to feel satisfied and safe. They decide whether each can bring something to the arrangement that will attain this mutual goal. If so, they then proceed, playing with the illusion of "forced captivity" and making it seem more fearsome than it actually is. But each watches for the other to play the role in a specific way, so there's a continuous and subtle circulation of power.

The dominant person finds pleasure in mastery while the submissive one enjoys the feeling of surrender. They help each other to explore their fantasies by each giving what the other needs to complete his or her idea about the desired feeling. The experience pushes them both closer to primal needs, which reportedly creates a flow of energy that neither can experience alone. Oddly enough, a delicate equality is achieved between the one who shoulders power and the one who is willingly stripped of it.

The most extreme form of this dynamic is sadomasochism, which involves consensual violence. One person may want to be burned, whipped, have a loaded pistol put to his head, or be cemented into a bathtub so he can't move. The "master" inflicts pain and humiliation to help the "slave" reach emotional catharsis, and both enjoy their parts in the scenario. Sadomasochism, according to practitioners, eroticizes mental and physical pain by synthesizing the body with mind and spirit. These rituals make the fantasies they both desire concrete. And while they're not essentially about genuine harm, some people are drawn to this world because of their penchant for violence—even murder.

John Robinson started his criminal career committing white-collar crimes and went on to use his knowledge of technology to lure victims over the Internet. He is considered the first known serial killer to do so. Born in Chicago to a blue-collar family, he'd been an Eagle Scout and had attended seminary to become a priest. Yet he turned toward new ambitions and became a forger, thief, embezzler, and liar. While in jail for a petty crime, he learned computer technology and exploited its potential for swindling unwitting people. He became romantically involved with a married woman, Beverly Bonner, who worked in the prison library. When he was released in 1993, she went with him and was never heard from again. A mother and daughter also fell into his net, and Robinson collected the daughter's disability checks to the tune of more than $150,000.

He then found women via the Internet, where he would enter bondage-oriented chat rooms as "Slavemaster." He soon had women signing sexual slave contracts that granted him total control over them. In 1997, he developed a relationship with a student at Purdue University named Izabela Lewicka, who was interested in the sexual world of sadomasochism. At Robinson's behest, she went to Kansas City and filed for a marriage license before she disappeared. Then he started an online relationship with Suzette Trouten, and in the typical pattern, no one heard from her again either.

Thanks to tips from her friends and family, the authorities watched Robinson, and in April 2000, a psychologist named Vickie Neufeld moved to Kansas City to pursue a relationship with the man. She ended up filing a complaint with the police, and after they questioned her for several hours, they arrested Robinson on the charges of sexual assault and theft.

Linking him via items in his possession to the missing women, they had a forensic computer expert go through his files and e-mail.

Warrants were obtained for Robinson's storage units and for property at La Cygne, Kansas. There, cadaver dogs led the investigators to two eighty-five gallon drums by the side of a pole barn. The drums proved to contain human remains, which dental records linked to Suzette Trouten and Izabela Lewicka. In Robinson's storage units, they found three more barrels, which contained the remains of Beverly Bonner, Sheila Faith, and her daughter, Debbie.

In Kansas, a jury found Robinson guilty of murder just before Halloween in 2002 and sentenced him to death. For the Missouri charges, he pleaded guilty in exchange for admitting to five murders, including two for which authorities did not have bodies. He was fifty-nine, among the oldest serial killers ever convicted. Then in 2004, Kansas overturned an old law that gave prosecutors an advantage in death penalty cases, and Robinson's sentence was commuted to life.

Unless they understand just what the appeal of this lifestyle is, investigators will fail to appreciate the motives for people who voluntarily participate—and might not view them as true victims when they are, such as in the case above. (Or in one case, the police decided that the willing "slave" was a victim and arrested her partner; publicly exposed, he committed suicide.) For the masochist, the violent loss of control, coupled with fear, translates into a powerful psychic orgasm and a feeling that the self has been momentarily obliterated. It reportedly feels like a radical transformation into a sense of openness and full existence. Let's look at what some experts have said is the basis for this.

Supposedly, the inner conflict produced by the scenarios that participants have choreographed can amplify the sensuality of their experience. Tension adds intensity, so bondage and spanking can develop an intimate mind/body bond. The concept of being forced to consent may seem confusing, even contradictory, yet the complexity of the human psyche makes it work. Psychologists describe it as an essential mechanism of self-deception, and B&Ders fully exploit it.

We all possess the capacity to initiate and immerse ourselves in an activity to such a degree that we can actually forget we set it in motion. We can thus believe we had no choice in the matter. In B&D, the "slaves" willingly surrender to the "masters," who force them with constraints and perhaps with pain or humiliation into a physical sense of their bodies, enabling them to explore capacities for pleasure and surrender that they might resist on their own. To make it work, both participants understand that consent makes it happen, but once things are in motion the memory of having been willing recedes. The intense role-playing produces an altered state of consciousness in which the captive does feel forced. That is, under auspices of having "no choice," one person gains erotic benefits from the illusion of becoming forcefully enslaved to another's will. If there is no risk of serious harm, the slave agrees to be dominated in unpredictable ways so that fear in the right measure can produce the most intense stimulation.

The idea of being pushed into something one both fears and craves sparks a fierce tension that draws body and mind together in a heightened state of arousal. The body teaches that pleasure is life's prize: Whatever engages the senses and makes one feel alive should be actively exploited within a safe framework. Applying restrictions to the body in the form of bondage or discipline brings attention to the body's capacity for extreme sensation. It's an absolute surrender to full impact of the flesh, and the individual's ego boundaries are transcended into something larger. Pain deconstructs the ego and when personal identity is thus challenged, people cease to be reluctant to perform actions heretofore considered inconsistent with who they believe they are.

Playing with imbalances of power through risk and surrender involves psychological stretching. Forced into their deepest anxieties and shame, captives must draw on inner strength to endure and overcome their fears. Often they gain a more heightened sense of themselves. They become stronger, wiser, and more self-aware. Paradoxically, it seems, things that inhibit desire can under certain circumstances also enhance it. Since arousal physiologically raises one's pain threshold, what might otherwise hurt can actually increase pleasure, i.e., what we fear or abhor may be what makes us hot.

This dynamic is not generally understood, certainly not by police officers or detectives. But investigators rely on reports from associates of offenders, as well as from witnesses, so cultivating a willing witness or informant from within any of these subcultures requires the ability to look past their differences and learn what they're about. In some cases, interpreting evidence actually requires some specialized knowledge of how the subculture is formed or operates, so it's best to get it from those who know it well. (And to contact psychologists or sociologists versed in it, since even the participants might not be articulate about the appeal of the rituals and perceptions of the subculture.)

Whether the subculture be clowns, furries, Goths, ghost hunters, or UFO fanatics, they have their own "language," and the investigator who can become multilingual, so to speak, will have important advantages in the quest for a quick case resolution.

Yet one doesn't have to brush up against a subculture to discover the need for specialized knowledge. Other areas of crime investigation also require it to such a degree that some investigators get a significant amount of extra training to become experts. Let's return to the "normal" world of crime investigation and examine one of these areas.

CHAPTER EIGHT

Accidents Happen

In police work, accident investigations (traffic-related and otherwise) are frequent, but they're not all what they seem. Some incidents are staged to look like accidents, while others just have complicating factors that prevent all but the savviest experts from figuring them out. In addition, people fearing prosecution may hit someone and flee the scene, leaving police to try to figure out who did it.

In several *C.S.I.* episodes, an incident required the skill of accident reconstruction, such as when a skateboarder was found in a car that had crashed into another car on *CSI-M*'s "Game Over." It turned out that he'd first been electrocuted and the "accident" was a cover-up. Even with a genuine accident, law enforcement often must solve issues of responsibility. In one episode, "Crash and Burn," on *CSI-LV*, an elderly woman crashed through the window of a restaurant, killing customers. The team had to look at her medical condition, as well as mechanical problems with her car. The cluster of facts, especially the drugs in her system, pointed to an intentional act of suicidal homicide: She ended her life but also targeted a group of people who ate at that restaurant. And Grissom's team also investigated an accident on a roller coaster in "Turn of the Screw."

Many police officers specialize in this area, which can be tricky, but it has become an important skill for resolving both civil and criminal litigation. From car and plane crashes to fatal falls, the ability to reconstruct what actually occurred is central to closing many cases.

VEHICULAR ACCIDENTS

Death by automobile accident is the sixth leading cause of mortality in America, after natural and unintentional deaths. That doesn't even account for the number of nonfatal injuries incurred. The most common causes of these events include excessive speed, failure to yield the right of way, disregard of a sign or signal, use of substances while driving, and improper passing.

There are two key types of personnel: investigators, who document the initial facts, draw diagrams, and take the photographs, and reconstructionists, who later apply engineering to the facts and photos to determine more precise data. To come up with accurate calculation of what happened between two vehicles or a vehicle and an object, the first group will note several key items:

- pre- and post-impact skid marks

- road and weather conditions

- lighting conditions

- time of day

- final positions of the vehicle or vehicles

- point of impact

- type of damage to the vehicle(s)/objects

- tire condition

- direction traveled

They'll also take verbal reports from the drivers, if possible, but will rely on engineering to get their final result (since some drivers might not know the speed, underestimate it, or have reason to conceal it). Key elements to be determined are speed, distance traveled, and lapsed time.

To determine responsibility, investigators will also learn what they can about the mechanical condition of the vehicle, and will note any contact mark between one vehicle and another or an object (a wall, a pedestrian). They will also collect eyewitness accounts, information about what to expect in terms of performance from the vehicle models, the date of the accident, and the placement of roadway markers that may have been implicated. Another factor will be the driver's history. These all go together into a file in the event that litigation will follow. In that case, a reconstructionist may be hired.

During one winter in New England, a fatal accident occurred involving a police officer hitting a tree. Responding investigators were at odds over what had happened: One believed that the primary factor was the cold weather and slick roads, making it an unfortunate accident. The other was certain, because there was no frost on the front windshield or windows, that there had been foul play and the scene was then staged to look like an accident. A reconstructionist examined such factors as the behav-

ior of frost under those conditions, the victim's driving record and potential substance abuse history, the skid marks on the road, the road conditions, and anything in the area that could account for him going off the
road. (Tracks from an animal might indicate a reason for sudden braking,
for example.) She also looked into the possibility that he had mentioned
having enemies or that someone he'd testified against may have been recently freed from prison. In the end, she determined that the car's heat
could have prevented frost formation under those conditions, and no factors were found supporting foul play, so it was ruled an accident.

A key problem for reconstructionists is that they do not see the scene
as it occurred. They usually arrive long after vehicles have been
towed or driven away. It might even be months since the accident occurred. Thus, they must rely on documentation from the initial investigators, so how expertly the accident was handled can impact on the
final report. The police will have an accident report, photographs, diagrams, access to the vehicles, witness statements, and statements of
survivors, if any. If the vehicle in question has been towed, altered, or
repaired, that must be taken into account as well. In addition, main-
tenance reports can be requested, as well as a history of the vehicle.

The reconstructionist's toolkit might include many different types
of screwdrivers, an extendable machinist's mirror, a set of sockets,
different types of metric and Allen wrenches, a jackknife, a 3-4-5 tri-
angle, a pad and drawing pencil, chalk, depth gauges, vehicle motion
rods, and a tape measure. They may also wish to use a tape recorder
for stating their observations for later transcription.

Reconstructionists who examine accidents must have good math-
ematical skills, as well as a background in engineering and machine
design. They also need to know how accidents impact human biological systems. Complex algebra can often be part of learning what ac-

tually occurred and converting the collected data into the right sequencing of events. They will also be able to "read" different types of skid marks. A "barber pole" pattern, for example, indicates that the tire that made it was going forward and sideways simultaneously.

The best information is the vehicle itself and where it came to rest. Investigators often work backwards to establish the incident chronology, including all other known facts. Then an engineering analysis is done to derive the speed at which the vehicle was traveling. This can be compared against available eyewitness reports.

The principal tools used to evaluate vehicular accidents involve the application of two laws: the Conservation of Energy and the Conservation of Momentum. Thus, there are two essential methods for reconstruction. The basic energy method utilizes the first law, which states that in a physical process, the total energy of the system at the start of the process is equal to the total energy at the end. The vehicle in motion has kinetic energy, and reducing it to zero when the vehicle is stopped requires that the kinetic energy take another form of energy. Kinetic energy is calculated according to the vehicle's mass and velocity, and reducing it to zero requires energy from brake friction, skidding, or hitting an object. There are equations available for a variety of scenarios, and certain clues, such as paint transfer from the vehicle, can help to determine who hit whom.

The momentum method relies on the law that defines momentum as velocity times mass. When vehicles collide, they exert opposing forces. Net momentum prior to the impact equals the net momentum after. Reconstructionists then apply formulas to the skid marks and depth of vehicle damages, among other things, to determine who or what might have been at fault, which vehicle was traveling faster, or just how fast an individual vehicle was traveling. In other words, the reconstructionist determines how much momentum was transferred from a vehicle in motion to something against which it impacted.

Both methods might be used at once for different aspects of the incident.

But even if it's determined that an accident occurred and no one is to blame, aside from weather or driver neglect, that might not terminate an investigation. An accident reconstruction can sometimes offer surprises.

Madison Rutherford, thirty-four, was a successful financial advisor from Connecticut. He went on a trip to Mexico one day in July 1998 to acquire a Brazilian mastiff, but he apparently struck an embankment while driving a rental car. Investigators who traced the car to him believed from a charred corpse found inside that he'd died in the resulting car fire. He had been insured for $7 million, so the Kemper Life insurance company, which had to pay out a large share of that money, wanted a more thorough investigation.

Dr. William Bass, a forensic anthropologist from Tennessee, was hired to go to Mexico to analyze the bone fragments—all that was left of the victim. Bass knew about the effects of fire on fracture patterns in bone. Looking through the car debris, he discovered the top of a skull, burned mostly on the inside. He decided that the head had probably exploded in the fire, thanks to the brain fluids expanding from the heat, but he thought its position in the car was odd: it suggested that at the time of the fire the victim would have been on the floor upside down. According to the reports, the driver had crashed into a ditch, but Bass did not accept that it would cause what he observed. In addition, the fire had seemed inexplicably hot—such as one finds with arson.

Despite the massive damage done to the body, Bass found sufficient material to determine from fracture patterns that the bone fragments were from a freshly dead body—not some older skeleton tossed into the car. From the cranium piece and from several teeth, Bass believed they could get a DNA analysis, but it proved difficult to acquire items for comparison from Rutherford's home. So the teeth provided another means via comparison to Rutherford's dental records. Yet even before the investigators asked for those records, Bass could tell that these teeth, worn down and full of unfilled cavities, had not belonged to an affluent, thirty-four-year-old Caucasian male. They were more consistent with an older native of Mexico. So was the skull fragment and the few spinal pieces that could be analyzed.

His analysis provided sufficient cause to open a more involved examination of this case, and the insurance company hired private investigators, who eventually tracked down the living, breathing Madison Rutherford, living under an alias in the United States. He had faked his death, stolen a corpse from a Mexican mausoleum to place in the rental car, crashed the car, torched it, and believed he would walk away a wealthy man. Instead, he went to prison for fraud.

In a similar incident in the United States, the investigator noted an absence of skid marks, which indicated that the driver had not had an accident. It turned out to be another faked insurance-related incident, with the theft of a corpse from a mausoleum.

When calculating for a hit-and-run, there may be transfer on the victim, such as imprinted bruises in the shape of a license plate or a special bumper, or paint transfer. In addition, if struck from the side, their leg may buckle, showing the shape of the car's bumper. The victim, when hit, will generally rotate and fly in a particular trajectory, and those reconstructionists with knowledge about cars will be able to calculate which front shape the offending car had.

If a suspect car were located, it could be compared with each of these things. If paint was left on the victim, investigators could utilize a car paint database to identify the make and model of car.

In any event, the points of contact between vehicle and pedestrian will be obvious on the victim. If the car broke skin (extremely likely, because such accidents usually break bones and even remove body parts), there may be blood spatter on the car. It's also possible that there will be imprints or threads on the vehicle from the victim's clothing.

To learn about how cars impact pedestrians, cadavers have often been used. One impact study showed the effects of different types of cars hitting human bodies, and some of the cadavers wore shoes and some did not. From the experiments, the researchers were able to calculate such things as frictional force between the sole of the foot and leather, trajectory distance and angle, impacts to the windshield, dents to the car, and the type of damage that would be done to the lower legs.

FORENSIC METEOROLOGY

Part of the reconstruction of accidents and other incidents may involve professional weather forecasters who can review weather patterns on the day of an accident and determine several factors. Environmental elements can have a dramatic impact on investigations, from determining time of death to breaking an alibi to supporting or negating a witness's recollection. From recorded data meteorologists can provide detailed weather reconstruction for many locales. They can also acquire and interpret weather forecasts from a given day, as well as address the effects of microclimates. If there was an unprecedented weather event on a day in question, they can calculate its impact on the incident under investigation. They can also devise computer graphics and visual exhibits for juries.

Forensic meteorology relies on such instruments as Nexrad Doppler radar for precipitation determinations, satellites for cloud-pattern mapping, lightning and tornado detection instruments, surface weather reports, and reports from storm spotters. They can then address both civil and criminal questions about such issues as damage done by weather, human negligence during weather events, windblown toxins, and moisture patterns that would be in place when an incident was going down.

In Wilkes-Barre, Pennsylvania, in 1986, Dr. Glen Wolsieffer was found by his brother, Neil, apparently attacked in his home. His wife had been killed upstairs. The doctor said that an intruder had broken in through an upstairs window, and a ladder positioned outside against the house seemed to support this. Yet suspicious circumstances eventually turned police attention to the doctor. When they pressed Neil about what he recalled, he committed suicide. Then evidence turned up that the marriage had been unhappy and that Wolsieffer had been repeatedly unfaithful. A pathologist also stated that the man's injuries appeared to have been self-inflicted. In addition, a meteorologist offered some telling evidence: Dr. Joseph Sobel examined the water vapor conditions on the night of the supposed break-in and murder. He said that there would have been enough dew that night that the intruder would have left clear footprints, but photos showed none. In addition, the doctor's car would have been damp with dew had it sat in the driveway all night, as he'd claimed. Instead, it was dry when investigators examined it. With this evidence and a good reconstruction of possible events, the prosecution managed to get a conviction of third-degree murder and Wolsieffer went to prison.

BIO-MECHANICS

Accident reconstruction is not limited to what occurs on a roadway, in a train, or on a plane. Many accidents occur at home, some of them fatal. On *CSI-LV*, Grissom's team investigated one such incident in "Bite Me," based on the following real-life event. In North Carolina, a man went on trial for the murder of his wife, and the key question was whether evidence supported a brutal fight or an accident.

Around 2:45 in the morning on December 9, 2001, an emergency call came in from 1810 Cedar Street in the Forest Hills section of Durham. Michael Peterson, a novelist and newspaper columnist, was calling frantically about his wife, who had apparently fallen and lay at the bottom of the stairs in their home. He was sobbing and breathing like a man in a state of panic. Paramedics responded at once and found Kathleen Peterson, forty-eight, dead and lying in the well of a stairway, with the walls covered in blood. Peterson, too, had blood on him, and was walking in circles. He asked if he needed a lawyer.

Although a medical examiner initially decided that the death was an accident, the police believed that the considerable amount of blood on the walls made the death suspicious. An autopsy of Kathleen Peterson indicated that she had seven scalp lacerations on the back of her head, as well as bruises on her face and head. Her manner of death was determined to be from blunt force trauma to the head that was inconsistent with a fall. The police got a warrant to search the home, seizing computers and more than sixty other items. Peterson hired attorney David Rudolf. He was arrested and released on bail. He returned to his home where Kathleen had died, and preserved every drop of blood within the staircase scene for his experts to examine.

In October, 2002, DA Jim Hardin, Jr., announced his desire to exhume the body of Elizabeth Ratliff, a former friend of Peterson and his first wife, who had also died at the foot of a staircase in 1985. A nanny had found her, but Peterson had walked her home the night before from dinner. The cause of death was determined to have been a stroke, but Hardin wanted a second autopsy, despite the fact that her body was still warm when found, many hours after Peterson had returned home. (He took over custody of Ratliff's two daughters and maintains a loving and supportive relationship with these girls even to this day.) This exhumation and autopsy was accomplished in April 2003, and the medical examiner concluded that Ratliff had been the victim of a homicide.

In July, Peterson's murder trial began, lasting four months. Hardin, joined by ADA Freda Black, insisted that Peterson, a former Marine, had battered his wife to death with a fireplace "blow poke" that had mysteriously disappeared from the home and then fabricated the story about his wife's fall. In light of the Ratliff autopsy results, Peterson's situation looked suspicious. Hardin said that he did not need to prove a motive, but he hypothesized that Peterson had not earned much that year from his writing and the couple was spending beyond their means. Killing Kathleen would gain him a 1.8-million-dollar insurance payout. Later in the trial, he would add another motive: Kathleen, eleven years younger than Michael, had learned about her husband's attempt to arrange a secret homosexual liaison and had fought with him over it.

The defense team, led by Rudolf, speculated that Kathleen's head injuries were not consistent with a beating. Rather she'd experienced an episode of hypoxia from head injuries related to a fall down the stairs. Her inability to help herself was influenced by a night of drinking at the poolside. As her husband stayed outside in the pool area, she climbed the stairs in flimsy plastic sandals, blacked out, and fell backwards and struck her head. She lay bleeding and then tried to get up. She slipped in her own blood, and hit her head again. She struggled there, trying to get up, coughing and wheezing, expelling blood all over the stairwell. Their experts indicated that this could have taken place over a stretch of time. Since there was no evidence of violence between the Petersons and good evidence that they had a warm relationship, it seemed unlikely that Peterson would just start beating his wife. Rudolf claimed that the prosecution did not even collect data to support their theory about motive until just before the trial, and in any event, there would not have been sufficient financial gain to justify the motive. He thought that the Durham police had a vendetta against Peterson due to columns he had written over a period of years criticizing the local police force for their inept handling of cases. So it was possible that they'd decided to skew the investigation toward implicating him.

The key factors in the trial were the amount and placement of the blood spatters (some 10,000 individual spatters), and the nature and number of lacerations on Kathleen's skull. (While police also claimed to have discovered bloody footprints going from the body to a utility sink and other places via the presumptive blood test, luminol, they failed to take photographs of them.) Also at issue was whether Peterson had done other things as his wife lay dying, rather than calling for immediate assistance, and why he had blood spatter inside the hem of his tan shorts. That meant involving experts on both sides to offer interpretations, which would tip the scales in favor of homicide or accident.

A paramedic who'd arrived at the scene said that he'd never seen so much blood. Some of it, he thought, was already dry. But he was not an expert and had only seen one other fatal fall incident. He thought Kathleen had died some time before he'd arrived, but the judge told jurors to disregard that comment.

The jury also saw a video of Kathleen lying at the foot of the stairs, which had been shot by a crime scene technician. In that footage, Michael's socks and shoes were sitting next to the body, as were bloody towels. They learned that Michael had grabbed Kathleen and held her, and that his son had pulled him away. Under cross-examination, the crime scene tech, Dan George, was forced to admit to a number of errors in processing the scene and allowing it to become contaminated. Key items were not taken into evidence, and a few other items were mishandled. Notes were brief or nonexistent, and the police had caused some of the contamination.

The prosecution's expert on Kathleen's injuries, Dr. Deborah Radisch, had performed the autopsy and also a second autopsy on Elizabeth Ratliff. Radisch testified to the similarities between the two deaths and said that based on her experience with wounds, she believed that Kathleen had been beaten to death, because the wounds were too numerous to have occurred during a fall. She said that Kathleen had defensive wounds on her hands and broken cartilage in her throat, which also indicated an attempt to strangle her.

Peter "Duane" Deaver, the blood-spatter expert from the North Carolina Bureau of Investigation, had run simulation experiments that got similar results; he said that three distinct patterns indicated that Kathleen had been bludgeoned with a weapon: blood spatter on the adjacent hallway wall as high as nine feet was possibly cast-off from a weapon being raised to hit again; other blood on the door molding indicated that Kathleen had been standing, and eight drops of blood inside Peterson's shorts was presented as proof that he was close to her when she was hit. Also, it appeared that a blood pattern on the stairs indicated that the weapon had been laid there. He concluded that Kathleen had been assaulted by someone using a fireplace blow poke to strike her, and that the points of impact were in space, not against the wall. This blow poke was allegedly given to the Petersons as a present by Kathleen's sister.

For the defense, Dr. Jan Leetsma, a forensic neuropathologist, indicated that the speed of the fall and the angle of the head, among other factors, could cause death without leaving the effect of a *contrecoup* injury, as expected from a blow to the back of the head. He had examined 257 beating deaths and believed that Kathleen's injuries were inconsistent with a beating. By his estimate, she had sustained four blows, not seven. In his opinion, a beating death with a blow poke was inconsistent with his pathological findings, while a fall down the stairs could have resulted in what he saw.

Then renowned criminalist Dr. Henry Lee said that the blood spatter was consistent with a finding of accidental death, as Kathleen's repeated coughing as she lay dying could have caused much of the spray patterns of blood on the walls around her. He could not rule out a bludgeoning, but did find inconsistencies with that theory. Most notably, there was a lack of the expected type of cast-off patterns, and/or damage to the adjacent surfaces by the forty-inch-long blow poke being swung in a confined area. In defense of criticism that he did not conduct his own point of origin exercise, he said that his experienced eye was as good as techniques using computers or string to find points of origin. Further, there was a belief that some of the pattern was altered by activities conducted by the state's crime scene investigators. He did not agree that the marks of blood high on the wall in the adjacent hallway necessarily indicated cast-off from a weapon, and bolstered his testimony by coughing and spitting diluted ketchup onto a white poster board to show different patterns.

Dr. Faris Bandak, a biomechanical research scientist indicated that Kathleen had experienced a ground-level fall. He had used Kathleen's height and weight, with the dimensions of the staircase and stairwell, to calculate the incident and used a computerized animation of what he speculated had occurred. The animation showed her walking up the steps, falling backward, and striking her head on a ridged molding on a doorjamb. Then her head grazed the wall as she fell, hitting a stair edge. She then tried to stand but slipped and fell again, with multiple impacts. He disagreed that an implement like the blow poke could have caused the injuries, but seemed unable to explain the facial bruising.

Rudolf also had a surprise in store. The prosecution had claimed that the murder weapon, the fireplace poker, was missing, but Rudolf produced a poker he indicated had been found in the Peterson's garage a few days earlier. It was an embarrassing moment for the investigators; they believed the poker had never been there. Nevertheless, it clearly had not been used in a beating death, and the prosecution had no alternate weapon in mind. Yet they did say that the blow poke that Rudolf produced was not the only one in the house.

On rebuttal, Dr. James McElhaney, an emeritus professor of engineering, testified that the injuries sustained were not consistent with a fall. He believed that something light and cylindrical had caused them, and he had calculated the velocity needed, which was more consistent with a beating than a fall. Still, he conceded that the defense scenario was possible.

Also, Dr. Saami Shaibani, a physicist, indicated that from experiments he had done where he asked subjects to fall backwards to see where they hit, that Kathleen could not have fallen. However, Shaibani's credentials came into doubt during the trial and his testimony was stricken.

Yet chief medical examiner John Butts, who supervised Dr. Radisch, indicated that Kathleen had not had a sufficient amount of blood in her lungs to have aspirated so much onto the walls. He did admit that Kathleen had consumed a sufficient amount of Valium and alcohol to cause a blackout and fall.

Hardin's closing emphasized the fact that the victim had sustained thirty-eight separate injuries to the face, skull, back, hands, and wrists, which he said that even two separate falls could not account for. He believed the defense's argument was counterintuitive. A fiction writer makes things up, and in this case, he'd fabricated the scenario of an accident. Hardin was defensive about the blow poke, and insisted that the two staircase deaths in Peterson's life were linked. He then discussed the motive of rage after Kathleen had grown angry over a homosexual liaison, and the fact that after finding his wife dead, Peterson had checked his e-mail—unexpected behavior for a grieving widower. The financial motive was not mentioned.

The defense witnesses had made some telling points as well. In closing, Rudolf offered ten reasons for doubt. Among them were that the supposed murder weapon had not been used; there was no credible motive and no history of violence; there was no brain trauma or skull fracture; the blood spatter on the walls was not created by blunt force impacts of Kathleen's head; there was no spatter on Peterson's shirt or glasses; the spatter on his shorts was in the back; the investigation was shoddy and the information from it unreliable; the state had used junk science; and the state had jumped to a conclusion and then gathered evidence to support it.

The jurors took six long days to come to their conclusions, as trial watchers debated the merits of both sides. Then on October 10, 2003, they convicted Michael Peterson of first-degree murder. He received life in prison without parole.

Tim Palmbach, director of the Forensic Science Program at the University of New Haven who had worked as a criminalist for the defense, believed that a "not guilty" verdict had been a reasonable expectation, and the verdict surprised him. He and Dr. Lee had worked on the case together, and for the testimony they'd each taken a separate area of responsibility.

"The core of the defense team," Palmbach said, "consisted of myself for the overall crime scene management and crime scene decision-making; Dr. Henry Lee for blood spatter analysis; Werner Spitz for pathology (although he opted out early and we didn't replace him); Jan Leetsma, a forensic neuropathologist; and the biomechanical engineering was done by Dr. George Bandak, which dealt with the question of whether the wounds were consistent with the facts of the energy and environment of the stairwell. We met many times as a team.

"My part was to work with Dr. Lee on the blood spatter, but I also looked at how law enforcement had treated the scene. How did they secure it, or didn't they? What did they choose to do relevant to imprint evidence, latent print evidence, fingerprint evidence, footprint evidence? How did they choose to handle it? Did they use the right collection methods and enhancement agents? Once they began to look at the evidence and develop their theory, did they do it holistically and objectively? In other words, did they follow a reconstruction model that would input all the correct data and properly develop a hypothesis, or did they just try to find a way to unscientifically bolster their limited theory of the case? Because Dr. Lee was the principal testimony piece for the defense for the blood spatter, I took the role of being the consultant on the cross-examination of Deaver. I helped in the defense's preparation of the blood spatter, but I also provided direct testimony for the evidence relating to the crime scene issues.

"I think we scientifically dismantled what they did and their 'hypothesis' and how they got there, and in the eleventh hour we demonstrated that the supposed murder weapon was not the murder weapon, but at the same time the defense strategy was primarily to take them apart and highlight the ambiguity. Through several defense experts a plausible theory, death attributed to a fall down the stairs, was established. However, much of what transpired within that stairwell remained a mystery. We didn't scientifically substantiate an alternate theory. Technically speaking, it works for reasonable doubt, but it didn't in this case. The blood was such a complicated series of patterns that it could only be explained by a complicated series of events.

"One of the main areas of the scene was the north wall, the bottom of the stairwell. That's where the vast majority of the spatter evidence was. Approximately four thousand blood droplets between one and three millimeters in size were on that one wall. It had a mixture of bloodstain patterns, contact transfer patterns, swipe patterns, void patterns, wipe patterns, spatter patterns, and even an overlay of what I believe was the luminol enhancement reagent, although they denied they used it there. So while you had all of this on one wall, their expert only attempted a very limited reconstruction. He said, 'I'm going to take a small selection of drops from that wall, string them, project them, and show you what the two impact sites are.' But our point was that he had selected forty-two out of four thousand droplets. We wanted to know how he was confident that his selection was a representation of the entire picture. If more than three thousand and nine hundred droplets didn't coincide with that picture, why didn't that mean something? You could see their confusion [during the investigation], because on the wall, there were some sixty circled droplets, and some were crossed out, while some were numbered the same as others and some weren't numbered at all. Some had lines, which is the two-dimensional indication of point of convergence, while others did not. For anyone who works in that field, it just appeared that they were confused or shortsighted.

"To me, that's where the science broke down. If you do it objectively, confused data is excellent data. You're testing a hypothesis that isn't working, and rather than saying you've failed, you say, 'That's not a plausible theory. Let me redefine my hypothesis.' Had they done that, I think they could have come up with the correct parameters of what took place in that stairwell, and that it was convoluted and took place over time. It was a series of events that had different dynamics. What Dr. Lee was trying to portray when he was coughing and flicking blood was that many of the events were not attributable to a physical beating of a human being, but someone who was bloody and trying to survive could account for a lot of what was there.

"In our team meetings, what Dr. Leetsma found was relevant to what we were saying. Because of the formation of red neurons, Kathleen had suffered a hypoxic event likely caused by her head injury, and she had survived for many hours. Leetsma was able to demonstrate that from a neuropathology point of view. We knew that many of the patterns had been created by Kathleen coughing, wheezing, falling into pools of blood, shaking her hair. That would take time for that to happen, and she did have the time to do that. Michael Peterson said he was out by the pool for about forty-five minutes after she came into the house, and no one else was in the house. Even if she was yelling for help, the pool was way off in the back of the house, down a path onto the back side of the property.

"I think our most telling point was that the wounds were not typical of a blow from a blunt-force rod-type injury to the head, and were more consistent with her head impacting a flat, wide, broad-based, hard substance. As we looked at the convoluted patterns of blood, the lack of correct type of cast-offs, the dynamics and limitations of the width of the stairwell, and their faulty theory of the forty-inch blow poke, it was unequivocally clear that there was no possible way that it happened as a blunt-force beating death. The further we worked toward that, the more firm that hypothesis became. That's not to say that the evidence precluded the possibility that Michael Peterson couldn't have gotten into a fight with his wife, and as he struggled with her, her head impacted the floor and the stairs. Could that have resulted in the wound patterns on her head? I believe so. They did not have a definitive cause of death. They had blunt force injury to the head, loss of blood, therefore death. But postmortem examination of her head injuries could not provide a sound medical diagnosis resulting in death.

"The jury bought into the motive of Peterson's bisexual relationship and that it was disturbing to Kathleen. They apparently thought that was a solid motive, though the state actually started with a financial motive. When they lost it so horrifically under cross-examination and rebuttal, they changed it. But Michael Peterson said that his lifestyle from before marriage had been bisexual. He'd never hidden it, and while his wife did not like it, she was aware of it.

"Duane Deaver built a staircase model. I thought that was an excellent idea. Then he set out to test his theory, but he did thirty-eight unconnected, disjointed experiments that didn't have any relevance to the state's explicit theory of the case. He didn't know how much blood he used—he just guessed. He didn't know why he'd used a particular weapon, except that he wanted to see what it looked like. The photograph at the end was the accumulation of all this activity, all thirty-eight events. And he was only able to create somewhere in the neighborhood of seventy-five hundred drops of blood. Yet they were willing to say that what transpired was the result of a series of impacts from a half-inch dowel to her head. He's showing with his results that he didn't even agree with that. But it didn't seem to show him that his theory was wrong.

"He actually said that he didn't take a single photograph or anything to document his work. Why would an objective expert not do that, unless you know it's not right and you do not want to be second-guessed? We confronted him with this wall and said, 'There are four thousand droplets here. You circled sixty droplets but only analyzed forty-two. What was that about?' And his answer was, 'I don't know what you're talking about.'

"The police also allowed Michael to go back into the stairwell, sit on a step above her, pull her back onto his lap, and hold her head, while he's crying, with the cell phone next to him. That's a huge mistake, and they eventually had to admit that some of the most difficult stains to evaluate were the stains on the inside of the bottom of the cuff of his shorts. But the second you let him hold her bloody head in his lap, it's over. The contamination is too significant to render any meaningful interpretation.

"And they didn't adequately process the prints. What if they found a number of Kathleen's bloody prints and none of Michael's? That would say a lot about who the moving entity was, but what if it were a mixture of the two? I think it could have potentially solved the case.

"For our reconstruction, we were bound by their errors. Whatever they did to the evidence, we had to live with it. To the extent that investigators won't tell us what they did, we have to guess at it, and wonder what may have changed because of what they did. They didn't document the process and didn't develop all of the pattern-related evidence. We had to say that there were a lot of unknowns that we couldn't account for, nor necessarily would choose to explore. That's the defense reality: If something might potentially hurt your client, you don't do your own testing. We had to do a limited reconstruction. You end up with a broad-based theory of the case that doesn't sound very conclusive. That, combined with a case that even if everything was done correctly would be so convoluted anyway, you'd never get a definitive result.

"Reconstruction is not just about experience. It's about using the scientific method objectively. Intuitive guessing is not good enough. For me, the failure of the case is that we have a system that allows anyone to approach a case with the mentality that they don't have to do it scientifically. That's dangerous.

"So why was the verdict seemingly contradictory to physical evidence and expert testimony relating to that evidence? The answer to that seems to rest with the way the jurors perceived the story that both sides told. Post conviction, several jurors were polled and provided an unexpected justification for their verdict. After having endured—or been genuinely engaged in—the expert testimony, they decided to summarily dismiss expert testimony in total. Their stated reasons included that it was confusing and technical. As to a motive, and without evidence that she even knew, they accepted the hypothesis that Kathleen Peterson had been so disturbed by a discovery of a homosexual affair involving Michael that they had argued and fought, concluding in Kathleen's death. Apparently that made the most sense to them.

"Most assuredly the jurors sought proof of a definitive cause of death. Since no direct evidence would meet that desire, it is likely jurors inferred a homicidal cause after learning of the death some twenty years earlier of Elizabeth Ratliff."

From this discussion, it's clear that resolving some cases requires far more than technical data, so let's turn now to the way ambiguous deaths are approached with the contribution of psychological analyses.

CHAPTER NINE

Complicating Variables

The second season of *CSI-M* opened with a case in "Golden Parachute," in which a female body was discovered several miles from where a small plane had crashed with the victim's former traveling companions. The scenario was ambiguous: It could have resulted from the plane's mechanical failure (an accident or sabotage), from the woman jumping out to kill herself (suicide), or from someone pushing her out (murder or manslaughter). The technique for investigating these angles is called psychological autopsy. Also known as "retrospective death assessment," "reconstructive evaluation," or "equivocal death analysis," the term refers to a specific method used for examining a person's life—specifically, the life of a dead person.

DEATH ANALYSIS

There are three key issues for death certifications: the cause, mechanism, and mode or manner of someone's death. The cause is the instrument or physical agent used to bring about death (a ligature, for example), the mechanism is the pathological agent in the body that resulted in the death (lack of oxygen), and the manner of death, according to the NASH classification, is considered to be Natural, Accident, Homicide, or Suicide. Sometimes, although the cause and mechanism of death can be easily determined, the manner cannot. Thus, it is known as an "undetermined" death, and among those, some may be labeled "undetermined, pending," meaning that further investigation is warranted.

In Tennessee, a hunter was found shot to death in the woods. By all appearances, he had accidentally tripped over a tree root and fallen in such a way that his gun had discharged, with fatal results for him. The police were ready to close the case as an accident, but the medical examiner thought that the wound and final position of the body did not look quite right for an accident. She thought it might possibly have been a suicide staged to look like an accident. That way, his family could benefit from an insurance payout. Yet the man had been a successful banker with no background of depression or suicide attempts. His family could think of no reason why he might have killed himself. Even so, when the medical examiner tried various experiments with people falling over the root, the mechanics were inconsistent with how the victim had been found and the wound trajectory. She could not bring herself to sign off the death as an accident, but she also could not prove that it had been a suicide, so she labeled it undetermined.

On *CSI-LV*, too, they used a dummy to try to learn the truth about the death of a man in "Who Shot Sherlock?" to attempt to learn if a man had been involved in a vehicular accident or was the victim of his own or someone else's hand. Often a reenactment can clarify if something is odd about an apparent accident, and if so, further steps can be taken to look into the victim's state of mind.

A medical autopsy generally establishes the cause of death by examining the physical condition of the body. In cases where the manner of death is unexplained and it's not clear what actually happened, a psychological autopsy may assist in clearing up the mystery. The idea of this procedure is to discover the victim's behavior and mental frame of mind preceding death, because the results may be needed to settle criminal cases, estate issues, malpractice suits, or insurance claims. When the circumstances surrounding a death can be interpreted in more than one way, psychologists can compile information retrospectively about past behavior, current psychological state, and potential motives.

Between 5 and 20 percent of deaths in the United States are considered equivocal, but most of them are undetermined between accident and suicide, with the potential for homicide being less frequent. In many cases, the manner of death matters. Any family would rather know that the death of an adolescent was an accident rather than a suicide, and sometimes with older people, insurance payments depend upon it. The psychological information can have an impact on the final determination.

The practice of psychological autopsy began with the frustrations of a coroner in 1958 in Los Angeles. The LA County Chief Medical Examiner, Theodore Curphy, was overwhelmed at the time with drug-related deaths. Often it wasn't clear whether these were suicides or accidental overdoses, so he enlisted the help of Edwin S. Shneidman and Norman Faberow, co-directors of the Los Angeles Suicide Prevention Center, to assist him. Shneidman then coined the term *psychological autopsy* in 1961 when he wrote an article and identified sixteen categories for inclusion in the process. Even with that, there were (and still are) no standard procedures to follow, although psychologists have developed a guide that lists twenty-six areas of significant focus. Among them are a change in eating or sleeping habits, suicidal threats, shifts in mental state, and behavior suggestive of bringing significant things to a close.

To consider a death a potential suicide, there must be evidence that a wound could have been self-inflicted and some way to determine whether the victim understood the consequences of what he or she was doing. That means compiling information about the person's last hours, days, and weeks. However, there are also autoerotic incidents, designed for maximum sexual gratification but dangerous enough to accidentally cause death. These incidents often appear to be a suicide, so much so that Nick Stokes on *CSI-LV* persuaded a wife that her husband had killed himself when he clearly had been involved in an autoerotic accident. So before finally deciding that a death has been intentional by the person, many factors must be considered.

A close examination of the death scene may indicate degree of intent and lethality—a secluded place and the use of a weapon indicating a higher degree than using slow-acting pills in a place where the victim is likely to be discovered. It may also be the case that people who knew the deceased have motives for concealing what may have happened, so the investigator needs to be proficient in deception detection as well. At times, the results will be clear, while at other times, the deceased's state of mind prior to death cannot be known with certainty.

A man was found in a cemetery in Pennsylvania, lit on fire. He died on the way to the hospital. The cause was carbon monoxide and the mechanism was damage to his lungs from inhalation. Initially, this incident was determined to be a suicide. The man had a history of mental illness and he lived near the cemetery. The assumption was that he went off his medication, had a psychotic break, and set fire to himself. However, people who knew him insisted this was a hasty assumption. Further questioning indicated that he'd been harassed earlier that week by neighborhood bullies for being gay. There was now a possibility that he had been murdered. It was also possible that he had set fire to himself by accident. As it turned out, he had done this act next to the grave of a relative, so it seemed most likely, from a comparison to similar cases, to have been suicide.

They're not all that simple. In *CSI-LV*, in the episode "Overload," a construction worker's death involves a mystery, as the team considers whether it was an accident, a suicide, or a homicide. There has actually been an incident in which the manner of death was believed at different stages to have been all three. Let's examine that case to see how difficult interpretations of a death event can sometimes be.

CONFUSION

In Portland, Oregon, a young couple went drinking one night in 1995. After David Wahl, twenty-seven, and Linda Stangel, twenty-three, had met, they had gotten involved, but the relationship was largely based, according to her, on drinking together.

On November 12 at three A.M., they decided to drive to the Oregon coast, to Ecola State Park, arriving mid-morning. The area has high cliffs, and it can be a dangerous place to go walking. More than three hundred feet over the ocean, the rocky path has no guardrail. Linda said that while they were sitting in the van, David had decided to take a short walk, saying he would be back in ten minutes. He wasn't dressed for much more than that on that brisk morning. He grabbed a can of beer and left.

She waited in the car. Ten minutes went by, then twenty. Linda said that she grew frustrated. She fell asleep, woke up, and discovered that David still was gone. She decided to drive home. There she checked the answering machine, expecting a call, but there was none. Around eight o'clock that night she called her sister to tell her what had happened and then called 911. David had been missing for seven hours.

Linda's mother understood. Her own husband, Linda's father, often did such things after drinking, disappearing for days at a time. Linda then called David's mother, who wasn't as understanding and who wanted to go to the coast to search for him herself.

The police, volunteers, and David's family went to the park, searching the entire area extensively, but there was no sign of him. Apparently Linda offered no assistance, and her behavior annoyed them. No one could believe that Linda would have just left him there without a coat.

A week went by and there was still no word. The police expected the worst. Linda left the state to be with her family in Minnesota. After two weeks, the search was called off.

It was fully a month before a headless male corpse washed ashore sixty miles north in Washington State. In May 1996, a fingerprint and partial jawbone were matched to David Wahl. His death was finally declared a suicide, with the assumption that he had gone into the ocean, either from the cliff or from the beach, on a day when it was far too cold to be swimming. He'd been inebriated, so perhaps he had not known what he was doing, but there was always the possibility that he'd been distraught over his relationship with Linda.

The Wahls were outraged at this finding. They insisted that David would not have done such a thing. At the very least, he had slipped and fallen by accident, but they insisted on a full investigation. They believed that Linda still knew something that she wasn't revealing. Since David and Linda had lived with them for a while, they knew that the two of them had been fighting and had nearly called off their relationship.

But Linda was out of reach of the police. She had already passed a polygraph so there was no good reason to insist that she return. But the Clatsop County DA's office wanted to get her back, so they lured her with the premise of a memorial service for David. She did as they hoped.

Under arrest, she was taken back to the park, now eight months after the incident, and asked to help reconstruct the events of that day. Two detectives had her climb the 340-foot-high cliff with them, urging her to tell them what had happened. Suddenly, up there on the cliff, she changed her story.

David had come back to the car, she admitted, and they had gone up the trail together. He had "fake-pushed" her to scare her and she had pushed him back, inadvertently causing him to lose his balance in a precarious place, and he had fallen to his death on the rocks below. She had kept quiet about it, fearing she would be blamed. She then repeated all of this on tape, and told it later to the DA.

Now David Wahl's death was being considered accidental. Still, his family was not happy with this and neither was DA Joshua Marquis. He charged Linda with manslaughter and bound her over for trial. She pleaded not guilty.

Yet at trial, Linda changed her recollection once again. She said that she had made up the story about pushing David because she was afraid of heights and she thought it was the only way to get off the cliff. Her attorney hired an expert to tell the jury that her confession was coerced via her extreme fear, and should be considered false. Linda retold her original story for the jury and explained why she had made up the second one.

They did not buy it. On January 16, 1997, they sentenced her to six years in prison for second-degree manslaughter.

So David Wahl's death had been deemed a suicide, then an accidental fall, and finally, a homicide. Even so, questions remain.

METHODS

Some mental health professionals estimate that a comprehensive psychological autopsy could take around twenty to thirty hours to develop, while others believe it takes much longer. The amount of time put in depends on the goal, and often on the time and funds available for it. To compose an understanding of a person's final days and hours, an investigator might use any number of the following sources, with the awareness that anyone he or she interviews may thwart as easily as facilitate the process:

- Interviews with eyewitnesses or police officers at the scene

- Medical autopsy reports (which can reveal things about the victim, such as substance abuse, that even close friends did not know)

- An examination of the death scene, at the scene or via photographs

- Journals/correspondences/suicide note associated with the victim

- Type of books victim read, music preferred, or video games played

- Behavior patterns noted by others, especially unusual recent behavior

- Records (school, military, phone, employment, medical, psychiatric)

- History of medication, if any.

They will then compile all the information to determine a number of factors about the person. For this they will need the person's basic information, details about the death, indications of the victim's familiarity with death methods and his or her access to them, their stress reaction patterns, and recent stressors in their lives. If they're known to drink or take drugs, this will become part of the study, as will any significant changes in routines. For example, if the person does not usually go to church but suddenly starts attending regularly, that can indicate thoughts about death. Changes in a significant relationship can also be a factor. On the other hand, if associates or relatives react strangely to news about the death, it could be something other than a suicide.

The final report should be a fairly accurate sense of the victim's personality, habits, and behavior patterns, specifically including any recent changes. Often the likely manner of death will emerge from these facts. The problem with ambiguous situations is that each new factor can shift the theory back and forth, and those who are being questioned may suffer.

In a bedroom of his mobile home in Kamiah, Idaho, Robert Perry was found shot to death on March 29, 2001. He was eighty-three and had been suffering from terminal throat cancer. Robert Perry's fifty-seven-year-old nephew, Craig Perry, claimed to have found him while Craig's girlfriend, Carol Flynn, called 911 to report a suicide. The police arrived and filmed the scene for analysis.

Robert Perry's body was in the back of the trailer. The Kamiah police chief described it: The body lay on the floor, facing the bed. Blood was coming from the back of the frail man's head and a .22-caliber long-barreled pistol lay near his feet. A deck of playing cards were scattered on the floor near him. Perry clutched an oxygen tube in his right hand.

Craig and Carol, who both lived there to help, gave their statements and seemed quite upset. Craig indicated that his uncle had made an earlier comment that he was going to end it, and Craig had tried to joke with him about it to dissuade him. They also said they'd found him on the floor, but then admitted they had found him slumped over on the bed, so close to the floor they couldn't believe he was still sitting. Carol indicated that Craig then went to embrace the man, and finding him dead, laid him on the floor.

Five months after the incident, Craig Perry was charged with second-degree murder in the shooting of his uncle. He took and passed a polygraph, but forensic science experts offered convincing opinion that the crime scene supported a finding of homicide. The prosecution said that Craig shot Robert. The defense insisted that Robert killed himself because he felt like a burden. Each side had to build its case with evidence that would resolve the ambiguity. They went back and forth on such aspects of the scene as blood-spatter-pattern analysis, wound analysis, and inconsistencies in the initial statements. And there were evidence problems. The pistol used was not tested for fingerprints, and no tests were done for gunshot residue in the bedroom or on Craig Perry, so important evidence for reconstruction was lost.

Several pathologists insisted that a man cannot shoot himself twice, and yet there is evidence that some people have done so. The defense's pathologist showed just how it could have been done.

In support of suicide, Craig claimed that he had no motive to kill his uncle. The man had no money and Craig loved him like a father. In fact, after his own father had died, his uncle had raised him. Medical records indicated that Robert's illness had grown worse, and his home nurse reported that he had rejected traditional cancer treatment. Two days before he died, he coughed up blood and went to the hospital, where doctors said they could do nothing more for him.

Hours before he died, Carol Flynn reported to his doctor that he was having trouble breathing. That same day, she called 911 to say he had shot himself. She claimed that he had been depressed.

Numerous character witnesses testified that Craig was a peaceful man who had loved his uncle and would not have shot anyone. He paid for all his uncle's expenses and took care of his needs, from feeding him to getting him into bed. There was no evidence that he considered his charge a burden. A nurse said that Craig had remained positive that Robert might survive, despite his poor prognosis.

In support of a finding of homicide, there was testimony that while Robert had grown worse, he was taking simple medicines and resisting making discussions about his will. He had demonstrated to his nurse that he was fierce about living. Police had found a newspaper article about assisted suicide in a suitcase, along with power of attorney documents. And a witness also testified that when she found the second cartridge under the playing cards, Craig threw it away, saying the police must not need it.

It was a tough case: There was no motive to kill the man, but a finding of suicide was not clear, either. In any event, on June 25, 2004, the jury acquitted Craig Perry of murder.

While no formal psychological autopsy was done on this case, it's not difficult to see what factors would have been important in the final conclusion: Craig's motive, his uncle's state of mind and physical health, the probability that a man shooting his uncle and staging it to look like suicide would be unlikely to shoot twice, and Craig's attitude about caring for the man. While assisted suicide is a strong possibility, outright homicide seems unlikely. All of the evidence was ambiguous and key evidence was not collected. The finding would have to rely on psychological factors, and they swing the balance away from murder.

Yet, given what we know about what courts require for scientific testimony, is the testimony from a psychological autopsy admissible? Not always, but it has been increasingly visible, especially in appeals courts. Problems with the lack of standards have been noted and little research has been done to prove that a psychological autopsy is a reliable scientific method. In fact, fourteen psychologists rejected the findings of a psychological autopsy performed by the FBI on an explosion in 1989 on the USS *Iowa*. Forty-seven sailors were killed and the investigation centered on Gunner's Mate Clayton Hartwig, who was thought to have exploded the bomb to kill himself over an emotional issue. The psychologists noted that the interpretation and subsequent finding of guilt had no basis in scientific methods. Thus, they could not support the degree of confidence with which it was written. Still, three accepted the navy's conclusions as appropriate. More than two years after the blast, the navy admitted that it had been an accident and issued an apology for Hartwig's family.

And then there are psychological analyses about a different aspect of a case; the manner of death may be clear but just how it came about could require some sleuthing that depends on special knowledge about human motives and character.

BACK STORY

On *CSI-LV* in "Coming of Rage," a boy is found bludgeoned at a construction site. Initially it's thought that one of the workers killed him. Then some kids are suspected. A girl offers a story of how suspects protected her from rape, but the evidence says otherwise. Sometimes an analysis of the manner of death is not sufficient, and the death event itself can shed important light on what needs to be done to seek the motive. That's because some cases defy expectations, as this one did.

The episode is based on an event in Philadelphia in 2003 that unfolded in a manner that shocked everyone who heard about it. Jason Sweeney, sixteen, had gone out with his new girlfriend, Jessica (not her real name). She was about to graduate from her eighth-grade class at a Catholic grammar school. She was a pretty, dark-haired girl from a good family, who had a lot of friends. Jason's mother considered this a positive turn in Jason's life, in line with his ambition to join the navy the following year and become a Navy SEAL.

He left his home in an area known as Fishtown around four o'clock that afternoon and never returned. On Saturday, someone found him in a weedy area, bludgeoned to death. According to Deputy Medical Examiner Ian Hood, the autopsy indicated that the victim's head had been crushed with multiple powerful blows. Every bone in his face was broken except for the left cheekbone, and he was unrecognizable. Pieces of bone were lodged in his brain. His head was so chopped up, his skull could be considered split in two.

The police contacted Jason's father, and he identified the body on Monday morning as his son. He couldn't imagine who would have done such a thing to his boy. Nor could anyone quite believe what unfolded.

Since Jason had been on his way to Jessica's, the police checked there. She offered nothing. They also learned from witnesses that Jason's friend, Eddie Batzig, and two acquaintances, Dominic and Nicolas Coia, had been with Jason recently. When the police requested that the boys come to the station as possible witnesses, two of them quickly confessed to the murder. According to a police transcript, under questioning Dominic admitted that Jessica had posed as bait to get Sweeney to the area. "We took Sweeney's wallet," he said, "and we split up the money and partied beyond redemption."

But Jessica was reputed to be a sweet girl in attendance at a Catholic school; it seemed impossible that she would have been part of this scheme. Still, the boys stuck to their story. Charged in Common Pleas Court as adults with first-degree murder, conspiracy, and related charges, the boys faced the death penalty. Detectives asked more questions and found out from an acquaintance of theirs, eighteen-year-old Joshua Staab, that he'd overheard their plans and had helped to wash out their bloody clothing afterward. He knew they were planning to kill Jason. They went out that evening, he said, and returned after failing to meet up with Jessica as planned. They called her and then went out again. Twenty minutes later they were back, but now in blood-covered clothes, telling Staab that they had killed Jason and could not believe that they had done it.

"They were shaking," Staab later added in court, in a way that implied they were exhilarated. They divided the money at the kitchen table. Each now had $125, and Jessica appeared, to him, to be happy. He said that she had called the whole incident "a rush." Staab noticed no signs in any of them of anxiety or remorse: "They seemed pretty fine." The ill-gotten gains were spent buying marijuana, heroin, cocaine, and Xanax.

What seemed to have occurred, once the evidence and statements were combined, was the following: As Jessica and Jason walked together into the woods, her cell phone rang. She allegedly answered with an angry retort: "What did you do, bitch out?" She then reportedly turned to Jason and suggested they have sex. They both began removing their clothes. Once Jason was vulnerable, the others attacked.

Eddie Batzip, who had been friends with Jason since the fourth grade, came at him with a rock. Following him were the Coia brothers. Batzig lifted a hatchet and struck the first blow to Jason's head. Dominic hit Jason in alternating blows with a hammer, slamming so hard that the hammer stuck in Jason's skull, and the younger Coia beat him with a brick he'd picked up in the trash-strewn area.

"Blood was spurting," Dominic later recalled. "We just kept hitting and hitting him." Supposedly, Dominic did not believe they were really going to do it, that it was just a game, but once Eddie struck the first blow, they all stepped in.

Even as Jason was fending off blows and begging for his life, he realized this had been a trap. His "girlfriend" had played him for a fool. His last words, according to confessions, were, "I'm bleeding," and then to Jessica he said, "You set me up."

They'd known that Jason would have money from his construction job with his father, because the boys later said they'd plotted this attack for over a week. For several hours that day as they waited, they listened to the Beatles' song, "Helter Skelter" more than forty times through. This was the song that had inspired Charles Manson to send his "family" on a murderous rampage in 1969 against actress Sharon Tate and her friends on one night, and against the LaBianca couple on another.

They kept beating Jason, ignoring his screams, until he choked on his own blood with a gurgling sound. One of them finished the job, using a boulder to crush Jason's skull. Their clothes were covered in blood, but their minds were elsewhere. Once they knew he was dead, they rifled his pockets for the money and got $500—his cashed paycheck. Excited, they joined together in a group hug. "It was like we were happy with what we did," Dominic said later to police.

The three boys who swung the hammer, hatchet, and rock that delivered the fatal blows were deemed guilty of first-degree murder, while Jessica was allowed to plead to third-degree murder in exchange for her testimony against the others. They received life in prison, while she'll be free before she's thirty-five. DA Jude Conroy admitted he'd made a deal with her so he could learn what had occurred.

Yet Jessica's post-crime correspondence to her cohorts hinted that there was still more to the story. "I'm a cold-hearted, death-worshipping bitch," she'd written, "who survives by feeding off the weak and lonely. I lure them and then I crush them."

While our knowledge of antisocial character disorders comes largely from incarcerated males, some researchers have examined children at risk for developing into adult psychopaths. Among the traits of concern are chronic deception, manipulation, lack of remorse, failure to accept responsibility for one's actions, cruelty, self-centeredness, and a tendency to blame others.

Jessica's behavior is revelatory. She said in court that she'd written her shocking letters because she wanted the boys to "accept" her and because she was afraid of them. Yet when asked to produce written threats, she said she had thrown them out. However, in one letter she mentioned having received no threats from Batzip. The appearance is that she has lied, blamed others, played a role for the court, and eluded responsibility.

In this case, only by seeing past the Catholic school girl façade and accepting that girls can be calculating and cold-blooded was the resolution of this incident brought to light. Fortunately, the boys involved turned on her and revealed her part. Otherwise she might have escaped punishment of any kind. In the *C.S.I.* episode, the evidence implicated the girl, proving her lies. In real life, the physical evidence would not have done so. Thus a psychological analysis of this girl's manipulative background was important to grasping her part in this terrible crime.

Usually, a psychological analysis occurs above the grave, but there are times when crime detection requires going into the ground or underwater to reconstruct what occurred. These are other areas of forensics that have played roles in *C.S.I.* episodes.

CHAPTER TEN

Into the Grave

On occasion, the teams have reason to exhume a body from a grave, or to dig up a grave to look for one that should have been there, as in "Friends and Lovers." In a suspected poisoning originally identified as a death by natural causes, Grissom's Las Vegas team had to reexamine the corpse with methods not used previously. This involved a specific protocol. So did the archaeological excavation of two Asian women in "Nesting Dolls" on *CSI-LV*, who were found dead and buried in tar in the desert. Generally a painstaking task, these extra complications make the ordeal harder, and there are always mixed feelings about disturbing the dead.

GRAVE DIGGERS

The word *exhume* means "take out of the ground." The procedure has several functions. It may be used to check historical records, locate someone in a mass grave, prove that the right person is in the grave, reexamine the deceased, or identify a missing person. Sometimes it's even done to grab a body to use for some nefarious purpose, such as an insurance scam.

First, we'll discuss the recovery of a crime victim. In the case of a missing person believed to have been buried, the first order of business is determining where to dig. In large areas, that may involve the use of cadaver dogs or ground-penetrating radar (GPR) to find anomalies below the surface.

> The GPR was created in 1929 in Australia to get readings from a glacier. It's comprised of a radar on a wheeled cart that has a digital control unit, which moves over the target terrain and generates a cross-sectional graph onto a computer screen of what's below the surface. No digging or drilling is necessary. While its antenna is rolled slowly along a surface, electromagnetic pulses are emitted into the earth. They detect soil disturbances and bounce off objects, returning to the system to be translated via the control unit into a visual image. The continuous subsurface profile appears as various contours that offer a cross-section of the measured area. In some loose soils, like sand, it may penetrate to a depth of twenty-five feet to provide parameters about the size, density, and shape of a buried object, as well as how deep it is and whether it differs electromagnetically from the surrounding soil. That way, the crew knows precisely where to start digging.

It's also possible to use a plane with forward-looking infrared to locate areas of ground disturbance or soil subsidence (a depression where decomposing remains have made the dirt collapse inward). And searchers might utilize metal rods, which they stick into the ground in different places to find softer soil and possibly to create an air hole through which decomposition odors can filter out. If the body is believed to be in water, other devices may be used, but we'll leave underwater forensics for later in this chapter.

With the help of these instruments, archaeologists usually map out the scene before any digging begins. The investigators must also document everything they find in the area, such as footprints, man-made items left behind, or tire treads. Then the area for digging is staked out. It's important to remove all of the soil from around the victim to be able to draw and photograph that person's position when buried, but it must be done carefully with hand trowels and brushes in order to preserve potential trace evidence. The archaeologists will document the various layers of soil as they dig deeper, because this will contain a record of weather events since the burial.

The soil that's removed is put through a sieve with screens large enough for the dirt to get through but tight enough to retain the smallest items—especially if the victim has been buried long enough to be only skeletal fragments. After everything has been photographed and documented, the body can be moved, examined, and put through procedures for identification.

After the U.S. invasion of Iraq in 2002 and the fall of Saddam Hussein, mass graves were found in the southwestern area of the country containing thousands of corpses. Archaeologists and anthropologists joined the teams sent over to excavate and preserve potential evidence in the event that Hussein was called to account for these crimes. In a grave outside Basra, sixty unearthed bodies were believed to have been those of Shiite Muslims massacred in 1991 after an uprising. The archaeological teams worked to identify them, determine how they were killed, and give them back their dignity as people. However, due to mutilations, decomposition, and burning of corpses, it was difficult to identify specific people and provide grieving families with closure. At best, they could show the conditions of such a massacre and hopefully deter other dictators from committing such atrocities in the future.

There are times in which remains are found unexpectedly. After they're exhumed, an investigation into the person's identification and history begins.

FORENSIC BIO-ARCHAEOLOGY

Dr. Thomas A. Crist is a forensic anthropologist and associate professor at Utica College in upstate New York. A former director of archaeological services at the Philadelphia-based consulting firm of Kise, Straw & Kolodner, Inc., since 1990 Dr. Crist has also served as the forensic anthropologist for Philadelphia's Medical Examiner's Office. He's also a member of the Homeland Security's National Disaster Mortuary Operational Response Team (DMORT), assisting with the recovery and identification of victims after the September 11, 2001, attack on the World Trade Center. He directs excavations of historical cemeteries throughout the United States, and each summer teaches a field school in forensic anthropology in Albania.

"What I do," Dr. Crist explains, "is bio-archaeology, where we use human remains to address questions about the past. It involves the excavation and analysis of historic-period remains, and the mortuary context in which you find them. We provide additional information about how people lived directly from their skeletal remains, rather than simply from artifacts that may or may not be associated with them."

Up until the 1970s, he points out, archaeologists rarely used human remains in a funerary context as a way to investigate historic questions about health and disease. Instead, they explored such themes as how burial practices might inform us about a decedent's social status. In recent decades, they've begun to use historic remains to understand the breakdown of labor activities among males and females, the type of diet people of a certain period had, and childhood vulnerabilities during that time. "The skeleton can tell us that information," says Crist.

That raises the issue of forensic taphonomy, which is defined as the discovery, recovery, and analysis of human remains in a context that has legal ramifications. The term derives from the Greek words for burial, *taphos,* and laws, *nomos.* People engaged in this activity deal with the many factors involved in excavating and preserving physical remains and documenting the ways in which death-related processes have affected them, differentiating biological processes from environmental factors. Over time, corpses undergo changes, and different conditions affect the way professionals may estimate how long they have been dead (from a few hours to several decades). These estimates may also have an impact on making identifications and figuring out the cause and manner of death.

"Taphonomy is a branch of archaeology," Crist explains. "It's a discipline that looks at the postmortem modification, natural or otherwise, of artifacts or remains."

A decedent's unique features will have an effect on taphonomic calculation, e.g., their height, weight, type of clothing they wore (or not), illness, use of drugs, and the physical properties of their bones. The type of burial rituals adopted by the culture that gives context to the remains, such as embalming methods, autopsies, and burial procedures, can also influence the findings. If there's been an injury to the bone, it's crucial to decide whether it occurred prior to death, during the immediate stage prior to death, or postmortem. That involves knowing the processes to which the bone was exposed and the appearance of specific types of damage in bones of the living versus the dead.

Dr. Crist was involved in a project in 2000 in Philadelphia, where his consulting firm excavated the remains of over 150 people from the burial ground of the former Second Presbyterian Church of Philadelphia, at Block 3 of Independence Mall, which is currently the site of the new National Constitution Center. While such excavations yield knowledge about earlier times, they may also contain surprises.

With graves dating from the mid to late eighteenth century, among the remains was a white man in his fifties who presented a classic gunshot entrance wound in his frontal bone, just above and between his eyes. The projectile was there as well, deformed from impact and embedded in his occipital bone. "We never expected to find someone with a gunshot wound to the head in a site like that," Crist says. Since it's clearly a murder, it's now a forensic issue and they are still attempting to identify him. Nevertheless, this man is now the earliest known gunshot victim found in Pennsylvania.

More recently, Dr Crist led a team of graduate students in the excavation of coffins found in the basement of an 1860s row home in South Philadelphia. Between 1732 and 1834, deceased residents of the city's almshouse were buried in a lot situated on the south side of Carpenter Street between Eleventh and Twelfth Streets. During renovations, the coffins were inadvertently discovered, providing an opportunity to explore the health status of infants and children from the institution. The team set out to establish the origin of the burials and document the demography and evidence of disease, trauma, and postmortem treatment of the individuals found there. Among the remains were the preserved skeletons of sixteen infants and children buried together in a single grave-shaft.

"Twelve had died before their first birthdays," Crist recounts, "including four premature infants and two newborns. Three were children between two and three years old. None of the individuals presented evidence regarding a cause of death. Of greatest significance, the heads and first two cervical vertebrae of three of the oldest children had been surgically removed prior to their interment."

In other words, the almshouse physicians had used these infants and children as anatomical specimens, an activity that had not previously been documented. The demography was consistent with the historical records regarding childhood mortality in America, "especially among those unfortunate enough to become almshouse residents, if only for a very brief time."

There are other types of unusual cases that require the services of a specialist in bio-archaeology. On June 21, 2004, the owner of the Canal Side Guest House in Weissport, Pennsylvania, built around 1820, discovered a plain white cloth sack and old clothing in an attic crawl space. To his surprise, the sack contained human remains but no documentation regarding their origin or identification. Unsure even how old they were, he contacted the local police, who turned the remains over to the Pennsylvania State Police. They called in Dr. Crist for analysis.

"It was an old general mercantile building located across an open area from the canal that runs through that part of the state," Crist recalls, "and the owner was renovating it to turn it into a bed and breakfast. He found the sack in the rafters."

Among the remains were an adult cranium; the anterior portion of a bilaterally resented mandible; all seven cervical vertebrae articulated with the cranium via desiccated soft tissue; a desiccated tongue;

the internal throat organs; one adult left hand; a female hip bone; and a female adult mandible without teeth. This unusual collection represented remains from at least two people.

Crist looked at these items and found that the skeletonized remains were dry, with no adherent soft tissue and no odor of decomposition. That gave him a pretty good clue about their prior handling. "The typical way that human remains were preserved for anatomical studies during the eighteenth and nineteenth centuries here in the United States was that they were often allowed to dry out. These remains were consistent with that. Many times, the arteries and veins were filled with different colors of latex paint. Arteries were filled with a red-colored substance and veins were colored blue. The jaws are typically cut so they are resected. It's a standard type of cut, along with the standard autopsy cut through and around the cranial vault, or the lid of the head, which comes right off. We also found that the bones of the left hand had been drilled through and they were all wired together, and we had a hand with wired bones, which is a classic representation of anatomical stuff. The left hip bone had a hole drilled through it, also a typical location for wiring the sacrum to the pelvic girdle.

"What I was looking for was evidence of standard types of anatomical preparation from that time. I wanted to see if the holes had been drilled professionally or if they'd just been hacked through. There was no evidence of hacking; they were professionally done with a real drill. The autopsy cut was standard. And then we had this desiccated soft tissue that covered the head. Inside one of the arteries I could see this material that was bright red in color. Blood exposed to oxygen turns brown, and this was a very bright red pigmentation. I'd seen it numerous times before with bona fide historic anatomical preparations, when I'd worked with the Mütter Museum and other anatomical collections in Philadelphia. We always check remains for cut marks, animal or rodent gnawing, and other types of postmortem change. These remains were mixed and might not have been from the same person, but they showed no evidence of rodent gnawing."

Indeed, Dr. Crist saw no evidence that they had ever been buried, either, due to a lack of roots or vegetation. "Once you're buried, especially during this historic period, roots like to make their way into human remains. It's fertilizer." From his experience, he was able to say that this method of postmortem preparation was most likely that of anatomical specimens dating to the early nineteenth century. "There's a slight possibility that back in the 1880s some crazy guy was killing people and making them look like anatomical specimens, and you never want to exclude that possibility 100 percent, but that's not the likely answer."

Helpful to his analysis was the fact that along with the remains, the property owner had also discovered several business letters and invoices from the late nineteenth and early twentieth centuries. "We need to assume that the letters and other dated material are actually in association with the remains. They were all found together in the cloth sack. We've found that a lot in Philadelphia, with its medical and dental schools, when people renovate older buildings."

One letter found in Weissport had an 1899 postmark and was addressed to Mr. J.K. Rickert, the builder of the structure in 1826. Two others with postmarks from 1909 and 1915 were addressed to Mr. Hiram Rickert, who apparently carried on the family mule and mercantile business. But there had never been a medical school or hospital in the area. "What makes this case so unusual," Crist points out, "is that there doesn't appear to be a good reason why someone would have anatomical specimens during that period in that area. We have no knowledge about it and probably will never have an answer." The origin of these bones continues to be a mystery.

When remains of this nature are found, the police initially treat the case as a homicide until proven otherwise, and some of the cases can be quite outlandish. When Crist was a graduate student at the University of South Carolina, he studied under the renowned Ted Rathbun, the state forensic anthropologist there. "We had a case of the remains of a three- or four-year-old child who had been placed on a base with a large metal rod going up, impaling the child, with its arms and legs splayed open, and his chest cavity opened up. These remains had been found by the Charleston police during a raid or arrest at some alleged criminal's house. The specimen was being used there as a hat rack. When they entered, they saw it and thought they had some crazy serial killer doing unbelievable things to children, so they brought the specimen to Rathbun, who correctly identified it as an anatomical specimen. The police did more research and found that the man had purchased the specimen at a flea market. They traced it beyond the flea market to Philadelphia, so it was likely that it had originated at one of the old medical schools or museums."

The police may also suspect a homicide before remains are found, and then do an excavation when they have the opportunity, relying on the help of a specialist like Dr. Crist. "I did one with a Pennsylvania coroner, Zachary Lysek, where there was an informant who came forward and said that a particular young man had been buried on a piece of property that some ten or fifteen years later, had been sold to someone else. That person was going to be building a new house on the property, so the police took advantage of the digging for construction to begin to explore the areas where they thought this young man had been killed and buried. Zack mobilized an army of people and equipment to undertake an archaeological excavation within a forensic setting. It went on for several days, and one of the state troopers found some bones. They thought they'd recovered animal bones, so they mailed them to me to analyze, and I told them that while most of it was animal bone, they had also found a human tibia.

So they went back out and found a good proportion of the rest of this individual. At one point, we were going through the remains at the morgue, and the trooper came in with a new bag of materials. In there, I found the left temporal bone, on the left side of the head, and in that bone was a classic gunshot entrance wound. They had suspected that something had happened to this man but hadn't been able to prove it. The man they suspected of committing the crime had moved out of the state, but with a body they now had a way to possibly bring him to justice."

When asked about this case, Lysek acknowledged the difficulties. "We couldn't use ground-penetrating radar because the ground was already disturbed. So we brought in cadaver dogs, which didn't work, because they smelled decomposition all over. To go through the massive piles of dirt, we used front-end loaders. This was approximately five acres of land, so there was no way we could sift all of that carefully the way archaeologists would have wanted us to. I estimate there was five hundred tons of dirt, so we used a power sifter. That's not the normal forensic standard, but that's what we did."

To figure out where to begin, they took aerial photographs and overlaid them onto old pictures of the property during the time when the suspect had owned it. He'd had a backhoe, and the tires were flat, so the investigators knew it hadn't been driven far. They started digging and going through dirt where it had sat. "We found the main torso of the body," Lysek reports, "and x-rayed it using digital x-rays. We found that the person had been shot in the chest, and we recovered the bullet." However, the suspect was long gone at this point, so going after him would require making a strong case.

"In the forensic setting," says Crist, "the bar is a lot higher when we find someone. We have to determine who they are, how they died, what happened to their body after death, and then be able to prove all of it beyond a reasonable doubt in a court of law. People's lives are at stake. But in the court of history, we have more opportunity for speculation. We are prepared to distinguish between historic and modern human remains, but we often never get the full history, and it can be frustrating. But it's rewarding work in many other ways. And everyone loves a mystery."

SETTING RECORDS RIGHT

Exhumation has also been used for historical purposes, although it is controversial, to identify remains as the person said to be buried in a specific place or learn if the historical records about the deceased are accurate. Among those who have been thus exhumed are civil rights victim Medgar Evers, assassin Lee Harvey Oswald, and former U.S. President Zachary Taylor.

One of the key figures in this business is Professor James E. Starrs, who teaches law and forensic science at The George Washington University in Washington, D.C. He's known internationally as the man who digs up the dead, and is famous for his exhumations of Jesse James and Albert DeSalvo. In a book about his most famous cases, *A Voice for the Dead*, he describes how he got his start after he went to Colorado in 1989 to attend the meetings of the American Academy of Forensic Sciences. While there, he decided to explore the area.

A local story that had always interested him was that of Alfred Packer, tried for the 1874 murders of five men in his mining party. Packer had claimed that he'd killed in self-defense, but he'd told so many lies and the circumstances had failed to support any of his stories, so the incident remained ambiguous. Starrs went to the town, talked to several people who knew the tale, and decided to organize an exhumation of the remains of the victims for anthropological analysis. He found them all and their bones were so well-preserved that his team of scientists managed to document numerous indicators

that these five men had died defending themselves rather than attacking Packer. For him, this scientific exploration was such a resounding
success that he turned his attention to other historical mysteries. To
date, he has performed more than twenty exhumations.

"I think about the fact," he says, "that we can do something a
hundred or so years after someone's death that would have been un-
heard of—unthought of—at that time." In addition, he is pleased to
help families find closure on cases that he feels may demand justice.
"It means so much to these people that they be told the truth as to the
death of their loved one. To me, that rubs off very easily."

When the family of murder victim Mary Sullivan sought help proving that
her killer was not Albert DeSalvo, as the police had believed since 1964,
Starrs assisted them to have her remains exhumed for examination. His
team also exhumed Albert DeSalvo, the so-called Boston Strangler. They
made headlines when they found that there were many inconsistencies
between DeSalvo's "confession" to the murder and Sullivan's remains,
and that DNA found on her did not match his. At the very least, it cast
doubt on DeSalvo's confession. Since he was never tried for the series of
murders attributed to him, his confession was the only evidence the police ever had. Not only were Sullivan's relatives affirmed in their belief
that her murder was still unsolved, but the team's findings exposed the
whole story as an American myth.

Before undertaking an exhumation, Starrs evaluates the potential case
against his requirements for doing an exhumation and autopsy (or re-
autopsy). For him, there must be a significant dispute to which science can make a contribution, as well as some type of new scientific
method available that was not present at the time the issue to be resolved arose. In addition, there must be more than a likelihood that

the remains will be in sufficient condition to be analyzed. That involves a variety of tasks, including testing the soil pH and mineral content where the remains are buried, determining the method and depth of burial, knowing the length of time since burial, gathering climatic and environmental data, and forestalling the disturbance of adjacent graves.

Once all of this has been established, the first task involves collecting all available historical documentation, which means looking into court records, newspapers, books, autopsy reports, and burial methods. Each state has its own requirements, so Starrs must learn what they are, and perhaps enlist an attorney. Once he has the case records in order and all necessary permissions from family or descendents, he determines whom he will invite onto the team from the various forensic specializations. "In some cases," Starrs explains, "it's anthropology, archaeology, and possibly tool-mark or firearms experts. In a case with flesh [on the bones], you have to have pathologists, and if there's poison involved, you need toxicologists for an analysis of the organs and tissues. You want to look under the fingernails for tissue, so you need a microscopist for that. The teeth are often impacted when people are killed in violent confrontation, so you need an odontologist—a forensic dental expert."

Projects often require months of work leading up to the exhumation and autopsy, as well as months of analysis afterward. But if family members of the deceased are satisfied, then Starrs believes he has done his job. Thanks to his renown, he has also gotten involved in investigating recent, as opposed to historic, deaths, and has been assisting people to get closure . . . or attorneys.

One area into which he will not lead an investigation is under water, and that's wise, because it involves a different type of approach.

UNDERWATER FORENSICS

When the Miami setting was introduced for a *C.S.I.* series, it meant learning about how investigators are trained for underwater search and recovery. Some of the investigators are experienced divers, as noted in "Blood in the Water" and "Dead Zone," and an underwater crime scene requires special training in recovery techniques specific to the effects of different types of water on evidence, including corpses. Such technicians must have extensive diving experience, knowledge about what to look for under water, and skill with the special equipment involved. But they must look for evidence systematically, i.e., according to the scientific method. As well, they must know how to document and handle it within the protocol for that context. There is a difference between rescue and recovery in a placid lake, for example, than in the ocean or in swift-running water.

In Kansas City, Missouri, Christine Elkins, thirty-two, the mother of two boys, had become a drug addict and was running drugs for her supplier, Tony Emery. Arrested, she agreed to turn state's evidence against him, but one day in 1990 she disappeared in her two-door Oldsmobile Cutlass.

Eventually an informant told investigators about the murder of a woman by Tony Emery and two other men. The victim had been beaten with a blackjack, rolled into a rug, and placed in a car, which was then sunk in a rock quarry. But searches of quarries failed to turn up Elkins or her car. In time, detectives learned that she had actually been pushed into the Missouri River. But that had been six years earlier, and since that time the river had flooded. There was no telling where the incident had occurred or if anything was left. The investigators enlisted the assistance of a team known as NecroSearch International.

Incorporated in 1991, NecroSearch is a volunteer organization of victim advocates comprised of biologists, geologists, chemists, meteorologists, geophysicists, plant ecologists, anthropologists, and other specialists who use the most advanced technology to help find bodies in difficult-to-search places. For this case, a team went out with special equipment to scour the Missouri River. They learned that in the target area the river was about twenty to thirty feet deep, and that the current was swift. Knowing the Cutlass's weight and composition, they collected their equipment: a magnetometer, a Global Positioning System (GPS), and nonmagnetic boats. The Coast Guard and Missouri State Water Patrol offered divers.

Using magnetic anomalies, they pinpointed seven potential locations for a submerged car. When the magnetometer failed, they switched to a gradiometer, which also measures changes in magnetic fields. With the GPS, they plotted a map.

Then divers went in, and at the second anomaly site, they found a two-door-style car. It proved to be the one they were seeking, so they brought it out of the water and looked inside the trunk. Rolled in a water-logged carpet, as the story had indicated, they found the remains of a human female. It was Christine Elkins, and her skull had been shattered from a blow. Emery was convicted of her murder and sentenced to life in prison.

According to Mack S. House, Jr., an experienced underwater forensics research diver (UFRD) who published *Underwater Forensics Research: Commercial Scientific Diving*, such investigators are trained with equipment that a C.S.I. who remains on land may never see. They might utilize a mask with lighting on it, for example, so they can use both hands. They might also have a video recorder with a remote monitor that allows people on the boat to see what they see. These divers, under the auspices of legal medicine, must know about courtroom procedure, evidence documentation, and proper evidence handling. But first, and foremost, they must understand the effects of being under water.

"Boyle's Mariotte Law," says House, "states that the volume and pressure of an ideal gas is constant given a constant temperature. It defines the relationship between the *volume* of the air space and the ambient *pressure*."

He points out two primary concerns for divers. First, he considers hyperbaric exposure, or pressure defined as greater than what occurs in normal atmospheric conditions at sea level (760 millimeters of mercury). It influences the behavior of gasses and air in a person's body. Small air-containing cavities, such as the sinuses, react to sudden pressure changes, as do larger air-containing organs, such as the lungs. Divers must pay attention to the effects of decompression and ensure safe working conditions. (These issues surfaced in *CSI-M*'s "Breathless" episode, when the team had to investigate these effects under water.) In addition, they must be able to intelligently document what they observe when encountering bodies under water.

"Breathing compressed air at depth," House explains, "results in an increase in gas pressure within the lungs, which is greater than atmospheric pressure. The greatest pressure change for the diver occurs within the first thirty-three feet. For example, a person who is free diving, with no compressed air equipment, has about two liters of air in his lungs before entering the water. By the time the diver reaches thirty-three feet, his lung volume is one liter.

"The problem for the scuba diver is in breathing compressed air. Let's say he's at a depth of thirty-three feet and ascends to the surface without exhaling. The lung volume, or pressure, will double by the time he reaches the surface. Noncompressed air will return the lung to the predive pressure. Compressed air diving will exceed the predive pressure."

Boyle's Law affects the diaphragm as well. "The greater the ambient pressure, the more the diaphragm is depressed against the delivery aspect of the regulator, thus requiring less negative inspiratory force."

The second issue for divers is "barotrauma," which House describes as physical damage to body tissues as a result of difference in *pressure* between an air space inside or beside the body and the surrounding *gas* or *liquid*. "Damage occurs in the tissues around the body's air spaces," he points out, "especially the lungs, because gases are compressible and the tissues—largely fluid—are not."

Added to diving concerns are protocols for evidence handling, whether it's for vehicles, weapons, clothing, trace materials, or bodies. Clear and detailed documentation of surrounding conditions is vital. While people are currently experimenting with the effective lifting of fingerprints from submerged objects, that has not yet been reliably accomplished. "It is the procedure for preserving an item in its original state that is imperative," says House. "There are considerable differences between the preservation procedures regarding 'latent fingerprints' and other evidence collection that occur in the underwater environment than those used for land, or surface, crime scenes. Containment, movement, current, water temperature, tools used, depth, lighting, and position of the evidence are important considerations when collecting evidence."

In addition, House says divers should be aware of long-term psychological effects from finding and handling the various states of decomposition in which victims may be found. There is both short-term stress and long-term burnout, in which the diver loses perspective and becomes withdrawn. Professionals who choose this specialized career need to know what to expect and prepare for it.

In the case of a missing person or a reported body dumping, if investigators have a general idea of where to look for a victim, they must consider several important factors.

"Safety first," says House. "A job hazard analysis must be conducted before anyone enters the water." Then, the depth of the water in the general area must be evaluated. "This often reduces the diver's exposure time and minimizes man-hours. It is not uncommon for a victim to 'drift' five feet horizontally for every five feet vertically. This is why many victims require an extended search time. If a victim drowns in sixty feet of water—a nominal current—the best procedure is to begin the search eighty feet from the suspected point of victim entry."

The medical examiner who will decide such things as time, cause, and manner of death will need to know as much as possible about the underwater conditions. Certain factors affect what happens to the body during decomposition:

- Refloat—the time it takes a body to float to the surface after having initially sunk

- Autolysis—spontaneous decomposition via internal enzymes

- Effects of scavengers—water life that consumes decaying organic matter

- Stages of decomposition—what bodies go through according to the environment in which they're left on their way to breaking down into basic elements

- Tissue preservation (adipocere)—conversion of fat into a soapy substance that can help to preserve the body in moist environments

- Prolonged immersion—the skin macerates and becomes vulnerable to peeling

- Cooling rate—the speed at which a body loses heat.

"Studies have shown," House states, "that a body will cool faster submerged in water than it will exposed to air." This is because of radiation, or the transfer of energy by non-particulate means, and convection, the transfer of heat from the victim to the surrounding water.

"Putrefaction is a rather unique event for the underwater victim," he continues. "There are many variables to consider. For example, what kind of medication was the victim taking; what did the victim eat prior to submersion; did the victim consume a malt beverage prior to submersion; was there a skin problem such as severe acne; what was the victim wearing at the time of submersion; and is the victim located in a cove or near a popular fishing spot? Depending on the weather and water environment, more often than not, the submerged victim will succumb to putrefaction at a greater rate than the surface victim. The effect that water has on a human body is a sort of 'hyper-hydration,' which facilitates the loosening of the skin as well as its exposure to the ever-present increase in bacteria. Keep in mind that bacteria levels in our lakes and rivers are becoming an environmental problem."

On Christmas Eve of 2002, Laci Peterson, eight months pregnant, disappeared from her home in Modesto, California. Her husband, Scott Peterson, reported her missing and said that he was out fishing that day. He gave several media interviews, and then a woman surfaced who claimed to have been his mistress. On April 13 and 14, 2003, the partial remains of a fetus and a woman surfaced off Point Isabella Regional Park in Richmond, California. Investigators made a careful recovery of them, but marine life had clearly been busy and not much was left. This was about two miles from where Peterson had said he was fishing. DNA tests confirmed that the remains were those of Laci and her unborn son Conner. Underwater divers also scoured the area where engineering and water current studies indicated that the bodies were likely dumped, to fnd any other evidence.

Arrested on April 18 near the border of Mexico, Peterson was found with recently-dyed hair, $10,000 in cash, and his brother's ID. He was soon charged with two counts of murder. Yet examinations of the remains, which had been under water for nearly four months, could not determine a clear cause or time of death. (He was nevertheless convicted and sentenced to death.)

With remains in such a condition, House points out, there are special problems in handling them. "[They need] documentation, such as photographic protocols and additional forms of documentation as instructed by the medical examiner," he indicates. "There must be a thorough search of the area for additional evidence, i.e., jewelry, fingernails, and clothing prior to moving any body part. The ideal process would include encasement of the victim or human remains in such a way as to preserve their condition. In addition, the handling of any victim must include procedures for protecting the diver, such as decontamination."

To become certified as a UFRD, some investigators take a Public Safety Diver course, but House believes there should be a program that focuses on many more subjects. Among them, he would include anatomy and physiology, psychology, human nutrition, the use of commercial diving equipment such as the Kirby Morgan EXO-26 BR, and Coast Guard regulations.

With all of these special conditions to consider, scientists and investigators continue to work together to improve equipment and develop innovations that will make investigation more efficient and sound. Let's look at some of those ideas and devices.

CHAPTER ELEVEN

Forensic Front Lines

With computer technology and the closer alliance of science with forensics, new techniques are being rapidly discovered. All of the *C.S.I.* shows rely on technological and scientific breakthroughs, and at times they even go over the line to offer techniques that cannot be performed. Perhaps, like science fiction, they're anticipating possibilities that may one day come to pass. They may also be alerting us to new dangers on the horizon, as well as how they would be handled. In what follows, we'll sample from a number of areas that have been featured and include profiles of professionals who have utilized some of these innovations. Let's start with a former detective who offers perspective on the multitude of changes.

ACROSS THE DECADES

Vernon J. Geberth, M.S., M.P.A., is a retired lieutenant-commander of the New York City Police Department, and was the commanding officer of the Bronx Homicide Task Force, which handled more than four hundred murder investigations every year. The recipient of over sixty awards for bravery and exceptional work, he has personally investigated, supervised, researched, and consulted on over 8,000 homicides. Over the past twenty-five years, he has offered a comprehensive flagship course in Practical Homicide Investigation, and law enforcement departments around the country, including the FBI, have collectively sent over 51,000 officers and agents to attend.

Geberth has devoted his life to the study of murder and was the first law enforcement professional to devise standard guidelines and protocols for proficient death inquiries. He is the author of the "bible of homicide," *Practical Homicide Investigation: Tactics, Procedures and Forensic Techniques*, and also published *Sex-Related Homicide and Death Investigation: Practical and Clinical Perspectives*. In addition, he's been the series editor for more than forty other textbooks for *Practical Aspects of Criminal and Forensic Investigations* since 1982.

Since Geberth has been involved in law enforcement for over four decades, he's witnessed a number of innovations. "We've come light-years in the last decade," he points out, "not only with the application of DNA technology to the investigative process, but just look at how we record and process crime scenes today, with virtual crime scene photography, including the Panoscan [a way to create 3-D crime scenes on the computer, as seen in *CSI-NY's* "Officer Blue"]. We also have the ability to do gunshot residue testing on a highly scientific level, which allows the examiner to do multiple copies at the same time, with ASPEX. We're better able to reconstruct the scene, and we don't walk into the scene like we did twenty years ago in our shoes and street clothes. We didn't know then that we were contaminating it, because there was no thought about microscopic contamination.

"We have come so far with our technology that we're able to find evidence now that we couldn't find before. It's easy to criticize older cases, but the truth is, we didn't have the capability of microscopic retrieval of evidence. As a result of this, many cases that we once couldn't even get into the system can now be solved. It's like comparing someone on a bicycle to someone on a rocket ship.

"Let's take the forensic laser, for example. Because of its size and construction, it was once confined to the laboratory. Now we have these little ALS [alternative light source] units, and some of them weigh less than five pounds. We can light up a scene now with these ALS units, find microscopic evidence, and retrieve it in ways we couldn't before.

"The downside is that television programs have picked up on the technology and they *always* find evidence. But the truth of the matter is that we don't always find evidence and we can't obtain fingerprints from some of the items that they 'process' on TV. Theoretically, the evidence should be there, but we may not be able to retrieve it for any number of reasons: time, environmental conditions, contamination by responders or the criminals who stage the scene and/or add or remove evidence, or things that took place at the scene before the investigators got there. It's a very complex path that we walk, full of twists and turns."

To keep up, investigators like Geberth stay attuned to the many advances in science and technology. "I make it my business to do research constantly," he affirms. "I attend forensic workshops as well as professional meetings. Not only do I have to be on top of the new technology so I can explain it to people in my classes, but more important, my ultimate goal when I was a homicide cop was to be the best murder cop in the world. That required a lot of homework. And I'm still doing homework."

Geberth believes it's important to know what's available and how to get it, and he shares this information with other investigators. Adopting a teamwork approach, which he also did as a cop, he offers others what he's learned so that they can become better investigators.

As for what may come in the future, Geberth views the Internet as having a significant role. "The Internet, which has been a great boon to those who do research," he comments, "also has a down side. It's a playground for the sexual offender, who basically has a whole new area in which to prey. Whether it's in the chat rooms where they attempt to meet potential victims or to reinforce some sort of deviant personality that they now can validate as they meet others with the same paraphilias, all of it will have an impact on law enforcement. More and more agencies will have to have computer cops in place. I don't just mean the people who go online and engage these offenders in conversation. I'm also talking about computer forensics, like the FBI laboratory and certain major departments have. A person's computer will become an additional element in search warrants, and it will offer a wealth of information."

And speaking of ALS, there have been several innovations in that field.

LET THERE BE LIGHT

Fluorescence makes things brighter, and any organic material can be made to fluoresce, as occurred when *CSI-NY* investigators used an ALS to find semen in "Tanglewood." But they also used it to derive a paint chip's "fingerprint" and to clarify initials and an emblem on a bag in "Blink." Fluorescent diagnostics helps investigators to see things more clearly than ever before, on a microscopic level. It's the result of colors absorbed and reemitted as warmer colors, so both absorption and emission spectra become key to the analyses. (On *CSI-M*, they used an ALS to examine a faked photo ID on "Spring Break.") The shift occurs via a transformation process from the blue end of the color spectrum, with shorter wavelengths (the farthest end being UV), to the orange and red end (infrared at the extreme). Fluorescence once provided only a surface read, which worked well for detecting trace evidence such as fibers and biological fluids, but now it can delve deeper, making it more valuable as an investigative tool.

Of the types of ALS units, those utilizing high-power light-emitting diodes (LEDs) have helped to refine their effectiveness, and they can offer better signals in presumptive field tests for the need for more sophisticated (and expensive) testing on an item or surface at a crime scene. Brightness varies with color, offering the Fluorescence Excitation Spectrum (FES). Because this is due to color absorption characteristics, it can help to spot and identify unknown substances, such as semen stains. A distinct fluorescent reading via an ALS can set semen apart from the fluorescent qualities of laundry products on the same fabric, so that the spot can be identified for what it is. The FES can also be set to preferentially excite the known color spectrum of the semen to make it stand out in greater contrast to the fabric. For this purpose, LEDs are more cost-effective than using lasers in ALS units, because they can be tuned to almost any color, they turn on and off quickly, and they're stable.

The fluorescence-reading units are used with a filtering system that allows one color to be seen while blocking others, typically in the form of fluorescence viewing glasses or goggles that intensify the fluorescence. Success comes from the right combination of light beam with colored filters. Yellow or red lenses block blue light, while orange blocks green and blue-green.

A type of ALS that gives a chemical-specific contrast is Fluorescence Excitation Radiometry (FER). In this system, LEDs that utilize combined blue and UV lights automatically alternate in quick succession, with a dial that increases or decreases the intensity of either of them. This device is useful in making fingerprints stand out in greater contrast to their surfaces.

But there's more to it than illuminating them. Some are difficult to lift, so scientists are looking at other methods for preservation.

FINGERPRINTS

In one episode in Las Vegas, "Mea Culpa," a clear thumbprint was found on a matchbook that had been processed five years earlier without it being picked up. While the technician considered it odd, he said that it was possible to have a print "process" itself over time in the climate in which it was stored (plastic), so evidence that was not available for the original trial was now in hand—and it changed the team's opinion about who was guilty. In other words, it processed more slowly because of the way proteins interact with ninhydrin, the substance used in that case to make the print visible.

While such incidents may not occur often, experts seek increasingly better methods to detect and clarify fingerprints, especially on surfaces that historically have been difficult to lift and even to photograph in a high-quality manner. Yet some researchers have found a way: For surfaces such as brick, skin, and blood, casting silicone can be used. Transparent silicone, often utilized for getting an accurate three-dimensional rendering of tool and impression marks, allows technicians to both preserve fingerprints and see them to make a comparison. It's safer than using chemicals and it's permanent. This method has even proven itself on curved surfaces.

But fingerprints are not the only useful means for identification. Biologists have closed in on several other helpful tools.

ID ASSIST

In the *CSI-M* episode "Stalkerazzi," the team finds sweat on the band of a hat used to murder a man, but they get no hits from a DNA analysis. In other words, they have no sources against which to match their evidence. So until they find a suspect, they can go no further with this type of identification. Still, they can narrow their leads with one more procedure: Amelogenin analysis. With it, they can learn, at least, if their suspect is male or female, as the New York–based team did in "Summer in the City."

Amelogenin is the major protein component of tooth enamel—about 90 percent of the developing tooth, and it produces X and Y chromosome–specific products. Coamplification of Amelogenin with the loci used for short tandem repeat (STR) in DNA testing provides a gender-identity test. STR procedures use nucleotide sequences that are only two to four bases long, which makes the procedures compatible with the PCR amplification process used on very small samples. More than 2,000 STR markers are practical for genetic mapping, with high reliability in making discriminations among individuals. Thus, even a small DNA sample can be subjected to a test that uses the Amelogenin STR to narrow a field of unknown suspects to male or female. The allele profile for female samples at the Amelogenin locus is X, X, and for male samples is X, Y. While this may seem too broad to be of much use, it was quite practical for a mass homicide incident.

Following the terrorist attacks on the United States on September 11, 2001, some 3,000 victims had to be identified, many of them piece by piece. Conventional DNA technologies sometimes proved insufficient for the task, which inspired several advances and new technologies. The Bode Technology Group from Virginia, the largest DNA testing company in the country at the time, worked with the medical examiners on site, but it became clear after the fire companies had hosed down the area, that human DNA in the rubble would be degraded. Also, many of the victims had been incinerated, so technicians had to work with only bone fragments, which do not yield easily to DNA analysis. Less than half of more than 12,000 fragments that went through an initial screening process provided useful information for identification purposes.

To improve upon these results Bode looked into developing other processes. One process involved using decalcification to isolate the DNA, which raised the success rate, and the other involved developing multiplex short tandem repeat systems, which included testing on the Amelogenin locus for gender identity. Amelogenin is the smallest of the STR markers, with about 115 base pairs. To meet the challenge, the company designed a way to make the tests more sensitive and appropriate for smaller samples.

In addition, Orchid Biosciences from New Jersey, which has done a lot of paternity testing, also made a contribution to the technology. They were using a specific type of stand-alone genetic marker and were asked to use it for identification of remains. Sometimes the only marker derived from a sample was Amelogenin, and on those samples, the company used its genetic test for genotyping information. They were able to find tissue samples from different locations around the affected area that matched one another. Their test was thus an improvement on the DNA analysis that required samples of higher quality and more markers.

Another method being developed is isotopic analysis of oxygen and strontium in tooth enamel. It can assist in the identification of cremated bodies where tooth enamel may still be intact, at least to indicate the general area from which the victims came. The type of water in a given region and the general habits of food consumption are factors in this analysis. Supposedly, the enamel stores a chemical record of the environment in which people spend their childhood—the time when the enamel forms. Since much of the oxygen that goes into the formation derives from the water we drink, the type of climate the person was exposed to will be stored in the teeth. Heavier isotopes come from warmer climates. Comparing the isotopes in the teeth with the water from different regions can offer a rough guess about a person's place of origin. Strontium analysis is related to the type of soil in which the food was grown. This method of enamel analysis applies more accurately to older cases, due to the greater distribution since the 1990s of bottled water.

Since we're on the subject of mass disasters, let's look at another type that *C.S.I.* has confronted.

RADIATION FOR GOOD AND ILL

An explosion in a club on *CSI-M*, "10-7," yielded clues to the possibility that this was no accident and no ordinary bomb. The first indication was the presence of a high level of potassium iodide (KI) in one victim's thyroid tissues, which may have protective value against radiation with iodide isotopes. Since the victim did not have a thyroid condition that explained it, the team believed that someone was working with radiation, and perhaps a dirty bomb. With the additional find of TNT, which can spread radiation, and a SKEW weather chart indicating optimal wind conditions, this threat loomed larger.

According to the U.S. Nuclear Regulatory Commission (NRC), which trains federal, state, and local agencies in the handling of such emergencies, a Radiological Dispersion Device (RDD), or "dirty bomb," combines conventional explosives like TNT with radioactive material. The first component is immediately lethal while the second one does its damage more gradually and in a wider area. The resulting contamination could generate birth defects, cancer, and other diseases. The NRC calls this a Weapon of Mass Disruption, because the effect of such a bomb is widespread panic, i.e., psychological terrorism. However, the NRC warns that "prompt, accurate, nonemotional information" could forestall such panic. An RDD is not like a nuclear explosion; it will generally contaminate a containable area—unless the terrorists do something like what the offenders had planned on the episode: explode the bomb in the air when the wind conditions are optimal.

While sources of radiation have been stolen and are currently unaccounted for, the NRC states that "the combined total of all unrecovered [United States] sources over a five-year time span would barely reach the threshold for one high-risk radioactive source."

Should a dirty bomb be exploded in any area, the precautions suggested on the NRC Website are:

- Move away from the immediate contaminated area

- Listen to the radio for advisories

- Remove clothing and place in a plastic container, saving them for testing

- Take a shower to decontaminate yourself

- Check with local authorities for exposure testing and protective procedures.

There are sophisticated programs in place, at least in large cities (the most likely targets) for predicting the direction in which the most lethal radiation plume will travel, and communication systems set up to alert people in affected areas. Thus, scientists have models in place for such emergencies. It remains for the government agencies to pay attention and efficiently implement them, as well as educate the public about them.

But sometimes radiation offers benefits to an investigation.

Forensic radiology is an area of medical imaging that uses radiological technology and methods to assist pathologists in determining the cause and manner of death in a context pertaining to investigation or the law. With refinements, such as the CT scan, ultrasound, and MRI imaging, radiology has become even more valuable for forensic purposes.

Wilhelm Roentgen discovered x-rays in 1895, and within a few months he was applying it to a case. A gunshot victim still had the bullet lodged in his leg, but it was unclear where. Using x-rays, the doctor was able to locate it, which assisted prosecutors to successfully resolve a case of attempted murder.

Foreign bodies show up on radiographs, and in one *CSI-NY* episode, "Creatures of the Night," investigators used radiographs to locate a rat from among hundreds of other rats in a building that had swallowed some evidence.

Specialists in this field work alongside pathologists and medical examiners in a variety of contexts, including offering guidance during the autopsy. For example, if a radiograph shows a new bone fracture in an unexpected area (not due to paramedics performing CPR, for example), they can draw attention to that area. X-rays that had been taken of a person while alive for some mishap, such as a broken leg, can assist in the identification of a John Doe who has the same injury.

Radiology can also help to determine if a child has been abused. A child with multiple fractures points to that possibility, and if a case is brought against an abuser, the radiographs serve as evidence. In other contexts, suspects can be screened via x-rays for transporting drugs inside areas of their body via specific types of packets meant to be expelled after they arrive at a destination.

Along these lines, x-rays have other purposes. On *CSI-NY*, investigators used a portable alloy analyzer, or handheld x-ray device, which indicates the presence, composition and grade of metal alloys on a handheld PDA. It's used to analyze soil composition, find metal in the environment, and offer geochemical mapping. The portability of x-ray technology, and its value for certain types of detection, firmly ground it in new directions for investigation.

Also in the future, radio frequency ID tags (RFID) will likely revolutionize our world. They consist of silicon chips and antennae that transmit data to wireless receivers, and they allow someone to track any type of item. They do not require line-of-sight reading, the way a bar code does, and many "smart tags" can be read at once. Reportedly, this technology will give computers much more power to "see." While many applications may be benign (restocking grocery shelves), as such technology becomes more useful and powerful, it may pose Big Brother–type issues.

In another area, a new type of forensic analysis is also providing a type of identification methodology.

GETTING THE DIRT

Scientists at the Institute of Environmental Science and Research (ESR) in New Zealand view soil and the bugs that reside in it as a type of "fingerprint" that will make investigating and solving crimes easier—all kinds of crimes. Environmentalist Jacqui Horswell developed a way to use DNA to analyze bacteria, such that a soil sample from an offender's shoe, car, or clothing might be matched to a particular site, proving his or her presence at a crime scene. Because the scientists can code the entire community of bacteria, he said, they can compare one soil sample with another (both of which contain bacteria), and decide with a high degree of accuracy whether there is a match.

They extract DNA from the sample to look at a gene labeled 16S rRNA, or a technique called terminal length restriction fragment polymorphism. Then they make copies via PCR amplification. Once the differing lengths are measured on a graph for a specific profile, they can submit it to a computer program that makes the comparisons and determines a match. They then have a visual result that can be shown to, and comprehended by, a jury. It's inexpensive, they say, and easily done by forensic scientists with background in molecular biology and access to the right equipment.

They hope to develop a database of the bacterial profiles in that country, so they can make reliable comparisons. That would give them the ability to determine the provenance of an unknown soil sample, i.e., to determine the type of environment from which it derived. Yet since the technology is relatively new to forensics, it has not yet been proven in that venue.

What they're doing in New Zealand parallels research at the University of Tennessee's Anthropological Research Facility (ARF), also known as the Body Farm. In *Death's Acre*, written by ARF's founder, Bill Bass, with Jon Jefferson, one researcher there has attempted to document the same thing. Dr. Arpad Vass, once a grad student at the ARF and now a research scientist at Oak Ridge National Laboratory, has been at work for years on an analysis of microbial measurements from decomposition found in soil beneath bodies. In this way, he's assisted with narrowing estimates of the postmortem interval—the time between when someone died and when the corpse was discovered. In addition, bugs that live in the soil go through developmental stages, and as they die and decompose, they, too, leave an imprint that helps with forming a PMI time line. During decomposition, bacteria evolves, and knowing more about those changes, coupled with the ability to compare them against information from a database, can assist investigators to answer many questions about a possible murder.

The New Zealand researchers hope to develop a kit for soil DNA analysis that will offer results acceptable to the court. Their goal is to assist investigators to make confident statements that an offender was at least present at a soil-specific site. While it's only one of many circumstances that would be necessary to determine anyone's guilt, a precise comparison of samples could be a rather powerful one.

Turning now to an entirely different area, let's look at odor as a tool for investigators.

THE NOSE KNOWS

A company called Electronic Sensor Technology has developed the zNose, a gas chromatograph that can capture and analyze odors and fragrances within ten seconds, based on "Surface Acoustic Wave" (SAW) technology. One model is portable and can operate outside, while a bench-top unit goes into a lab; three other types are in development. (On *CSI-LV*, they discuss the exorbitant cost and value of the electronic nose in "Bully for You.") This device has been adopted for homeland security, with the idea of installing fixed units in buildings as early warning alarms for chemical or biohazardous threats. According to the company's website, the device can recognize any type of vapor, toxin, or compound.

From nose to mouth, let's turn now to a scientific approach to how we talk.

ELECTRONIC STABILITY

Video imagery can be clarified in several ways, and NASA offers companies the opportunity to license its video stabilization and registration technology (VISAR). It was originally developed for investigating the bomb incident during the Summer Olympics in Atlanta in 1996, and it also helped to identify the Rider truck in the Oklahoma City bombing in 1995.

Two people died and 110 people were injured when a bomb exploded in Olympic Centennial Park in July 1996 during the Summer Olympics. There was a report of a suspicious package near the stage where a concert was going on at the AT&T Global Village. The police evacuated people from the area, but not everyone understood. Suddenly, the package exploded and shrapnel flew in all directions. During the concert and evacuation, people with handheld cameras took home videos, but they produced blurred and jittery pictures at best. There was an urgent need to enhance the images, to try to see who might have placed the bomb at its location. Law-enforcement officials asked for assistance from U.S. federal laboratories and, ultimately, NASA assigned the task to researchers who worked with solar image processing. They had developed the technology for stabilizing images taken across vast distances. VISAR was the result.

According to the VISAR Website, the technology stabilizes rotation and zoom effects, enhances the images for clarity, reduces video "snow," and smoothes jagged edges. It's good for video taken in moving vehicles, medical imaging, microscopic tracking, and security videos. It can improve moving images and extract still images from videos. The technology was later used in the trial of a man caught on a security video, kidnapping a young woman who turned up dead.

LANGUAGE BETRAYS YOU

We are what we say, and our personal use of language can be tracked right to us. Language-based author identification involves classifying patterns in written documents with rigorous methods that will reliably attribute the questioned text to a specific author. Some people attempt this identification via subjective interpretation based only in personal experience, while others have spent years grounding it in sound scientific methods and principles. Dr. Carole Chaski is among the latter. Having received her Ph.D. in linguistics from Brown University, she has been consulting in legal cases about linguistic analysis since 1992. Six years later in 1998, she founded the Institute of Linguistic Evidence, Inc. as a nonprofit agency to support research on the validity and reliability of language-based author identification and to refute techniques not based in science. Knowing the difference is important for forensic investigators.

"Forensic linguistics," Dr. Chaski explains, "is the application of linguistic theory to forensically-relevant questions. Linguistics is a social science, closely related to both cognitive psychology, which deals with questions about language structure, language processing and language acquisition, and sociology, which is about dialects, the history of languages, and subcultures. Any tool developed by linguists for answering these types of questions can be applied to forensic situations."

All of the sciences face the demands of *Daubert* qualifications for getting into court. To review, a judge determines whether the testimony is relevant to the case, the methodology is acceptable to peers, an error rate is known, and the method is testable. Before giving testimony, linguistic experts must know how to address this.

"As one of the social sciences," Chaski states, "linguistics is learned and taught within the normal scientific paradigm, which the *Daubert* ruling espouses. Any science is built on the idea that human error and bias has to be constantly guarded against through clear and repeatable procedures and multiple replications with similar findings. Science makes predictions based on known patterns. These predictions are only as good as they seem to be when tests show that they are correct at a certain rate in certain conditions, over and over again. Further, any science recognizes its own limitations. The most developed sciences have gathered enough replications to provide error rates."

Those linguistic procedures that fail a *Daubert* test have not been validated sufficiently in situations apart from litigation for an error rate to have been developed.

"The only forensic linguistic method that I know has passed the scrutiny of *Daubert*," Chaski points out, "is the syntactic analysis method for author identification, which I have been developing and validating since 1992. As a social scientist, I approached the problem in the normal scientific paradigm, so that I was prepared for the *Daubert* hearing when it occurred."

Nevertheless, there are many other linguists attempting to get into courtroom proceedings, and some are considered "junk science." Chaski recognizes that kind of testimony from various signals. For example, "experts" who use the term *forensic linguistics* but have not applied methods from linguistics. But there are other indicators as well: "Personal opinion, intuition, and experience without documentation are not scientific procedures," Chaski says. "I once read a report in which the analyst said that no blue-collar worker could write such a long document. This totally unsubstantiated, personal, and rather elitist opinion was later soundly refuted by the discovery that the blue-collar worker was a well-known and prolific author of internet pornography."

She also sees linguistic terminology being used in nonstandard or erroneous ways, which indicates that the analyst does not really know linguistics, although judges and juries might not realize this, since they don't have the technical knowledge to screen the vocabulary. "This is especially dangerous because it might impress a judge or jury with scientific terms."

Among the responsibilities for Dr. Chaski's profession is to watch for methods that have "no known limits in terms of the amount of text needed or the type of text needed," as well as for "the statement that any new data will not or could not ever change the conclusion." Another red flag is "a method that has no statistical analysis even though the conclusion is stated in pseudostatistical terms, such as 'highly likely' or 'probable.'" She believes this gives a false impression.

In addition, when an expert's training is closely related to literature and literary criticism, "there is an underlying literary approach dependent on the analyst's response to the documents. In literature and literary criticism, the normal scientific standard of replication is missing."

She dislikes any approach that applies "the kind of grammar we teach in schools about what a writer should or should not do," because it "indicates that the analyst is not well trained in linguistics. Pedagogic grammar is antithetical to linguistics. Further, pedagogic grammar mistakes are shared by most writers or there would be no reason to teach most writers not to produce those mistakes." To her mind, it's "illogical to think that such mistakes would identify individuals."

Another indicator of junk science, she says, is "a disregard for our legal system. I have seen this in several ways. First, I think, some ex-

perts have complained that the *Daubert* ruling is all wrong, that there
are different kinds of sciences, and that linguistics should not have to
abide by the normal science procedures of *Daubert*. I think that attitude is very dangerous for several reasons. It puts the expert in the
place of lawyers, and yet these are experts who are not legally trained
doing all the complaining. It denies the fact that both physical and social sciences are sciences, playing within the same worldview. It certainly cannot endear linguistics to judges. It delays the research that
needs to be done. It is simply a red herring for the fact that these com-
plainers have not done the research they need to do in order to be admissible under *Daubert*."

Yet, from what she has seen, there's an even more flagrant show
of disrespect, which would be true about any professional. "An expert who talks about an ongoing case is fine with me when that expert is not actively involved in the case and knows that s/he will not
be involved in the case. But an expert who talks about an ongoing
case in which the expert is providing, or has provided, evidence
analysis is flagrantly disregarding each citizen's right to a fair trial. I
consider this poisoning the potential jury pool, and testifying without
cross-examination."

Chaski's own method, syntactic analysis, is based on generative
grammar, a touchstone in linguistics for the past five decades, and she
utilizes a standard statistical test on which to base an opinion.

"After I had several cases in which my conclusion was validated
by the suspect confessing on the witness stand," she says, "I sought
research funding to pursue validation studies independent of any litigation. I won a research fellowship at the U.S. DOJ's National Institute of Justice, where I stayed for three years. I created a database of
known authors' writing samples so that I could run experiments. I
also tested hundreds of linguistic variables in these experiments. I
tested several different statistical procedures. This work is still ongo-

ing, but the current validation tests involving ten authors show that the current method assigns documents to the correct author 95 percent of the time."

She's sometimes asked to analyze suicide notes to determine if they were actually composed by the person found dead. When left on a computer, handwriting analysis is useless, so another method becomes necessary. "Syntax is the way that we combine words to create phrases and sentences," Chaski explains. "It is an automatic, unconscious process, which decays from memory in milliseconds. These facts are well-supported by almost forty years of psycholinguistic experimentation, but anyone can recognize their truth by simply trying to repeat verbatim what has been said in a conversation: The very fact that it takes extra effort to do this shows that the normal processing of language is not focused on syntax, but on meaning. Because syntactic structures are unconscious and automatized, they are difficult to imitate. So, first I analyze any document for the syntactic patterns, then analyze the counts of these patterns statistically, and base my conclusion on the statistical results. I have authored computer software to automate most of the syntactic analysis and I use commercially available statistical software."

One of her earliest cases illustrates the point.

In 1992, twenty-three-year-old Michael Hunter, a computer programmer, was found dead in his bed. His roommate, Joseph Mannino, made the emergency call. An autopsy indicated that Hunter had died from a mixture of several over-the-counter drugs and an overdose of Lidocaine, an anesthetic. The pathologist found an injection mark on his arm. Since it seemed unlikely that he'd have given himself such a drug, and in any event, couldn't have done so and removed the needle before he died, the police decided to investigate.

They soon learned that Hunter shared an apartment, and his romantic life, with two men: Mannino, twenty-six, and Garry Walston, thirty. Walston was a landscape architect and Mannino, a medical student. Since triangulated relationships often spawn emotional difficulties, and since Mannino could have gained access to Lidocaine, it was surmised that he might have had reason to kill Hunter. Walston confirmed that Mannino and Hunter had been angry at each other, and Walston had sided with Hunter. Mannino had been in the process of breaking things off with them and moving out.

When police confronted the suspect, he denied any wrongdoing but told them he'd given Hunter Lidocaine for migraine headaches. Mannino also implied that Hunter had recently discovered he was HIV-positive, so he'd probably found the Lidocaine and used it to kill himself. In short order, Mannino offered a computer disk that appeared to contain several suicide notes to friends and relatives. Since they were typed, there was no way to do handwriting analysis. That's when the police turned to Dr. Chaski.

"While I was a professor at North Carolina State," she recalls, "I was contacted by W. Allison Blackman, a detective with the Raleigh Major Crimes Unit, concerning the authorship of suicide notes left on a home computer." For making comparisons, she received numerous samples of both Hunter's and Mannino's writing. Then she applied her computer program to the samples and the alleged suicide notes, and offered statistical information about grammar and phrasing. It turned out that the author of the suicide notes had several unique stylistic habits, notably to join long sentences and to overuse adverbs. None of Hunter's known exemplars exhibited these things. "I analyzed the syntax of the documents," says Dr. Chaski, "applied a statistic that compared the counts from the questioned documents to the known potential authors, and determined that there was an extremely low probability that the decedent had actually written the notes, but there was no significant difference between the questioned documents and the other potential author."

That author was Mannino, and he was arrested. The linguistic analysis supplied proof of Mannino's involvement in at least writing the notes,
and he also had a motive and access to the murder weapon. Once the suicide notes were shown to be phony, Hunter's body was tested for HIV. He
was in fact not infected with the AIDS virus.

Mannino went to trial, and admitted on the witness stand that he had
written the suicide notes, but since the jury thought that Hunter might
have been complicit in getting the injection for a migraine headache, as
Mannino had indicated, he was found guilty of involuntary manslaughter.
He received seven years in prison. Dr. Chaski went on to write about the
case, and subsequently added many more that continued to prove the
quality and reliability of her methods.

HEARING VOICES

Many types of audio technology are explored on *C.S.I.*, with an emphasis on computer programs that can clean up recordings, clarify
sounds sufficiently to be recognized, and separate out certain noises
from background to better identify them. Aiden, on the *CSI-NY*
team, for example, analyzes a spectrographic sonogram on the voice-
mail of a victim to isolate and clarify background noise. Enhancement software is used for this purpose. Forensic analysts can also
recover damaged recordings, determine if there was any tampering or
editing, stabilize voice patterns, and identify the sources of voices via
voiceprint technology.

Voiceprints are charted graphs that illustrate various qualities in
someone's voice. The size and shape of the vocal cavity, tongue, and
nasal cavities contribute to this, as well as how that person coordinates lips, jaw, tongue, and soft palate to make speech. That's all done
on a sound spectrograph, and a number of exemplars are required for
a positive identification between a recording and a suspect. The ana-

lyst listens for the way someone speaks, pauses, breathes, inflects words, and repeats phrases or idiosyncrasies, such as "ya know?" But *CSI-LV* tried out another technique in a rather daring episode that drew criticism from forensic scientists.

In "Committed," Grissom brought equipment into a psychiatric institution to try to solve a murder, and when Sara saw it, she mentioned "acoustic archaeology." Grissom acknowledged that she was correct. He went on to describe research done during the 1960s on paintings and clay pots, in which scientists were able to capture the sounds of the creative process from these seemingly impervious and silent material substances. The process is not unlike a gramophone, used as a mechanical transducer to produce music when a stylus hits the grooves of a wax record in which vibrations of sound are stored and amplifies them.

But can we walk up to any stone edifice and find out who's been talking nearby? Can the earth absorb such clearly recognizable sounds? And even if so, can we actually translate them into a coherent communication?

In *Stone Age Soundtrack: The Acoustic Archaeology of Ancient Sites*, scientist Paul Devereux took a series of measurements of monolithic places such as Stonehenge, the temple of the Feathered Serpent, and other prehistoric ceremonial sites to see if he could coax from the stones the sounds of the rituals. He used a computer and laser optic transducers to calculate frequencies and timbres, hoping to learn how the echoes in these places might have enhanced ritual music. He did indeed find evidence that these sites may well have been constructed because of their facility for acoustic amplification: "The structure and order and size and shape and controlling human logic are such that we can reasonably conclude sounds were part of its ancient purpose." The rock face was possibly viewed, he thought, as an "interface" between the physical and spiritual worlds. Some places apparently resonated at the range of a male baritone; add hallucinogens during religious rituals, and that echo may have seemed even more mystical.

On the episode, with a Doppler laser and an optical transducer, they managed to pull the sound of a word from a clay pot, which had been thrown on a wheel while two people were talking. That takes us to yet another area of science, interferometry, which combines two or more input points of a data type to form a more intense or higher resolution manifestation. The principle is that two waves that coincide will amplify each other. The components involve a light source (such as a laser), a detector, two mirrors and a semi-transparent mirror. This provides two paths for the light sources to travel to the detector.

The laser supposedly read the sound off the clay grooves as the pottery rotated. A noncontact optical probe such as this allows a visual imaging process with items below a surface (e.g., ground, skin) that generates acoustic waves when heated by a laser pulse and transported by light diffusion within the tissue. A dual-beamed common-path interferometer provides detection of surface movement—it develops the image of an absorbing object. The transducer receives the electromagnetic energy from the environment and converts it into bioelectric signals that the human brain can comprehend.

Researchers are attempting to apply the technology and they claim to be getting results, primitive as they may be. The *C.S.I.* writers, seeking unique new ways to solve crimes, may have stretched into science fiction, but it's just possible that in doing so they've suggested something to an investigator somewhere who will pick up the idea and run with it. That remains to be seen.

Certainly, innovators are those who spot applications that no one else has yet recognized, and they take steps to set it in motion. Among other inventions or developments we may see in the future are:

- Portable DNA machines and more precise methods for extracting DNA and for determining a DNA reading from minute samples, with decreased risk of corruption

- An electronic device for duplicating the way a cadaver dog detects odors of decomposing remains (some devices are close but not yet that good)

- Microbial forensic technology for anticipating and tracking biological terrorism

- Computer programs for improving such activities as background extraction algorithms and incident simulation

- Accurate computerized threat assessment programs

- More precise methods for physiologically-based deception detection.

Professionals are at work in these and other areas. The interface of science and forensics has become an exciting arena, with room for many innovations. Pathfinders are needed to make ideas realities, such as the people we meet in the next chapter who founded programs or agencies for developing unique angles on forensic situations.

CHAPTER TWELVE

Unique Applications

Although there's plenty of scientific activity in mainstream investigations, *C.S.I.* has presented several side issues as well, which generally require the utilization of special teams or talents. Let's take this fascinating detour.

COUNTERFEIT CURRENCY

Counterfeiting involves printing fake money and passing it off as real. In several cases, the teams have been confronted with counterfeit schemes, including the robbery of a security truck in Miami that contained only counterfeit bills in "Money for Nothing." We learned then how people tell the difference between real and fake money.

Genuine currency bears a watermark that can be seen in a certain type of light, and counterfeit bills not only lack this mark but may have another, which can help investigators to identify the type of paper used. Thus, document examination skills come into play as well. In the real world, the investigators might have called in a federal team to assist them (or take over).

Since 1865, the job of the Secret Service had been primarily to investigate and stop counterfeiting and fraud against the government. In 1883, they became a distinct organization within the Treasury Department, and eleven years later were assigned the job of protecting the president. Eventually some agents were transferred to the Department of Justice, and that became the FBI. By 1915, the Secret Service agents were investigating espionage. Then they also began to protect former presidents, the vice president, and their immediate families. In 1984, Congress enacted legislation that made the fraudulent use of credit and debit cards a federal violation, and soon the Treasury Police Force merged with the Secret Service.

According to the Secret Service's Website: "The types of criminal cases we work are mainly concerned with safeguarding the nation's financial security. . . . We spend a lot of time investigating counterfeit money both in the United States and overseas. Additionally, we currently investigate credit card fraud, computer fraud, and financial institution fraud. Even though we now rely on computers to help us, we still go out and ask questions of victims, witnesses, and suspects. . . . We also investigate people who make threats against the president, vice president, or any of our protectees."

Thanks to advances in computer technology and desktop publishing that allow color printers and copy machines to reasonably imitate actual currency, counterfeiting has become a more serious problem: Digital technology has even allowed counterfeiters to dupe large banks. An international ring stole a corporate dividend check from a California-based bank, scanned it, and altered the amount and the name of the recipient. The bank paid out a quarter of a million dollars.

To protect the currency, the U.S. Treasury added features to American bills to make them more difficult for counterfeiters to duplicate. On a $20 bill, for example, if held up to light or under a microscope with Andrew Jackson's face looking up, to the right side is the watermark, in refined and vivid detail. On the left side is a security strip, which runs horizontally. In addition, the numbers are dyed in such a way that they will appear to be a different color when looking straight down on them than from the side, and under a microscope, other features can be found, such as microprinted lettering. Ultraviolet light activates fluorescent ink and fibers used in the bills (and other government documents), and the notes will have a slight magnetism; they also react chemically with a specific substance that, when applied, will change to a certain color and eventually fade from sight. Yet still, counterfeiters persist in finding ways to enrich themselves at the government's expense.

For several years, the Secret Service had been on the trail of James Mitchell DeBardeleben. They called him the "Mall Passer," because he was quite successful at passing counterfeit bills in various suburban malls. In one year, traveling through thirty-eight states, he managed to pass about $30,000. He'd go from store to store, using fake twenties to purchase low-priced items he didn't need, like socks or greeting cards, in order to get change back in real cash. The agents tracked him and lost him on several occasions, but eventually managed to accurately predict where he'd go next.

On April 25, 1983, the forty-three-year-old con artist went into a targeted (and alerted) mall and bought a paperback at B. Dalton. He spent $4 and got $16 back in change. The clerk watched him go across to a toy store and make a purchase, and then called mall security. They tracked DeBardeleben through several stores and out to the parking lot, where they got his car make and license plate number. They also had him on videotape passing bad bills. He went from there to several other states, dropping false twenties in each. Agents staked out several more malls where they expected him to turn up, and alerted relevant personnel.

A month later in Knoxville, Tennessee, the "Mall Passer" arrived in a car registered in two states with license plates stolen in Virginia. He went into several stores in a local mall and was recognized by a store clerk, who reported him. By the time he realized he was being followed, he was already caught.

A search of his car turned up guns, counterfeit bills, numerous license plates, prescription drugs, a police badge, nine fake driver's licenses, and a substantial stash of pornography. Then agents suspected that DeBardeleben had not only printed fake money but may have raped and murdered several women. He was associated with four such incidents. The investigators located his printing press, and after six trials in several jurisdictions that resulted in convictions for counterfeiting, he was sent to prison for life. Given the fact that he would not be eligible for parole until he was over one hundred years old, the other jurisdictions declined to press further charges.

LOCKING THEM OUT

In "MIA/NYC—Nonstop," linked cases in Miami and New York brought Horatio Caine into contact with Mac Taylor and spun off the New York series. Central to solving the case was knowledge of keys and locks, and the crucial information was that duplicate keys have a red sheen that sets them apart from the master key. But the specialty practice of forensic locksmithing is a more complicated art than that.

The International Association of Investigative Locksmiths offers a set of standards for lock analysis via scientific means. They have an examination process for certification, training programs, and a review board to ensure that members are properly qualified in proven tool mark analysis and investigative procedures.

Since criminal acts often involve breaking a lock, whether for entry into a home, business, car, or safe, forensic locksmiths can assist by examining a lock to determine whether surreptitious entry was tried or gained. They first note the type of lock they're dealing with.

The most common is the pin and tumbler lock, which usually includes five or six pins that make the lock work. The tumbler is the cylinder that goes through the lock from front to back, with the pins positioned at the top. A key is inserted into the tumbler, pushing the pins upward and allowing the tumbler to move to open the lock. The typical lock uses rounded pins, while high-security locks have a more involved setup, such as pins with indentations on them. They can be bypassed but it's a much more difficult process, reserved for the most experienced intruders or thieves.

Picking a lock involves pushing the pins upward without a key. The pick is usually a narrow-pointed metal bar with a tip that can provide leverage or grip. The job also utilizes a tension wrench, which is an L-shaped tool. Between them, pressure is applied to the locking mechanism such that the wrench acts like a key. There are also electronic picks and pick guns that operate in the same way.

To determine if an attempt has been made to pick a lock, the forensic examiner observes the lock's external appearance for indicative markings. Often the plate has been scratched. But a more thorough examination requires removing the lock and dismantling it to look for scratches on the pins. This may involve looking at them under a microscope, but the right keys do not leave scratches, so any scratches would indicate a break-in attempt. Electronic picks also leave characteristic indentations.

Getting past combination locks involves a technique that acquires the right combination . . . or else just blowing up the door that bars access. Padlocks are generally cut with heavy-duty cutters, which isn't difficult for experts to assess as a break-in. Forensic locksmiths may also offer services to customers on which lock would work best for their purposes.

COLD CASES

In "American Dreamers," an episode of *CSI-NY*, a skeleton is found on a tourist bus and identified as the remains of a young man who'd been missing since 1987. It's determined that he had died from a blow to the head, so the hunt was on for a murderer. The main hurdle to solving the case was the amount of time that had passed since his death, since any crime scene would likely be difficult, if not impossible, to process (and perhaps never even identified) and evidence that may once have been on the remains was long gone. Nevertheless, new technologies these days have solved cases ten, twenty, even fifty years old. In fact, there are special teams known as Cold Case Squads devoted specifically to looking for new leads in cold cases.

On December 8, 1999, in Chicago, Illinois, Larry Vincent found the skeleton of a child while digging in his garden. With it were a homemade dress, sweater, and pajama top. The forensic anthropologist called into the case indicated that the remains were of a female and that she had been buried for at least a decade, probably longer. She'd also been abused, showing several broken ribs and a fractured lower jaw.

The detectives used a run number from the pajama top to find its manufacturer, who told them that the design was from 1968. Thus, the child had been buried for three decades. Neighbors from that time offered names, and from the files at the Chicago Board of Education, detectives located a boy from that family. Tracking him down, they persuaded him to reveal his mother's address. Although he could not recall having a sister, he told them, he'd heard his parents argue over someone named "Holly." With that information, detectives found a birth certificate. They then located the mother, who was on her death bed. Just before she died, she admitted to the murder. This young victim finally received an identity and a proper burial.

The Cold Case Squads were formed as the result of a drop in the number of violent crimes. From 1960 until the mid-1990s, the U.S. murder rate steadily rose, and police departments added personnel. By 1985, the Department of Justice had documented nearly 20,000 homicides, and a decade later, it was even higher. Complicating the investigations was the fact that stranger homicides—the most difficult to solve—had become an increasingly larger percentage, accounting for roughly half of them. It seemed that things would only get worse, but by the middle of the 1990s, the murder rate began to decline. Thus, police departments found that they now had resources that they were not utilizing. Since there were many cases on the shelves, the detectives could return to some of these older crimes. They were called "cold cases."

With dramatic new developments in forensic science and technology, especially DNA analysis, the solution to some looked promising. A new breed of detective developed who learned about scientific resources and computer technology, and figured out how to put these things to work for investigative purposes. Seminars were offered by experienced detectives for brainstorming and resource-swapping, and databases were made available to these efforts.

Over the past decade, the cold case units around the country have cleared hundreds of backlogged cases, putting offenders behind bars who believed they'd escaped detection. In addition, many innocent people who did not belong in jail were exonerated and freed. But these investigators can't take on every cold case. They must prioritize, and the key to case selection involves "solvability factors." For example, there would be reason to believe that a witness, once uncooperative, might now be willing to talk (perhaps due to a divorce or the pressures of a guilty conscience). Or, perhaps a suspect was still alive or a new technique relevant to the case had never been tried. In addition, key evidence must be preserved and available for testing: biological evidence can be tested for DNA profiles or fingerprints can be entered into databases that receive new prints every day.

Cold case detectives have access to the FBI's National Center for the Analysis of Violent Crime, the U.S. Marshals Service, military investigative services, organized groups of retired professionals, and crime investigation volunteer groups that offer unique services. Their successes have been documented in television programs, books, seminars, and journal articles, and even if the crime rate goes up again, it appears that the cold case units are making too great a conribution to ever dissolve them.

CRIME SCENE CLEANERS

In *CSI-LV*, the crime scene cleaners arrived in "Swap Meet" while Nick and Warrick were still at the scene, giving viewers a glimpse at a unique profession that may also become part of a murder or suicide incident. These professionals may even arrive after a death by natural means, if the deceased has been there a while.

In New Jersey in 2004, police went to a home from which an offensive odor exuded and found the remains of an eighty-two-year-old man who had been dead for several weeks. He still lay in his bed, but shockingly, an

entire family had continued to live in the home. Even more disturbing, the adult couple who were foster parents to three children had forced their thirteen-year-old to bring food in each day to the decomposing corpse. They knew the man had died, yet they continued this bizarre behavior. They were arrested and charged with child cruelty and elder neglect.

While forensic technicians take samples and photographs when cases like this require investigation, they don't do the clean-up. But somebody has to.

Crime scene cleaners are entrepreneurs who do the job that most people want no part of: restoring a room, car, home, business, or the street to the way it was after a murder has been committed or a body has badly decomposed. In other words, they remove the physical signs that a tragedy or unpleasant death has occurred.

The first service solely dedicated to sanitizing the aftermath of such incidents opened for business on the East Coast in 1993. Trauma scene marketing soon became a lucrative industry across the country and into Canada. These professionals appeal to families who have experienced tragedies and do not wish to clean up the place themselves or are simply not equipped to handle biohazardous material. Even a janitorial service may not know how to properly dispose of the waste.

The job requires a protective biohazard suit, mask, gloves, and extensive training in HazMat procedures, as well as knowledge of the right cleaning solvents to use in various environments. Enzymes, for example, remove bloodstains, but sometimes that's not enough. A carpet soaked all the way through must be disinfected completely, and the flooring beneath it treated. An inside job will need strong deodorizers. There's clearly a science to it.

Crime scene cleaners don't remove the bodies—that's the job of a coroner or medical examiner—but once a scene has been released, they can see fairly clearly what happened: blood spatter and brain matter on a wall, a pool of blood on a floor, purged biological fluids from a liquefying corpse. It's not uncommon with a gun-related death that tiny bits of blood and brain matter will be all over the floor, walls, and ceiling. It may be on books and bedspreads as well. Sometimes what remains behind is still wet, but after it's hardened, it can prove a real challenge to clean up. And they must also deal with the odors. A body that has long decomposed or decomposed in a hot area can leave a putrid stench that no one wants to approach. The deceased can also have maggots and other insects on or in it.

After a building or vehicle gets a thorough going-over, the waste products must be dealt with as well. They can't just be tossed into a local Dumpster. They must be incinerated, like a cremated corpse, so such crime cleaners must be registered with a licensed medical waste treatment facility.

People do remain in or purchase houses where terrible things have happened or where someone has simply passed away quietly, and they often don't realize its history. That's because someone has come along in the aftermath and restored the place in preparation for the living. They also assist with documentation for insurance claims.

In addition to responding to the public's need for such a service, these crews may also clean police vehicles that have transported biological evidence. Or they may assist in removing contaminated furnishings from distressed properties, or clean up the remnants of an illegal methamphetamine lab.

There is a certification process, via the Certified Alliance of Trauma Practitioners, as well as training programs for those who wish to enter this field as registered practitioners. Training centers set up simulated scenes in order to give people hands-on experience. They learn that they must keep their eyes open while cleaning a scene, because it's possible that the technicians failed to find something, such as a bullet beneath some playing cards or a severed finger that flew across the room. They must also look in less obvious places for biological fluids, such as on an overhead fan blade or in cracks in a floor, and they need to learn how to handle it as potential evidence.

Crime scene cleaners also must know how to interact with surviving family members, talk with law enforcement, and deal with pets left in the home. In addition, they have to watch for the danger signs in themselves and their comrades from exposure to life's darkest side: what people do to themselves and each other. The stress can be overwhelming, and good trainers use techniques to help these professionals distance themselves from the life that's been lost. A key part of the training should prepare them for surprises, because people can do some rather odd things.

In Queens, New York, in July 2005, the police received complaints of a terrible smell exuding from a specific building. When they went to the apartment from which it originated, a woman opened the door, then slammed it. When they finally gained entry with the assistance of a building supervisor, they discovered the decomposed body of an elderly woman lying on the floor in a hallway outside a bedroom. It looked as if she'd been there for several weeks, and it turned out that indeed she had died in the apartment she had shared with two sisters and a niece. Apparently they had coexisted with the remains. Understandably, the living were all sent for psychological testing.

MASS DISASTERS

When the United States came under a terrorist attack on September 11, 2001, a special team was in place to respond. Members of that team were deployed to Georgia when several hundred bodies were discovered on the grounds of a cremation business and grieving relatives demanded to know if their deceased loved ones were among them. (*CSI-M's* "Forced Entry" was inspired by this incident.) This team also organized the resources needed at the site of the 1995 Oklahoma City bombing, with 168 fatalities and more then 700 people injured, and they assisted with the aftermath of a tornado there. Mass disasters can take many unexpected forms, and thanks to the vision of a few key people and the devotion of a special breed of professionals, the Disaster Mortuary Operational Response Team (DMORT) is ready.

Disasters leave surviving families and friends with a sense of loss, shock, and disbelief. Someone needs to assist them with coping and getting answers about their loved one's disposition or remains. During the 1980s, the National Funeral Directors Association noted this need and initiated a committee to form a plan for responding to mass fatalities. It wasn't long before such a plan was activated.

Near the end of January in 1990, Tom Shepardson led a group of volunteer professionals to assist the local medical examiners with seventy-three fatalities at the crash site of Avianca Flight 052 on Long Island. Shepardson set up shop in a hotel ballroom and coordinated other agencies overnight to develop a plan to assist grieving families. Two months later, he and his team were called to another disaster.

On March 25, 1990, Julio Gonzales, thirty-six, was fuming over the behavior of a girlfriend, Lydia Feliciano. After seven years, she had broken up with him. Since he believed he owned her, he decided to teach her a lesson. Feliciano worked at the Happy Land social club, located in the Bronx area of New York City. It was a place where people could dance all night, though the building was substandard for such gatherings. There was only one functional door, located on the ground floor, so in the event of a fire, there was only one way out. People upstairs would essentially be trapped.

That night, Gonzales had made one final attempt with Feliciano at reconciliation and had been rejected. He was asked to leave, but he vowed that he would be back. Around three-thirty in the morning, he purchased gasoline from a gas station near the club, carried it to the building, and poured it around the bottom of the door. Then he lit a match and went across the street to watch the wooden structure catch fire.

Only five people managed to get out, while sixty-one men and twenty-six women died from being trampled in the panic, from smoke inhalation, and from terrible burns. Feliciano was not among them. She had already gone home, entirely escaping the night from hell meant for her. Gonzales was arrested, and under interrogation, he said, "I got angry. The devil must have gotten into me and I set the place on fire." He was charged with eighty-seven counts of murder. A jury convicted him of them all, and he received twenty-five years to life for each count.

While law enforcement dealt with Gonzales, others had to confront the task of identifying the dead. The body count was far too great for the local resources to handle, even for a city as large as New York. They asked Shepardson and his volunteers to step in, and they were up to the task. Afterward, Shepardson developed a mass fatality response course, sponsored by the National Foundation for Mortuary Care, through which he trained private citizens with relevant skills on how to respond to a mass disaster. These volunteers had to be prepared to respond at a moment's notice and go wherever they were needed. This initial effort grew into trainings in other places and the organization of multifaceted teams that coordinated a diversity of skills. In 1992, DMORT was born and members became paid federal workers, with Shepardson as the first commander.

DMORT is a federal program placed under the Federal Emergency Response Plan within the Department of Homeland Security, according to a history written by forensic odontologist David Williams. Their responsibilities, he says, include setting up temporary morgue facilities, search-and-recovery efforts, assisting in victim identification, and processing, preparing, and determining the disposition of human remains. They also offer a support staff for team members who may need counseling or stress reduction.

The organization has roots in the Office of Civil Defense Planning, formed in 1948. Official programs for large-scale emergencies went through several permutations under successive presidents, and after September 11, 2001, President Bush drew together several agencies, including DMORT, into the Department of Homeland Security. DMORT is part of the medical response system, now organized into ten regional teams that correspond to the ten districts for the Federal Emergency Management Agency (FEMA).

Its first official task as an organization was the aftermath of a flood on the Missouri River on July 31, 1993. A cemetery in Hardin County, Missouri, was washed out and 769 graves decimated, including some that were more than a century old. When the DMORT members arrived, they saw a seventy-foot-deep lake in the middle of the cemetery, and caskets appeared to be floating all over the place, posing health problems to local communities and more grief to relatives. Some caskets were whole, some broken open, and many half-rotted. In fact, the graves' contents had dispersed over 65,000 acres. Caskets, both in and out of vaults, were found as far as thirty miles away, and corpses floated away from where they'd been interred. One by one, those that could be recovered were pulled in.

DMORT set up a morgue and brought in anthropologists, dentists, pathologists, funeral directors, and embalmers to place those remains that they were able to identify into new caskets. They also met with concerned families faced with the task of reburial. Some of the deceased were identified by dental records or from the description of a relative, and most of the modern caskets had serial numbers that had been recorded with the name of the deceased. Bodies and body parts were placed into new caskets and reinterred. It took five months, but finally 607 of the corpses that had been disturbed by the flood were restored to what was hoped would now be their final rest. (While not as ambitious as this incident, *CSI-M* also took on a washed-out cemetery in "Crime Wave.")

With the Oklahoma City disaster in 1995, DMORT set up a series of stations to assist with victim tracking and identification. First was the documentation of injuries for cause of death; then there was a station for photographs and fingerprints; then radiology, and another station for dental x-rays. There were also therapists to help with grieving families. It proved to be an efficient system, so it remained in place.

TWA Flight 800 crashed into the Atlantic Ocean on July 17, 1996, with 230 fatalities. This time, DMORT was not officially activated, but Shepardson went to the scene anyway, and he told a poignant story for a Discovery channel documentary. The family of one female victim, whose remains were considered unviewable, was grief-stricken that they could not see her to get closure. Shepardson saw that one arm was whole, so he arranged to have the remains placed into a body bag, with that arm and hand available for the parents to touch and hold for their last contact.

In 1999, the crash of an Amtrak train in Louisiana inspired the use of the Disaster Portable Morgue Unit (DPMU), with workstations, autopsy tools, x-ray machines for a full-body scan, victim ID tags, medical supplies, and an entire mobile computer network. When a catastrophe like this overwhelms local resources, they have the DPMU brought in. During that period as well, forensic scientists, rather than just mortuary officers, were considered for the position of Team Commander. By then, a St. Louis–based dentist, Dr. James Mc-Givney, had developed a computerized database system, WinID, for entering dental information about victims to facilitate matches. In fact, as the organization is deployed, each member strives to stay current in disaster management to provide whatever he or she can to improve the emergency response.

DMORT member Joyce Williams, R.N., M.A., is a diplomat of the American Board of Medico-legal Death Investigators and a forensic nurse examiner for the state of Maryland. She describes the organization's development.

"DMORT individuals or teams respond at the request of four different modes," says Williams, "the Public Health Act, Federal Disaster Declaration, Aviation Disaster Family Assistance Act, and a Memorandum of Understanding (MOU) with a Federal Agency. DMORTs respond to aviation accidents, floods, fires, and any incident where the local resources cannot handle its magnitude and have the proper activation method utilized."

Initially, DMORT had no forensic component, but with mass disasters becoming potential crime scenes, such as the Happy Land social club, evidence handling took priority, so professionals trained to observe and collect it were needed on the teams. Sometimes local law enforcement could do the job, but with overwhelming or multisite incidents, such as the attacks of 9-11, outside resources became necessary. Team members work for the local authorities, but they know their jobs well. They may be involved in search and recovery or employed at one of the sites in the temporary morgue, where bodies are triaged. "Following this," Williams explains, "they move through the various stations where the identification process is carried out. Antemortem and postmortem data comparison is completed in many of these sections. From here the body or remains are identified. Not all identifications are completed at this point, especially if DNA analysis is required—as would be the case in fragmented remains [explosions, airline disasters]. Additionally we have a Family Assistance Center, where the families of the victims wait for updates on identifications. Here DNA is taken, if necessary, for comparison, as well as victim information to facilitate the comparison of antemortem data. Embalming may also take place following the identification. All of the records are then turned over to the local authorities for permanent record-keeping and issuance of death certificates."

The ten regional teams have different requirements for filling positions, and DMORT now supports over 1,200 members. "Additionally," says Williams, "there is a core team that responds with the DPMU and those who set it up. They are often referred to as the 'Red Shirts'."

To get into these units requires some training. "Team members maintain [professional] licensure and certification in their state of residence, and during activation [local] licensures are recognized by all states. There are federal requirements to maintain each year, and courses are provided by the National Disaster Medical System (NDMS) followed by an examination. FEMA offers courses, as well as annual team training via lectures, demonstrations, and hands-on training. Specialty groups also have additional training and there is an annual NDMS conference where the teams from across the country meet en masse to learn the latest advances. Many members belong to the American Academy of Forensic Sciences, where presentations provide a variety of advancements and experiences in disaster/victim identification methods."

After participating with DMORT in some disaster responses, local professionals sometimes wish to become part of the national effort, as do people who hear about DMORT on news or documentary programs. So what would they do?

"Requirements are initiated," Williams points out, "by completion of an application found on the Internet. This is then forwarded to the team commander and administrative officer, where position availability is assessed. NDMS approves all applications and issues the identification badges required for access to a disaster site once a team member has been activated. Each regional team may have special requirements, such as the dentists who take the AFIP Identification Course, which is offered each year in March."

So in the event of an emergency, FEMA would notify the proper agency of resource needs, and DMORT would come under the jurisdiction of a Management Support team, which in turn would process requests from the local medical examiner or coroner. A commanders' conference facilitates the twice-yearly training and the fluid movement, if needed, of one team into another's region. In short, in the event of a large-scale disaster, DMORT offers an integrated emergency management system with high-tech capabilities and professional standards. "They provide communities with confidence that everything humanly possible is being done," Williams added, "to recover, identify, and return victims to their families."

This second volume about science and forensic investigation has gone beyond the basics to explore more sophisticated areas. New discoveries are being made all the time, and as science has learned its application in the legal arena, more researchers are eager to be involved. There are still more frontiers to explore, and even within the areas we've described, more refined methods are being devised and tested. The *C.S.I.* programs, growing from one to three, and enduring for several years, offer solid proof that science and investigation have formed a productive partnership in the name of justice. The need for new material will send the creators into ever more innovative areas of research, and while the presentations may not always be accurate, they will most certainly continue to ignite interest in millions of people in the forensic sciences. The *C.S.I.* Effect, for good or ill, is here to stay.

Forensic Glossary

Accident Reconstruction An approach to vehicular and related accidents that involves engineering and knowledge of the laws of motion for reconstruction of what occurred.

Acoustic Archaeology A method for recording sounds from ancient monuments to determine if the stones retain the rhythm of past rituals.

Actus Reus One of the two requirements for a finding of criminal responsibility; this one involves the capacity to have physically performed the act. *See also mens rea.*

AFIS Automated Fingerprint Identification System, a computerized database for storing and making rapid comparisons of fingerprints.

Age Progression A method in forensic art used to estimate and depict what a person would look like at a time much later than his or her last known photos.

Aggravating Circumstances Conditions that make a crime more serious, such as knowing the risk involved that may have led to injury or death.

Algor Mortis Cooling of the body after death.

ALS Alternative light source, used for bringing out latent fingerprints, blood, fibers, and other trace materials that are difficult to see under regular light conditions.

Amelogenin Gene Locus of the chromosomes that can be analyzed with a DNA analysis to determine gender for human remains too far decomposed to reveal this in other ways.

Amplification The procedure used in the polymerase chain reaction method for replicating a DNA sample exponentially.

Antemortem Prior to death.

Antisocial Personality Disorder As defined in the *DSM-IV*, it emphasizes antisocial behaviors such as deception, manipulation, and breaking the law.

Arsenic Mirror A test for arsenic detection devised during the nineteenth century that relied on a highly reflective deposit.

Autoerotic Accident A death that occurs from the hypoxia produced by asphyxia during masturbatory rituals.

Automatism One of the defenses offered to mitigate criminal responsibility, it involves proposing that a defendant committed a crime while sleepwalking, and thus did not possess the requisite state of mind to be aware of the behavior.

Autopsy The medical examination of a body to identify cause of death.

Behavioral Evidence Forensic evidence suggestive of certain behaviors, generally used for criminal profiling.

Beyond a Reasonable Doubt The degree of proof that will convince the trier of facts to a near-certainty that the allegations have been established. This is the highest of the three standards of proof in a courtroom, and it's used in all criminal trial proceedings.

Bio-archaeology An area of archaeology concerned primarily with human remains, such as learning from a historic cemetery what the burial customs were.

Brain Fingerprinting A device said to measure the brain's stored memory of being at a certain place, notably a crime scene.

Burden of Proof The necessity of proving a fact in dispute, according to the standard of proof required in a specific proceeding. In criminal trials, for example, it's beyond a reasonable doubt.

Case Linkage Finding links among two or more cases.

Cause of Death An injury or disease that produces a condition in the body that brings about death; it's usually stated on a death certificate.

Chain of Custody The method used to keep track of who is handling a piece of evidence, and for what purpose.

CODIS Combined DNA Index System, the FBI database of genetic material.

Cold Case Unsolved case no longer under active investigation, but still open; many can be solved with today's sophisticated technology.

Competency Sufficient ability to participate in proceedings, such as to stand trial, to waive rights, and to testify.

Computer Animation Reproducing the way a crime actually occurred as a visual for the jury or investigative team.

Computer Forensics The discipline that interfaces computer technology with the legal process, specifically for investigation and evidence.

Computer Simulation An interpreted reconstruction, based on collected data, of how an incident might have occurred.

Coroner In some jurisdictions, the person in charge of the death investigation; might be a medical examiner or an elected official.

Corpus Delicti Essential body of facts that indicate that a crime has occurred.

Crime Reconstruction Using location of evidence and position of bodies, if relevant, to determine the sequence of actions involved in a crime.

Criminalistics The science of analyzing physical evidence from a crime.

Criminal Profiling The use of observation of the crime scene and pattern of crimes to determine characteristics of the perpetrator that are relevant to an investigation; it guides police in narrowing the field of suspects and devising a strategy for questioning.

C.S.I. Effect The influence of popular crime shows on the culture, specifically with regard to possibly miseducating viewers who are potential jurors.

Cyber-crime Crimes that occur with the use of a computer, most often on the Internet, such as identity theft, hacking into protected systems, and dispensing child pornography.

***Daubert* Standard** A recent standard used in federal and many state courts for deciding the admissibility of scientific evidence, redefining the Frye Standard.

Deposition The pretrial statements, given under oath, by any witnesses in a proceeding.

Depravity Scale The device used to launch a study and thereby derive a consistent standard for the courts regarding aggravating factors defined as depravity or other forms of evil.

Digital Data Information in digital form, such as photographs and computer files.

Diminished Capacity A psychological defense indicative of an inability to appreciate the nature of a crime or to control one's actions. Not used in all states.

Dirty Bomb *See* Radiological Dispersion Device.

Discovery The process through which parties in dispute find out facts about the case.

Dissociative Identity Disorder (DID) The name given to what was once known as Multiple Personality Disorder, diagnostic of people who seem to have fragmented personalities such that some seem to be entire people coexisting in the same body.

DMORT (Disaster Mortuary Operational Response Team) A federal organization of diverse professionals, organized under FEMA by areas, that deploys for emergencies involving mass fatalities.

DNA (Deoxyribonucleic acid) Genetic blueprint found in every cell in the body and unique to every individual.

DNA Profile The blueprint of a person's physical identity, as determined by his or her genes.

DNAPrint A type of DNA test that provides information about ethnicity.

DSM-IV (The Diagnostic and Statistical Manual for Mental Disorders, 4th edition) The bible of modern psychiatry and psychology for the diagnosis of specific forms of mental illness.

Due Process Guaranteed steps in a legal proceeding.

Equivocal Death Analysis *See* Psychological Autopsy.

Evidence Documents, statements, and all items included in the legal proceedings for the jury's sole consideration in the question of guilt or innocence.

Exhumation The process of removing human remains from a grave.

Expert Witness A person with specialized knowledge about an area, or with a special skill that is germane to the proceedings, such as hair analysis, DNA, or a mental illness. This person's role is to assist the fact finders in understanding complicated information.

Fact Finder The person (judge) or persons (jury) who weigh the evidence in a trial to determine a verdict.

Felony A serious crime for which the punishment in federal law is generally severe, including capital punishment.

Fluorescence When molecules absorb electromagnetic radiation, the energy can be used to excite the electrons, and when they decay back to their original state, they emit energy with a lower wavelength for as long as the source that excited them is present.

Folie à Deux A delusion shared by two or more people, generally initiated by one person who truly believes it and can persuade others to do so, too.

Forensic Archaeology A professional discipline that focuses on the location and excavation of human remains for legal purposes.

Forensic Art The use of artistic methods such as drawing and sculpture for legal purposes, such as suspect posters or identifying missing persons.

Forensic Linguistics A scientific analysis of the manner in which individuals speak, such that samples of a piece of writing of unknown origin can be matched to a suspected author.

Forensic Locksmithing A professional discipline that involves activities for the court such as determining if someone has attempted a break-in via triggering a lock.

Forensic Psychology The interface between professional activities in psychology, such as formal assessment, counseling and research, and the legal profession.

Frye Standard A test that governs the admissibility of scientific evidence, such that evidence entered into a case must be generally accepted by the relevant scientific community.

Gas Chromatography The method used to break down compounds into their component parts; *See also* zNose.

Gene A segment of DNA that codes for the production of a specific protein.

Ground Penetrating Radar (GPR) A device that measures the depth and density of shapes beneath the ground's surface.

Homicide A death caused by another person.

Identity Theft The illegal act of appropriating another person's identity for the purposes of stealing their credit and resources, or for posing as them for some criminal purpose.

Impression Evidence Anything that leaves an impression at a crime scene that links someone to the crime; tire tracks, footprints, fingerprints, tooth marks, and bite marks.

Indictment Accusation issued by a grand jury that charges an individual with criminal misconduct.

Informatics The systematic organization of computerized data.

Innocence Project An effort based in Cardoza University that uses DNA testing on biological samples from crimes to find out if the person convicted of doing it is in fact guilty. As of August 2005, sixty-one men had been proven not guilty.

Insanity A legal term for a mental disease or defect that if present at the time of a crime, absolves the person of responsibility.

Interrogation The art of getting suspects to talk, possibly to confess.

Intent Mental state ranging from purpose to awareness of consequences.

Junk Science Research or methodology falsely posed as science that is offered to the courts for testimony.

Jurisdiction The authority to exert power over individuals or legal matters within a defined geographic area.

Latent Fingerprints Prints left on something that aren't visible, but can be made visible with certain techniques.

Livor Mortis Discoloration of the body after death, when the red blood cells separate and settle to the lowest point of gravity. Also called lividity.

Marsh Test A nineteenth-century test, invented by James Marsh, which was the first reliable procedure to detect the presence of arsenic in human tissues.

Mass Spectrometry A way to identify elements of a compound, by bombarding it with electrons; this device can identify constituent parts too small for the gas chromatograph to detect.

Medical Examiner In some jurisdictions, the person who runs the death investigation; also the person who does the autopsies for the death investigation.

Mens Rea One of the two requirements for criminal responsibility; this one has to do with having the requisite mental state for intent and awareness of what one is doing. *See also Actus Reus.*

Misdemeanor A lesser crime than a felony, generally punished by a fine or a short sentence in jail.

Misinformation Effect The phenomenon found with eyewitness research that indicates that people exposed to erroneous information may incorporate it into their memory schemes and report it as fact.

Mitigating Circumstances Factors such as age, motivation, duress, or unstable home life that can diminish the degree of guilt in a criminal offense.

Modus Operandi **(MO)** An offender's method of carrying out the offense.

Murder A type of homicide that involves killing another person illegally; the degree is decided by the type of evidence, with premeditated first-degree murder being the most serious.

National Center for the Analysis of Violent Crime (NCAVC) A subdivision of the FBI's Behavioral Science Unit, which also runs the VI-CAP and profiling programs.

NecroSearch An organization of professionals who are hired to assist in finding missing victims in difficult terrain.

Paraphilia A disorder or deviance based in unusual sexual preferences, such as fetishes.

Perimortem The time interval just before death.

Polygraph A machine used to determine through changes in physiological functions whether a person is lying.

Polymerase Chain Reaction (PCR) The method used to replicate small amounts of DNA so it can be further tested.

Portable Thermo Alloy Analyzer X-ray fluorescence device that indicates the presence and composition of alloys.

Postmortem Interval (PMI) The time since death, as determined by several factors.

Preliminary Hearing A hearing held before a judge to decide whether there is sufficient evidence to go to trial.

Prosecutor The attorney who represents the government in a criminal proceeding.

Psychological Autopsy Methods used to determine state of mind of a person where a suicide is questionable.

Psychometric Testing The activity of psychologists and psychiatrists when hired to do an assessment of an individual about to stand trial; they will use formal tests and instruments to determine such things as competence, organic disorders, and mental illness, especially at the time of the crime.

Psychopathy Personality disorder defined by long-term antisocial behavior by a person who feels no guilt or remorse and is not inclined to stop the behavior; often predatory, exploitive, and manipulative.

Psychosis A major mental disorder in which a person's ability to think, respond, communicate, recall, and interpret reality is impaired. They show inappropriate mood, poor impulse control, and delusions. Often confused with insanity, which is a legal term, and psychopathy, which is a character disorder.

Query by Example The procedure used to access databases to get matches.

Radiological Dispersion Device The use of conventional bomb components such as TNT with radioactive materials added.

Renfield's Syndrome A syndrome based on a character from *Dracula* in which a person believes they need blood and may try taking it from animals or people.

Restriction Fragment Length Polymorphisms (RFLP) The original method for getting a DNA profile, which splits the molecule and cuts it into pieces.

Rigor Mortis The stiffening of the muscles after death.

Serial Crimes Any type of crime occurring in a pattern that indicates a single offender.

Serial Killer Someone who kills three or more people and has a psychological cooling-off period in between murders.

Serology The analysis of body fluids like blood, semen, and saliva.

Short Tandem Repeats (STR) A method for getting a DNA profile after replicating it with PCR.

Signature Analysis The method used to "read" crime scenes that indicate a serial offender who leaves a personal mark.

Spectrometry The detection of various wavelengths of light, which can be done with different pieces of spectrographic equipment. Some measure wavelengths emitted, some measure wavelengths absorbed.

Subpoena A command to appear at a certain time and place to give testimony on a certain matter.

Syntactic Analysis A scientific approach to how someone speaks that uses a statistical program for analysis and comparison with samples.

Taphonomy The systematic study of human decomposition versus environmental factors to determine the postmortem interval.

Testimonial Evidence What an eyewitness says about a crime.

Time-stamping A method that puts a definite time and date on digital data when it's created so that it cannot be manipulated to appear to have been created at a different time.

Toxicology The section of the lab, and the discipline, that tests tissues or products for contamination by drugs, poisons, and alcohol.

Trace Evidence The smallest pieces of evidence at a scene, including fiber, hair, grass fragments, seeds, dust, and soil.

Variable Number of Tandem Repeats (VNTRs) Polymorphic DNA regions that repeat themselves, and are unique to individuals.

Verdict The decision of a judge or jury after hearing and considering the evidence.

Violent Criminal Apprehension Program (VICAP) The FBI's nationwide data information center, designed for collecting, sorting, and analyzing information about crimes.

Victimology A study of victim information to find clues about the offender's opportunity and selection process.

Virtual Autopsy The use of CT scans and computers to attempt to make diagnoses about cause of death for certain cases without cutting into a body.

Voice Stress Analyzer A device that purportedly measures deception via stress in the voice, but has been found to be less than satisfactory.

Voir Dire The process of qualifying jurors prior to a trial; it's also used to qualify experts.

zNose A gas chromatograph that captures and provides information about odors and fragrances in the air.

Selected Sources
and Resources

Baden, Michael, with Marion Roach. *Dead Reckoning: The New Science of Catching Killers*. New York: Simon & Schuster, 2001.

———with Judith Hennessee. *Unnatural Death: Confessions of a Medical Examiner*. New York: Ivy Books, 1989.

Bass, Bill and Jon Jefferson. *Death's Acre: Inside the Legendary Forensic Lab the Body Farm*. New York: Putnam, 2003.

Beavan, Colin. *Fingerprints*. New York: Hyperion, 2001.

Bell, Suzanne. *The Facts on File Dictionary of Forensic Science*. New York: Checkmark Books, 2004.

Benedict, Jeff. *No Bone Unturned*. New York: HarperCollins, 2003.

Berlow, Alan. "The Wrong Man," *Atlantic Monthly*, November 1999.

Brenner, John C. *Forensic Science Glossary*. Boca Raton, FL: CRC Press, 1999.

Butler, John M. *Forensic DNA Typing: Biology, Technology, and Genetics of STR Markers, 2nd Edition*. San Diego, CA: Academic Press, 2005.

Casey, Eoghan. *Digital Evidence and Computer Crime: Forensic Science, Computers and the Internet, 2nd Edition.* San Diego, CA: Academic Press, 2004.

Chaski, Carole. "Forensic Cases in a Murder Trial," linguisticevidence.org.

Cleckley, Hervey. *The Mask of Sanity* (rev. ed.). St. Louis, MO: C.V. Mosby, (1941), 1982.

Clement, John G. and Murray K. Marks. *Computer-Graphic Facial Reconstruction.* San Diego: Academic Press, 2005.

Devereux, Paul. *Stone Age Soundtracks.* London: Vega, 2001.

"Digging the Dirt on Criminals," *The Guardian,* May 26, 2005.

Douglas, John, Ann W. Burgess, Allen G. Burgess, and Robert K. Ressler. *Crime Classification Manual.* San Francisco: Jossey-Bass, 1992.

Douglas, John and Mark Olshaker. *Mindhunter: Inside the FBI's Elite Serial Crime Unit.* New York: Scribner, 1995.

——*Cases That Haunt Us.* New York: Scribner, 2000.

Dowling, Paul, with Vince Sherry. *The Official Forensic Files Casebook.* New York: Simon & Schuster, 2004.

Doyle, James M. *True Witness: Cops, Courts, Science and the Battle Against Misidentification.* New York: Palgrave Macmillan, 2005.

Evans, Colin. *The Casebook of Forensic Detection.* New York: John Wiley & Sons, 1996.

——*Murder 2: The Second Casebook of Forensic Detection.* New York: John Wiley & Sons, 2004.

Faretta v. California, 422 U.S. 806. (1975).

Fisher, Barry. *Techniques of Crime Scene Investigation, 6th Edition.* Boca Raton, FL: CRC Press, 2000.

Fridell, Ron. *Solving Crimes: Pioneers of Forensic Science.* New York: Grolier, 2000.

Frye v. U.S. 293 F.1013, 34 A.L.R. (DC Circuit 1923).

Geberth, Vernon J. *Practical Homicide Investigation, 3rd Edition.* Boca Raton, FL: CRC Press, 1996.

——*Sex-Related Homicide and Death Investigation.* Boca Raton, FL: CRC Press, 2003.

Haglund, William D. and Marcella H. Sorg. *Advances in Forensic Taphonomy: Method, Theory and Archaeological Perspectives*. Boca Raton, FL: CRC Press, 2002.

Hare, Robert. *Without Conscience*. New York: Pocket, 1993.

Houde, John. *Crime Lab: A Guide for Nonscientists*. Ventura, CA: Calico Press, 1999.

House, Mack S., Jr. *Underwater Forensics*. Bloomington, IN: AuthorHouse, 2005.

Inman, Keith, and Norah Rudin. *An Introduction to Forensic DNA Analysis*. Boca Raton, FL: CRC Press, 1997.

"Investing on a Whiff: Chemical Spray Shows Power as Trust Booster," *Science News*, Vol. 167, no. 23, June 4, 2004.

James, Stuart H. and Jon Nordby. *Forensic Science: An Introduction to Scientific and Investigative Techniques*. Boca Raton, FL: CRC Press, 2003.

Kurland, Michael. *How to Solve a Murder: The Forensic Handbook*. New York: Macmillan, 1995.

Lee, Henry C. and Howard A. Harris. *Physical Evidence in Forensic Science*. Tucson, AZ: Lawyers & Judges Publishing Company, 2000.

Lee, Henry C. and Frank Tirnady. *Blood Evidence: How DNA Revolutionized the Way We Solve Crimes*. Cambridge, MA: Perseus, 2003.

Loftus, Elizabeth. *Eyewitness Testimony*. Cambridge, MA: Harvard University Press, 1979, 1996.

————"Our Changeable Memories: Legal and Practical Implications." *Science and Society* Vol. 4: March 2003.

————"Misinformation and Memory: The Creation of New Memories," *Journal of Experimental Psychology*: General 118 (1), March 1989.

Loftus, Elizabeth and Pickrell, J. E. "The Formation of False Memories," *Psychiatric Annals*, 25, 1995.

Lovgren, Stefan. "Artful Software Spots Faked Masterpieces," *National Geographic News*. November 23, 2004. news.nationalgeographic.com

McCrary, Gregg, with Katherine Ramsland. *The Unknown Darkness: Profiling the Predators Among Us*. New York: Morrow, 2003.

McCuthcheon, Chuck. "Solving Old Mysteries: Exhumations on the Rise," newhousenews.com, June 9, 2005.

McNally, Richard J. *Remembering Trauma*. Cambridge, MA: Belnap Press of Harvard University, 2003.

Melton, Gary B., John Petrila, Norman Poythress and Christopher Slobogin. *Psychological Evaluations for the Courts, 2nd Edition*. New York: Guilford Press, 1997.

Morris, Mill. "Casting a Wide Net: Lifting Fingerprints from Difficult Surfaces," *Forensic Magazine*, Vol. 2, No. 4. August/September 2005.

Nickell, Joe and John Fischer. *Crime Science: Methods of Forensic Detection*. Lexington, KY: The University Press of Kentucky, 1999.

Noll, Richard. *Bizarre Diseases of the Mind*. New York: Berkley, 1990.

Nordby, Jon. *Dead Reckoning: The Art of Forensic Detection*. Boca Raton, FL: CRC Press, 2000.

Perkins, Sid. "Seeing Past the Dirt," *Science News*, Vol. 168, No. 5. July 30, 2005.

Platt, Richard. *The Ultimate Guide to Forensic Science*. London: DK Publishing, 2003.

Ramsland, Katherine. *Inside the Minds of Mass Murderers*. Westport, Connecticut: Praeger, 2004.

——*The Forensic Science of C.S.I*. New York: Berkley Boulevard, 2001.

——*The Human Predator: A Historical Chronicle of Serial Murder and Forensic Investigation*. New York: Berkley, 2005.

——*The Science of Cold Case Files*. New York: Berkley, 2004.

Randall, Brad. *Death Investigation: The Basics*. Tucson, AZ: Galen Press, 1997.

Rhine, Stanley. *Bone Voyage: A Journey in Forensic Anthropology*. Albuquerque, NM: University of New Mexico Press, 1998.

Roane, Kit R. "The C.S.I. Effect," *U.S. News & World Report*. Vol. 138, No. 15, April 25, 2005.

Rosenhan, J. "On Being Sane in Insane Places," *Journal of Abnormal Psychology*. 84, No. 5, 1975, pp. 442–452.

Schechter, Harold. *The Serial Killer Files*. New York: Ballantine, 2003.

Scheck, Barry, Peter Neufeld, and Jim Dwyer. *Actual Innocence*. New York. Random House, 2000.

Starrs, James E., with Katherine Ramsland. *A Voice for the Dead*. New York: Putnam, 2005.

State v. Crisafi. 128 NJ 499, 510–12 (1992).

Taylor, Karen T. *Forensic Art and Illustration*. Boca Raton, FL: CRC Press, 2000.

Trestrail, John Harris. *Criminal Poisoning*. Totowa, NJ: Humana Press, 2000.

Van Kirk, Donald J. *Vehicular Accident Investigation and Reconstruction*. Boca Raton, FL: CRC Press, 2001.

"Virtual Autopsies May Cut Scalpel Role," cnnhealth.com. December 4, 2003.

Wingate, Anne. *Crime Scene Investigation*. Cincinnati, OH: Writer's Digest Press, 1992.

Welner, Michael and Katherine Ramsland. "Behavioral Science and the Law," in *Forensic Science and Law: Investigative Applications in Criminal, Civil, and Family Justice*, edited by Cyril Wecht and John Rago. Boca Raton, FL: CRC Press, 2006.

Wrightsman, Lawrence S., Michael Nietzel and William Fortune. *Psychology and the Legal System, 3rd Edition*. Pacific Grove, CA: Brooks Cole Publishing, 1994.

Index

Dr. Katherine Ramsland has a master's degree in forensic psychology from John Jay College of Criminal Justice, a master's degree in clinical psychology, and a PhD in philosophy. She has published twenty-seven books, including *Inside the Minds of Mass Murderers, The Science of Cold Case Files, The Criminal Mind: A Writer's Guide to Forensic Psychology*, and *The Forensic Science of C.S.I.* Her *Vampire Companion: The Official Guide to Anne Rice's Vampire Chronicles* was a bestseller, and she has been translated into nine languages. With former FBI profiler Gregg McCrary, she coauthored *The Unknown Darkness: Profiling the Predators Among Us*, and with law professor James E. Starrs, *A Voice for the Dead*. In addition, Ramsland has published more than three hundred articles on serial killers, criminology, and criminal investigation, and was a research assistant to former FBI profiler John Douglas for *The Cases That Haunt Us*. She writes forensic articles for Court TV's Crime Library, contributes editorials on forensic issues to the *Philadelphia Inquirer*, and teaches forensic psychology as an assistant professor at DeSales University in Pennsylvania.